Academic Life in the Measured University

While a life in academia is still one bestowed with enormous privilege and opportunity, on the inside, its cracks and fragility have been on display for some time. We see evidence of this in researchers bemoaning time spent applying for grants rather than doing research; teachers frustrated at the ways student feedback data are deployed to feed judgements about them; and doctoral students realising that they have little chance of securing full-time academic work. Yet in the public policy domain, the opposite appears true: academics left to their own devices in their elite ivory towers, rarely ever do enough.

This collection addresses the fact that academic life deserves to be rigorously researched. Its emphasis on the *measured* university traces *how* academic life had ceded itself to the logics of perverse measures, and raises questions about whether the contemporary university may well have become *too measured* to adequately counter the political times now upon us. The contributors explore the ways in which measurement inhabits paradoxical positions in these spaces. It sketches the contours and consequences of mismeasurement, including the personal costs to academic staff. It examines our desires and fumbled efforts at institutional transformation, and it puts on display our own ethical conduct. The collection concludes with a call to chart a course for a revitalized moral economy of academic labour.

This book was originally published as a special issue of *Higher Education Research & Development*.

Tai Peseta is a Senior Lecturer in the Learning Transformations team at Western Sydney University, Australia. Her current research interests include the development of teaching cultures in academia, stewardship in doctoral curricula, the idea of the university, and the scholarship and ethics of academic development.

Simon Barrie is Pro Vice-Chancellor of Learning Transformations at Western Sydney University, Australia. He is responsible for leadership of strategic educational innovation and collaboration to shape the University's commitment to ensuring its students fulfil their potential to become influential global citizen-scholars in a new technology-enabled world.

Jan McLean is a Senior Lecturer in the Institute for Interactive Media and Learning at the University of Technology Sydney, Australia. As a higher education researcher, she is particularly interested in the effects of the changing higher education context upon academic life and practice as well as student belonging and learning.

Academic Life in the Measured University

Pleasures, Paradoxes and Politics

Edited by
Tai Peseta, Simon Barrie and Jan McLean

LONDON AND NEW YORK

First published 2019
by Routledge
2 Park Square, Milton Park, Abingdon, Oxon, OX14 4RN, UK

and by Routledge
52 Vanderbilt Avenue, New York, NY 10017, USA

First issued in paperback 2020

Routledge is an imprint of the Taylor & Francis Group, an informa business

© 2019 Higher Education Research and Development Society of Australasia

All rights reserved. No part of this book may be reprinted or reproduced or utilised in any form or by any electronic, mechanical, or other means, now known or hereafter invented, including photocopying and recording, or in any information storage or retrieval system, without permission in writing from the publishers.

Trademark notice: Product or corporate names may be trademarks or registered trademarks, and are used only for identification and explanation without intent to infringe.

British Library Cataloguing in Publication Data
A catalogue record for this book is available from the British Library

ISBN 13: 978-0-367-58293-7 (pbk)
ISBN 13: 978-1-138-36953-5 (hbk)

Typeset in Minion Pro
by RefineCatch Limited, Bungay, Suffolk

Publisher's Note
The publisher accepts responsibility for any inconsistencies that may have arisen during the conversion of this book from journal articles to book chapters, namely the possible inclusion of journal terminology.

Disclaimer
Every effort has been made to contact copyright holders for their permission to reprint material in this book. The publishers would be grateful to hear from any copyright holder who is not here acknowledged and will undertake to rectify any errors or omissions in future editions of this book.

Contents

Citation Information vii
Notes on Contributors ix

Introduction – Academic life in the measured university: pleasures, paradoxes and politics 1
Tai Peseta, Simon Barrie and Jan McLean

1. Higher degree research by numbers: beyond the critiques of neo-liberalism 6
   Liam Grealy and Timothy Laurie

2. The paradox of collaboration: a moral continuum 20
   Bruce Macfarlane

3. Measures of success: cruel optimism and the paradox of academic women's participation in Australian higher education 34
   Briony Lipton

4. Counting on demographic equity to transform institutional cultures at historically white South African universities? 46
   Masixole Booi, Louise Vincent and Sabrina Liccardo

5. The mismeasure of academic labour 59
   Angelika Papadopoulos

6. Rendering the paradoxes and pleasures of academic life: using images, poetry and drama to speak back to the measured university 74
   Catherine Manathunga, Mark Selkrig, Kirsten Sadler and (Ron) Kim Keamy

7. Made to measure: early career academics in the Canadian university workplace 89
   Sandra Acker and Michelle Webber

8. Fear and loathing in the academy? The role of emotion in response to an impact agenda in the UK and Australia 103
   Jennifer Chubb, Richard Watermeyer and Paul Wakeling

9. Challenging a measured university from an indigenous perspective: placing 'manaaki' at the heart of our professional development programme 117
   Nell Buissink, Piki Diamond, Julia Hallas, Jennie Swann and Acushla Dee Sciascia

10. Measuring the 'gift': epistemological and ontological differences between the academy and Indigenous Australia 131
    Jonathan Bullen and Helen Flavell

CONTENTS

11. Target-setting, early-career academic identities and the measurement culture of UK higher education   145
    Jan Smith

12. The missing measure? Academic identity and the induction process   160
    Jennie Billot and Virginia King

13. Lost souls? The demoralization of academic labour in the measured university   173
    Paul Sutton

    Index   185

Citation Information

The chapters in this book were originally published in *Higher Education Research & Development*, volume 36, issue 3 (May 2017). When citing this material, please use the original page numbering for each article, as follows:

Editorial
Academic life in the measured university: pleasures, paradoxes and politics
Tai Peseta, Simon Barrie and Jan McLean
Higher Education Research & Development, volume 36, issue 3 (May 2017), pp. 453–457

Chapter 1
Higher degree research by numbers: beyond the critiques of neo-liberalism
Liam Grealy and Timothy Laurie
Higher Education Research & Development, volume 36, issue 3 (May 2017), pp. 458–471

Chapter 2
The paradox of collaboration: a moral continuum
Bruce Macfarlane
Higher Education Research & Development, volume 36, issue 3 (May 2017), pp. 472–485

Chapter 3
Measures of success: cruel optimism and the paradox of academic women's participation in Australian higher education
Briony Lipton
Higher Education Research & Development, volume 36, issue 3 (May 2017), pp. 486–497

Chapter 4
Counting on demographic equity to transform institutional cultures at historically white South African universities?
Masixole Booi, Louise Vincent and Sabrina Liccardo
Higher Education Research & Development, volume 36, issue 3 (May 2017), pp. 498–510

Chapter 5
The mismeasure of academic labour
Angelika Papadopoulos
Higher Education Research & Development, volume 36, issue 3 (May 2017), pp. 511–525

Chapter 6
Rendering the paradoxes and pleasures of academic life: using images, poetry and drama to speak back to the measured university
Catherine Manathunga, Mark Selkrig, Kirsten Sadler and (Ron) Kim Keamy
Higher Education Research & Development, volume 36, issue 3 (May 2017), pp. 526–540

Chapter 7
Made to measure: early career academics in the Canadian university workplace
Sandra Acker and Michelle Webber
Higher Education Research & Development, volume 36, issue 3 (May 2017), pp. 541–554

Chapter 8
Fear and loathing in the academy? The role of emotion in response to an impact agenda in the UK and Australia
Jennifer Chubb, Richard Watermeyer and Paul Wakeling
Higher Education Research & Development, volume 36, issue 3 (May 2017), pp. 555–568

Chapter 9
Challenging a measured university from an indigenous perspective: placing 'manaaki' at the heart of our professional development programme
Nell Buissink, Piki Diamond, Julia Hallas, Jennie Swann and Acushla Dee Sciascia
Higher Education Research & Development, volume 36, issue 3 (May 2017), pp. 569–582

Chapter 10
Measuring the 'gift': epistemological and ontological differences between the academy and Indigenous Australia
Jonathan Bullen and Helen Flavell
Higher Education Research & Development, volume 36, issue 3 (May 2017), pp. 583–596

Chapter 11
Target-setting, early-career academic identities and the measurement culture of UK higher education
Jan Smith
Higher Education Research & Development, volume 36, issue 3 (May 2017), pp. 597–611

Chapter 12
The missing measure? Academic identity and the induction process
Jennie Billot and Virginia King
Higher Education Research & Development, volume 36, issue 3 (May 2017), pp. 612–624

Chapter 13
Lost souls? The demoralization of academic labour in the measured university
Paul Sutton
Higher Education Research & Development, volume 36, issue 3 (May 2017), pp. 625–636

For any permission-related enquiries please visit:
http://www.tandfonline.com/page/help/permissions

Notes on Contributors

Sandra Acker is a Professor Emerita in the Department of Social Justice Education at the University of Toronto, Canada. Her research interests focus on women and higher education, and on careers and workplace cultures of teachers, graduate students, and academics.

Simon Barrie is Pro Vice-Chancellor of Learning Transformations at Western Sydney University, Australia. He is responsible for leadership of strategic educational innovation and collaboration to shape the University's commitment to ensuring its students fulfil their potential to become influential global citizen-scholars in a new technology-enabled world.

Jennie Billot is an Associate Professor and Head of Researcher Development at Auckland University of Technology, New Zealand. Her personal research interests include leadership, academic identity, higher education and postgraduate education, and supervision.

Masixole Booi completed a Masters Degree in the Department of Political and International Studies at Rhodes University, Grahamstown, South Africa. He has been involved in student and community activism and served in different leadership positions.

Nell Buissink is a Senior Academic Advisor in the Centre for Learning and Teaching at Auckland University of Technology, New Zealand. She provides professional development and recognition for all AUT teaching staff. Her primary interests are in the well-being of staff and students and in understanding their experiences of being in a university.

Jonathan Bullen is a Sessional Academic in the School of Psychology at Curtin University, Perth, Australia. He has published articles in *Higher Education Research & Development* and *The Australia Educational Researcher*.

Jennifer Chubb is a Postdoctoral Research Associate in Research Policy and Responsible Metrics in the Faculty of Social Sciences at the University of Sheffield, UK. Her teaching expertise includes research impact, ethics, and integrity.

Piki Diamond is an Academic Advisor at Auckland University of Technology, New Zealand. She is skilled in research, indigenous education, and professional learning. She has a history of developing bicultural curricula for higher education and finding creative solutions for developing teachers and learning environments.

Helen Flavell is a Coordinator in the Faculty of Health Sciences at Curtin University, Perth, Australia. She is the co-author of *Academic Leadership for Course Coordinators Program: A Guide to Coordination and Facilitation* (with Beverley Oliver, Rick Ladyshewsky, and Sue Jones, 2008).

NOTES ON CONTRIBUTORS

Liam Grealy is a Postdoctoral Research Fellow at the University of Sydney, Australia. He is working on the project 'Housing for Health: Fixing Infrastructure and Housing Policy in Indigenous Australia and Beyond', funded by the Henry Halloran Trust, and led by Associate Professor Tess Lea.

Julia Hallas is an Academic Developer in the Centre for Learning and Teaching at Auckland University of Technology, New Zealand. She is skilled in research, teaching, higher education, and educational technology.

(Ron) Kim Keamy is an Associate Professor (and Honorary Professor) in the College of Arts and Education at Victoria University, Melbourne, Australia. His professional experience includes teaching in primary education, special education, community education, vocational education, and higher education.

Virginia King is HLS Senior Research Associate in the Centre for Global Learning, Education and Attainment at Coventry University, UK. Her current research interests include academic identity, the staff experience, staff development, collaborative learning, the PhD experience, and academic writing.

Timothy Laurie is a Scholarly Teaching Fellow in the School of Communication in the Faculty of Arts and Social Sciences at the University of Technology Sydney, Australia. His core research interests include cultural theory, popular music studies, and gender and sexuality studies.

Sabrina Liccardo is a Research Psychologist and Lecturer at the University of Pretoria, South Africa. She has drawn extensively upon multidisciplinary insights deriving from psychosocial studies, hermeneutic phenomenology, narrative theory, life writing, critical race feminism, cultural geography, and the visual arts.

Briony Lipton is a PhD candidate in the School of Sociology at the Australian National University, Canberra, Australia. Her thesis explores how key discourses of feminism, neoliberalism, and leadership constitute academic performativity and identity in the contemporary Australian university.

Bruce Macfarlane is Professor of Higher Education and Head of the School of Education at the University of Bristol, UK. He specializes in developing concepts for understanding the ethical dimensions of what it means to be an academic.

Catherine Manathunga is an Honorary Professor in the College of Arts & Education at Victoria University, Melbourne, Australia. She is a historian who draws together expertise in historical, sociological, and cultural studies research to bring an innovative perspective to educational research, particularly focusing on the higher education sector.

Jan McLean is a Senior Lecturer in the Institute for Interactive Media and Learning at the University of Technology Sydney, Australia. As a higher education researcher, she is particularly interested in the effects of the changing higher education context upon academic life and practice as well as student belonging and learning.

Angelika Papadopoulos is a Lecturer in the School of Global, Urban and Social Studies at RMIT University, Victoria, Australia. Her supervisor interests include higher education policy, contemporary Australian social policy and practice, and social theories.

Tai Peseta is a Senior Lecturer in the Learning Transformations team at Western Sydney University, Australia. Her current research interests include the development of teaching cultures in academia, stewardship in doctoral curricula, the idea of the university, and the scholarship and ethics of academic development.

NOTES ON CONTRIBUTORS

Kirsten Sadler is an Honorary Fellow in the College of Arts & Education at Victoria University, Melbourne, Australia. She works across the college to assist staff with securing funding, conducting research, and producing research outputs, particularly early career researchers.

Acushla Dee Sciascia is a Senior Research Officer at Auckland University of Technology, New Zealand. She interested in research that has a specific Māori or Indigenous focus, which seeks to transform and develop an Indigenous people and culture.

Mark Selkrig is a Senior Lecturer in the College of Arts & Education at Victoria University, Melbourne, Australia. His research and scholarly work focuses on the changing nature of educators' work and how educators navigate the ecologies of their respective learning environments.

Jan Smith is a Faculty Member in the Centre for Academic Practice in the School of Education at Durham University, UK.

Paul Sutton is a Senior Lecturer in Sociology in the Faculty of Education and Social Sciences at the University of St Mark & St John, Plymouth, UK.

Jennie Swann is an Academic Advisor in the Centre for Learning and Teaching at Auckland University of Technology, New Zealand. She works with lecturers, helping them to develop and facilitate their courses online.

Louise Vincent is a Professor in the Department of Politics at Rhodes University, Grahamstown, South Africa. She is a qualitative research methodologist and consultant, who researches in fields including narrative research, discourse analysis, action research, research proposal development, academic writing, content analysis, and coding of data.

Paul Wakeling is a Professor in the Department of Education at the University of York, UK. He is a sociologist of education with particular interests in higher education, especially access to postgraduate study, and in social inequalities.

Richard Watermeyer is a Reader in the Department of Education at the University of Bath, UK. He supervises PhD candidates in the areas of higher education policy, management and governance; academic practice and identity; science and society; and STEM education.

Michelle Webber is a Professor in the Department of Sociology at Brock University, St Catharines, Canada. She publishes on various aspects of higher education including, contingent faculty, tenure and promotion, and academic identities.

INTRODUCTION

Academic life in the measured university: pleasures, paradoxes and politics

The theme of academic life in the measured university has felt especially pressing to us. As co-editors, we have aimed to work together in ways that matter to us while still meeting numerous deadlines along the way. In curating this issue, we have shared and savoured many moments of intellectual pleasure together. One that stands out is the precious thrill invited by a slow encounter with a beautifully argued piece. Yet at other times, the editorial work has cast the paradoxes of our own academic lives and workplaces into sharp relief. Like so many others, we wrestle with our location in the measured university: endless cycles of organizational restructure promising liberation from past inefficiencies; our capacities being counted in ways that exclude our participation from the process and the final outcome; and the constant accounting for the worth of our thinking and the quality of our judgements. We are not special: these are the academic lives of many of our colleagues too. Working on this issue together has reinforced all the more that academic life is a peculiar kind of difficult work. It is tough for an outsider to see past the privilege, and even harder for them to empathize with our difficult work. Yet we see this issue as joining a conversation with the many others seeking to make meaning from, and develop alternatives to, what an academic life has become today.

In the time since the 2016 Academic Identities Conference – the genesis of this issue – the politics of higher education have radically altered. Brexit – England's momentous decision to leave the European Union – happened only a few days before the conference started, plummeting a handful of visiting delegates into unknown futures all the while knowing full well that their academic colleagues back home would be anticipating plights of the very worst kind. Many of us were glued to our devices looking for explanation, analysis and consolation, hoping that the conservative decision would not extend to the US presidential election. We now know the outcome of the latter, and it is clear that universities will be grappling for some time with the consequences of a climate that has reified populism over expertise, and post-truth over evidence and scholarship. It is not that these aspects of sociality and civic discourse are particularly new; rather, it is that elevating their status to high office (and watching their flow through social media platforms) lends them an altogether different posture of credibility and speed that centuries of patient and meticulous inquiry will struggle to keep up with. Indeed, we may see the revitalization of the activist public intellectual and/or we may see the qualities of the post-fact world begin to wheedle their way into what gets measured in academic life, how and by whom, drastically transforming the nature and conduct of academic inquiry. Whatever future is on the horizon, the work of teaching, research and scholarship is going to get much more thorny.

Against this backdrop many people have told us that our emphasis on measurement is both welcome and timely. The demand to count, measure, rank, quantify, evaluate and judge the work of universities (along with those who labour and study in them) haunts virtually all aspects of our work: from the quality of research, to targets for income generation, counts of patents, citations of articles and public testimonies of policy impact made visible and likeable online; from the quality of curriculum, to teaching with technology, responding to student feedback, watching the employment destinations and salaries of graduates as a comment on the value of their education; to whether a university is healthy, sustainable, sufficiently globalized or doing enough to position itself as the world leader in this or that discipline. Every day, our conduct is being shaped to procure a commitment to institutional indicators, targets, standards and benchmarks that help us to diagnose ourselves (and others) as worthy and successful academics. At the same time, universities repurpose our labour to shore up their market distinctiveness in ways that are likely to surprise, shock and repulse us. Ocean and Skourdoumbis (2016) remind us that we are already well schooled in the language of measurement's 'discursive accompaniments: failure to measure up, failing to count, cutting and letting go, what the numbers say' (p. 442). And far from being benign, '[m]etrics hold real power: they are constitutive of values, identities and livelihoods' (Wilsdon et al., 2015, p. iii).

And yet there is another argument in circulation too: that the appeal to measure – which often draws on mountains of numerical data derived from the increasing surveillance of workloads, decision-making activity, performance reviews and enterprise systems analytics – is an altogether reasonable response to the complexity of the higher funding education environment and the bombardment of bureaucratic reporting associated with public accountability. On this logic, as Liam Grealy and Tim Laurie note in their contribution to this issue, 'while numbers do not necessarily produce well-informed ideas about education, there are many ideas about education that can only be promoted through the institutional force of measurement practices'. Even those of us committed to equity, social justice and ethical practices need measures to mount persuasive arguments that advance the projects we are attached to. Nonetheless, compelling objections remain. Is it the fact that measurement has encroached so brutally into the domains of academic life by pushing forms of political reason that accomplish its inevitability, and that lead to the suspicion and erosion of expertise? Is it primarily that measurement is numerical and reductionist in that it offers uncomplicated accounts of lived worlds as facts? Is it the mismatch between the crude tool and its effects – outcomes that lodge themselves in systems and collective consciousness as real rather than representations of the real? One such example might be the ubiquity of student satisfaction as a proxy for learning. Is it that the communal discussions we participate in with good will and that are intended to nurture nuanced and complex measures are routinely dismissed or ignored by those in senior institutional positions or in government? Is it that others are defining our vocabularies of value and so violating our autonomy to craft narratives about our own work? Is it the way measurement works through, and on, our bodies, psyches and conduct, instantiating a panopticon-like surveillance and competition among individuals to be seen, to be performing, to be adding value? Or is it that the judgements resulting from measurement spill out from their original context and end up as categorical pronouncements about who we are and what we do in ways we do not recognize and have not consented to?

Whether in isolation, or taken together, these objections signal a need for caution. Moreover, many of the measures we are pressed to believe in as academics – those which antagonize and inspire us in equal parts – support a fallacious belief that past performance is the best predictor for future success even when the partiality of measures is writ large. In presenting those imperfect measures publicly – to society, to prospective students and to future colleagues – we (mistakenly) scale up their significance. We empower others to breathe life into those measures. We fashion stories of students' futures around them. We evaluate the successes and failings of our academic lives in relation to them, and we appraise the moral compass and business acumen of the university against them. Not only do we need to keep a keen eye on the measures themselves and their material entanglements, effects and affects in the world, there is an intellectual duty to make a spectacle of the logics in play.

In his 2010 book *Good education in an age of measurement: Ethics, politics, democracy*, Gert Biesta argues that a measurement culture takes root *as if it is education* because we are no longer sufficiently engaged with what a good education is and what it is for. In his view, the question of purpose has fallen from the public gaze. Departing slightly from Biesta, the trouble for us is not so much that there is an absence or dismissal of 'purpose' (purpose-talk in universities is everywhere and nowhere at once); it is that academic life is now confronted with a multiplicity of purposes that are in deep contradiction. The danger, as Ball (2012) has written, is that we become 'malleable rather than committed, flexible rather than principled, essentially depthless' (p. 31). In this scenario, our academic subjectivities are shaped by, and belong to, the institution. Paul Sutton, another of the contributors to this issue, has a striking way of putting it: 'the creation of this new organizational actor takes place when academics come to want what is wanted from them'.

From the 80 or so submissions we received in response to the original call, we are delighted to bring 13 together in this special issue. As individual papers they address a fascinating range of higher education practices unsettled by the prospect of measurement: the ongoing struggle to take seriously the experiences of academic women, the potential for indigenous knowledges to transform the university, the contradictions of transparency in formulating academic workloads are just some of them. And they come to us from a range of national contexts too – Aotearoa New Zealand, South Africa, Canada, Australia and England – each one wrestling with related challenges in local ways.

On the whole, we have noticed an interesting pattern among the contributions. Each of the three opening papers – Liam Grealy and Tim Laurie on the neo-liberal framing of measurement in research degrees, Briony Lipton on the consequences of mainstreaming of gender equity for academic women and Bruce Macfarlane on the need to be more perceptive about the moral nature of academic collaboration – bring to their object of interest a fresh insight on the ways measurement inhabits paradoxical positions in these spaces. On the one hand, there is the tantalizing satisfaction in 'getting things done' (Grealy and Laurie) while on the other, an alertness to the 'cruelty of our attachments' (Lipton).

The next two contributions sketch the contours and consequences of mismeasurement. From post-apartheid South Africa, Sabrina Liccardo and colleagues show just how enormous the task is in recruiting and retaining black academics especially when institutions attend mostly to measures entrenching the very situations those academics are intended to address. In a different vein, Angelika Papadopolous analyses data from nine Australian universities' workload models, alongside the results of a survey regularly commissioned by the national academics' union. Claiming that workload models operate as policy technologies, Papadopolous not only advances a case that these models seldom begin from real empirical grounds, but she also displays how these models obscure the very 'thing' they aim to be transparent about.

Unsurprisingly, the personal costs in being relentlessly measured feature in the special issue. While Catherine Manathunga and colleagues outline how an art-based postcards project afforded a space for resistance, rejuvenation and fellowship, their description of writing about it is heartbreaking: 'our stomachs clench, our foreheads knot, our shoulders tighten. We feel sick as we struggle to sketch in what has come to count in the entrepreneurial university'. By comparison, Sandra Acker and Michelle Webber's portrayal of seven early career Canadian academics caught up in preparations for tenure seems far more muted. To be clear, there are costs evident – work–life balance, time away from children, deciphering inconsistent institutional messages about success – but it may well be that, in Canada, metrics are still skating across the top of academic life as an upshot of the absence of a national approach to research assessment or teaching evaluation. To close this theme, we turn to the contribution by Jennifer Chubb and colleagues who, in interrogating the variety of emotional responses to the research impact agenda in the UK and Australia, assert that we ought to be more circumspect about the accuracy, prevalence and hyperbole of *only* crisis accounts. Interestingly, they advocate for a distinction between being a 'public intellectual, the notion of public accountability, and performance-related auditability'.

From there we move to four contributions grounded in the desire for institutional transformation. The first two turn our minds swiftly to the experiences of doing indigenous knowledge work and being indigenous workers in an academy whose measures are entirely western. From Aotearoa New Zealand, we glimpse into Nell Buissink and colleagues' institution-based efforts where they have partnered with the UK-based Higher Education Academy (HEA) to place the Māori value *manaaki* at the heart of professional learning for all university teachers. The piece describes why and how their university extended the professional standards of the HEA Fellowship Scheme as a radical act of care, hospitality and kindness. In the second article, Helen Flavell and Jonathan Bullen draw on Rauna Kuokkanen's logic of the gift and Martin Nakata's commitment to the cultural interface to expose how the measures and machinations of quality often work against universities' espoused obligations to Indigenous studies, and to projects intended to indigenize the curriculum. The context in question: a large first-year interprofessional unit on Indigenous cultures and health. For them, the quality measures associated with this unit constitute an act of epistemic violence.

The next two contributions – from Jan Smith and Jennie Billot and Virginia King – are no less significant in their appeal for universities to conduct themselves more ethically. Smith takes aim at the UK process of academic probation, specifically, the task of setting targets and moulding oneself to meet them despite deep institutionalized uncertainty. In Smith's research, the intellectual horizons of early career academics on probation are being driven into safe terrain precisely because they have been individualized and over-surveilled. And in a related way, Billot and King's focus on a process of academic induction that joins together formation, socialization and agency reminds us there is the potential to design professional learning activities and spaces inside the academy where human flourishing can be imagined and made practical.

We leave our closing contribution to sociologist Paul Sutton who resurrects the humanism of Karl Marx to encourage an academic life with adequate moral energy for the language of love and the desire to cultivate care for our souls. While Sutton has long surrendered to the measurement of academic labour, he finds hope and prosperity in well-being measures that are 'hedonic, eudaimonic, and evaluative'. For him, these examples chart a course for a new moral economy of academic labour. And, we add, of academic life.

As is customary in all issues of *HERD*, we include a Book Review and Points for Debate piece, both intended to further elaborate our theme. Tai Peseta takes us on a tour of two books: Maggie Berg and Barbara K. Seeber's *The slow professor: Challenging the culture of speed in the academy* (2016) and Les Back's *Academic diary: Or why higher education still matters* (2016). And, in *Being an academic is the key to who I am – a memoir* (our Points for Debate), Canadian sociologist of education Sandra Acker examines the addictive rhythms of academic work and reveals what keeps her engrossed in retirement.

As this is the last special issue commissioned by the former *HERD* journal editorial team led by Executive Editor Barbara Grant, we want to make special mention of three Associate Editors – Stephanie Doyle, Tamsin Hinton-Smith and Lisa Thomas – who assisted in the preparation of this issue. They bore the brunt of many interactions with patience, grace and humour. Our thanks, too, to the reviewers (both College members and others) whose anonymous and free labour is rarely ever rewarded enough. We also want to acknowledge the labour and creativity of the many researchers, scholars and teachers who subjected their thinking and writing to peer review but whose scholarly efforts do not appear here. And finally, we extend a special note of love and appreciation to Managing Editor Diana Nicholson who has shepherded us to the end in the most efficient and humane way possible.

References

Ball, S. (2012). *Global Education Inc. New policy networks and the neo-liberal imaginary*. London: Routledge.
Biesta, G. (2010). *Good education in an age of measurement: Ethics, politics, democracy*. London: Paradigm.
Ocean, J., & Skourdoumbis, A. (2016). Who's counting? Legitimating measurement in the audit culture. *Discourse: Studies in the Cultural Politics of Education, 37*(3), 442–456.
Wilsdon, J., Allen, L., Belfiore, E., Campbell, P., Curry, S., Hill, S., … Johnson, B. (2015). *The metric tide: Report of the independent review of the role of metrics in research assessment and management*. doi:10.13140/RG.2.1.4929.1363.

Tai Peseta
Simon Barrie
Jan McLean

Higher degree research by numbers: beyond the critiques of neo-liberalism

Liam Grealy and Timothy Laurie

ABSTRACT
This article argues that strong theories of neo-liberalism do not provide an adequate frame for understanding the ways that measurement practices come to be embedded in the life-worlds of those working in higher education. We argue that neo-liberal metrics need to be understood from the viewpoint of their social usage, alongside other practices of qualification and quantification. In particular, this article maps the specific variables attending measurement in higher degree research programmes, as the key sites that familiarize students with measurement practices around research and teaching. With regard to the incremental reframing of doctoral study as a utilitarian pursuit, we suggest a need to better identify the singular and immeasurable features of long-term research projects, and argue for a revitalized notion of failure. In this context, this article suggests that many critiques of neo-liberalism do not sufficiently advance alternative ways to think about the purposes and limitations of higher education.

Introduction

Like the category of obscenity in art, neo-liberalism seems to obey a maxim that ensures its regular circulation within university folklore: we know it when we see it. We know something neo-liberal is happening when generous colleagues fail to have their contracts renewed because they do not meet obscure metrics for research performance derived from Key Performance Indicators (KPIs). We know neo-liberalism has taken hold when, rather than pursuing their interests or talents, students make course choices based on perceived benefits for future employment incomes to repay higher tuition fees resulting from sector-wide marketization and deregulation. We know that we belong to neo-liberal institutions when the carefully formed languages of specialist disciplines are replaced by the languages of management, such that a research project acquires value only through its outputs, its impacts, its scalability, its 'innovations', or its potential to produce further growth. And yet, we do not always know what a unifying concept such as 'neo-liberalism' adds to all of this knowing.

Many contemporary commentaries on neo-liberalism could be classified as what Eve Sedgwick, following Silvan Tomkins, calls 'strong theories'. Strong theories claim to be 'capable of accounting for a wide spectrum of phenomena which appear to be very remote, one from the other, and from a common source' (Tomkins, quoted in Sedgwick, 2003, p. 134). For example, Marxist political economists have been accused of being overly 'functionalist' in their accounts of neo-liberalism, by attributing multiple transformations to a single causal factor – the struggle between capital and labour (Flew, 2014, p. 58). Calling Marxism a 'strong theory' does not mean saying that it is false, only that its most common articulations involve moving from an unstable multiplicity of effects to a more stable continuity of causes. But cultural accounts of neo-liberalism can also contain similarly 'strong' impulses. For example, competitive reality television programmes or self-help books have been described as neo-liberal because they participate in the common logic of individual self-determination, even if competitive games and popular psychology have entirely different cultural origins. Elsewhere, neo-liberalism has been identified in the ideology of 'linear time' subtending European colonialism, thereby linking the critique of neo-liberalism to a strong theory of global- and post-coloniality (Shahjahan, 2015, p. 491). These strong theories present contrasting narratives about the historical duration and geographical scope of neo-liberalism, but they do share a commitment to distinguishing between neo-liberalism as a unitary cause and social interactions as derivative effects. This raises the following questions: when we use neo-liberal as a modifier – neo-liberal society, neo-liberal university, neo-liberal subject – do we mean that these phenomena would not exist without neo-liberalism? Or, do we mean that neo-liberalism has merely modified already existing phenomena?

This article argues that the strong theorization of neo-liberalism does not provide an adequate frame for understanding the local circumstances attending one of its most recognizable components: measurement. We do so by examining contemporary pressures on, and techniques employed in, higher degree research (HDR) programmes. It is an educational truism that the most exciting learning experiences are hard to measure, and that the experience of being measured is hardly exciting. The experience of completing a PhD dissertation brings this issue into sharp relief, as graduates frequently encounter a mismatch between the intellectual and emotional work required to complete a thesis, and the performance indicators used to sort applicants for academic positions, which may only have a tangential relationship to the substantive achievements of the thesis. But singular learning experiences are difficult to incorporate into staff meetings, curriculum reviews or institution-wide policy initiatives. Measurement can therefore arrive as a way of 'getting things done' in finite decision-making environments, even when this involves drawing upon impoverished representations of lived experiences. Rather than understanding measurement practices according to the criteria of naturalism that would seek to represent the world 'as it is', we understand such practices as material signs with varying degrees of embeddedness in social and institutional worlds. In this context, the article argues that many critiques of neo-liberalism do not sufficiently advance alternative ways to think about the purposes of higher education, and that correspondingly, 'neo-liberalization' does not exhaustively explain the issues attending increased measurement and surveillance practices in HDR environments. We therefore want to focus on the worlds that measurements bring into being, and on the criticisms made of these worlds in contemporary sociological research on higher education.

Measurement is examined here from three distinct viewpoints. Firstly, we revisit contemporary studies of the neo-liberal university, and consider the high premium placed on measurement as the privileged technology of institutional progress. The article suggests that metrics often become mobile sites of powerful collective investment, and that even those sceptical about the purposes of metrics can come to care about and desire certain numbers. Secondly, we focus on specific concerns raised around measurement regarding HDR. Postgraduate environments are considered by many to be the final bastions of passionate intellectual inquiry protected from the continuous measurements that attend most undergraduate programmes. The incremental reframing of doctoral study in Australian universities as an outcomes-driven pursuit places heightened pressure on educators to clearly identify those features of long-term research projects that may have immeasurable outputs. Finally, as a gesture towards imagining alternative ways of thinking about learning outcomes, the article argues that pedagogical environments need to find ways to make HDR 'failures' – non-submissions, abandoned projects, flawed ideas – institutionally worthwhile and intellectually generative. It may be that measurement cultures are best inhabited by learning how to fail well.

Measurement and higher education

The relationship between quality and quantity has widespread significance for organizations interested in measuring 'quality' practices and objects (see Anderson, 2006). In simple terms, qualities are properties that allow one thing to be distinguished from another thing. For example, blue is a quality that can be distinguished from red. Some qualities have direct quantitative correlates (blue has a wavelength of 450–495 nanometres), but many concepts describe non-quantifiable qualities. For example, the musical notion of 'timbre' has been used to describe composite variables, where no single quantity – amplitude, pitch, resonance – is completely essential to the concept. By contrast, quantification presupposes exactness in the units quantified, and there is no quantity that does not require a fixed separation between qualities. However, numerical measurements can easily become unmoored from the experiential world of qualitative differences, producing differential numbers with no sensible referent. For example, the birth rate in Australia in 2012 was 1.93 children per Australian female, and although qualities are required to distinguish one birth from another, one cannot imagine 1.93 children. Furthermore, a changing annual birth rate may be detectable only across a large-scale population, and a national shift from 2.03 to 1.93 may go unnoticed within any particular community. Used in this way, measurement practices may risk alienating or disempowering those to whom they are applied, either because the objects being measured cease to be tangible in everyday experience (1.93 children), or because metrics may suffer from scaling effects, where extremely broad trends contain little explanatory power at a local level (2.03 to 1.93). The development of proxy indicators and probabilistic inferences (see Shachter, 1988) to measure large groups – students, workers, voters – can often produce measurements more useful for the governance of a population than for assisting the practices or improving the well-being of any particular individual within that population. This opens onto the issue of the organizational structures that coordinate measurement practices.

Within institutional settings, disagreements about the purposes, frequency and effects of measurement can reflect structural conflicts between various stakeholders in the production of quantitative data. Measurement practices simultaneously reflect and modify relationships between those who measure and those who are measured. In a variation of commodity fetishism, the aura of objectivity acquired by measurement practices can mask the social power relations between managers and the managed. This may also mean that key metrics come to be defined not by their utility to individual practitioners, but by their capacity to travel upwardly through an organizational administration. Numbers begin signifying more easily as reliable 'proof' once they circulate beyond an original 'circle of belief' – that is, those who actually produced the numbers (Kamuf, 2007, p. 257). Issues of this kind are regularly raised regarding the measurement of 'learning' and 'research' in the Australian tertiary sector, and such measurements have particular impacts on HDR students.

We can only offer a sample here of the measurement practices that attend HDR programmes in Australian universities, but they are broadly indicative of wider trends. Firstly, students are evaluated for entry into research programmes and eligibility for scholarships. For example, RMIT University's 'Model to determine merit-based selection' establishes a candidate's score based on their highest qualification (up to 55 percentage points), a school allocated score (up to 15), and either a combination of recent degree (20) and publications (10) or publications (10) and relevant professional experience (20) (RMIT, 2011, p. 1). In this formula, a Master's degree by research is equivalent to 20 years' relevant professional experience, and a refereed article in a scholarly journal is equivalent to an original creative work of international significance. Once enrolled, doctoral candidates are measured at regular intervals within their candidacy, often through discrete and ordinal indicators such as satisfactory, less than satisfactory, unsatisfactory. Although many doctoral candidates will not be able to pursue stable academic careers (see Mayhew, 2014), many will learn to recognize the KPIs used to measure academic performance, especially those that could shape future employment opportunities: publication outputs and the H-Index, student evaluation scores, 'impact' scores and so on. For the measurement of cohorts or populations, university administrations frequently mobilize recruitment rates, completion rates and post-doctoral employment rates. Differentiated metrics produce a logic of continuous improvement, where strong performance is not measured according to a fixed standard (60–70, 70–80), but is oriented instead towards infinite growth and expansion (e.g., 2% per annum).

Finally, any metric whatsoever can be subsumed within a system of ordinal measurements, or rankings. Ordinal rankings for programmes, institutions, journals and publishers can have a significant impact on what Guy Roberts-Holmes (2015) calls 'data chains', with institutions modifying postgraduate recruitment practices to improve the rank attached to programmes, faculties or entire universities, and to reduce any penalties attached to HDR candidates who fail to complete (this is relevant for the distribution of Australian Postgraduate Award scholarships). Unlike interval variables, ordinal variables do not require any specification of the gap between each placement, such that trivial differences between individuals can acquire a heightened sense of symbolic meaning (see Bowman & Bastedo, 2011, p. 441). Tacit logics of ranking may also shape the interpretation of data intended to be criteria-based. For example, the Excellence in Research for Australia (ERA) framework claims to evaluate programmes 'against national and international benchmarks', but the resulting numbers frequently circulate among potential postgraduate students as proxies for 'best' or 'worst' programme (on the ERA, see Redden, 2008).

Sociologists of higher education have amply shown that measurement practices across universities worldwide can produce distorted understandings of teaching, learning or research.[1] We want to focus less on criticisms concerned with true or false representations, and consider instead how measurement practices actively modify the worlds they seek to measure (see Burrows, 2012; Redden, 2015). As studies of standardized testing have shown, learning environments cannot be subject to continual measurement without bringing into being new professional practices and anxieties responsive to metric cultures (see Redden & Low, 2012). In some contexts, metrics used to determine teaching performance or research quality may even come to be treated as compliance-based games abstracted from pedagogical or intellectual purposes (see Anderson, 2006, p. 171). For this reason, in order to better understand forms of continuity and change in conceptions of HDR, the following section examines the overlapping critiques levelled at measurement under the concept of neo-liberalism. In the final section of this article, we link various effects of the forms of measurement that attend contemporary PhD programmes in Australia.

Four critiques of neo-liberalism in the university

Contemporary scholarship on measurement in higher education has been profoundly shaped by the concept of neo-liberalism (e.g., Ball, 2015; Gill, 2016; Redden, 2015). According to David Harvey's influential approach, neo-liberalism holds that 'the social good will be maximized by maximizing the reach and frequency of market transactions, and it seeks to bring all human action into the domain of the market' (2007, p. 3). Harvey acknowledges that neo-liberal economic practices have developed 'unevenly' across the globe, and that state-sponsored neo-liberal policies have been 'partial', 'lopsided' and 'tentative' (p. 13). Nevertheless, despite the highly disparate phenomena now labelled as neo-liberal, Harvey suggests that the emergence of neo-liberal thought can be attributed to a broad historical situation: the crises of over-production in industrial and post-industrial economies that culminated in the early 1970s (pp. 11–14). This politico-economic explanation has faced numerous challenges, and Terry Flew (2014) notes that at least six distinct theories of neo-liberalism now circulate in sociology and economics. Among these, Michel Foucault's lectures on neo-liberal techniques of government have become highly influential. Across his broad *oeuvre,* Foucault traces the development of state-based institutions – schools, hospitals, psychiatric wards, the police force – that bring forth subjective dispositions through direct intervention into everyday habits, routines, desires, anxieties and so on (see Donzelot, 2008; Foucault, 2008). Rather than describing a re-articulation between capital and labour, Foucault's account of neo-liberalism focuses on its ethical prescriptions and epistemological presuppositions, including neo-liberal reconceptions of human behaviour, interest and justice. While Marxists and Foucauldians share an understanding that neo-liberalism seeks to marketize all manner of social relationships, the former tend to emphasize the erosion of collectivized labour rights and working conditions, while the latter take a greater interest in new forms of selfhood and ethical conduct that cut across class positions and socio-economic hierarchies. Such differences are reflected in the spectrum of criticisms weighed against neo-liberalism in higher education, which can be divided into four broad themes: commensuration, incentivization, corporatization and alienation. We will consider these criticisms in turn, before returning to the broader questions raised around metrics and HDR.

Firstly, there is a critique of commensuration, or the subsumption of diverse activities within a single quantitative calculation. Roger Burrows suggests that academic use-values were once properly distinguished from other value systems, such as aesthetic and commercial values, and that this distinction dissolved with the 'metricization' of the academy, which has 'flattened' culture through 'economic imperatives' (2012, p. 355). One example is the H-Index for academic citations, which combines 'the number of papers – as an aspect of quantity – and citations – as a supposed aspect of quality, into a single number' (p. 361). The H-Index as a proxy indicator for research 'quality' or disciplinary 'impact' allows universities to compare publications from diverse disciplines as if they each contribute to a solid mass of something called knowledge. Structural analysis of the H-Index algorithm shows that it tacitly rewards publishing quantity over quality, partially as a result of its failure to signal the diversity of ways that intellectual labour can produce institutional or disciplinary value (see Costas & Bordons, 2007).

Secondly, scholars have criticized incentivizing metrics, or those intended to promote workplace competition and constant self-improvement (Ball, 2015). From a Foucauldian perspective, neo-liberal governance through metrics requires remoulding subjects as competitive individuals, and therefore builds on cultural myths of self-determination and autonomy (see Stevenson, 2010). Rosalind Gill describes the calculative, neo-liberal university as 'an overheated competitive atmosphere in which acts of kindness, generosity and solidarity often seem to continue only in spite of, rather than because of, the governance of universities' (2016, pp. 46–47). While many new metrics are advertised as reflexive resources for monitoring and improving individual performances, competitive workplace environments inevitably position KPIs within a comparative frame: another's success becomes a possible sign of one's own failure. In the context of HDR programmes, fine-grained differences between students can acquire a cumulative institutional force. For any given individual, slight under-performance relative to a cohort can mean decreased eligibility for awards, scholarships, teaching opportunities and so on.

Thirdly, scholars have criticized the corporatization of universities as a response to funding shortfalls in neo-liberal climes. Henry Giroux (2011) argues for the continuing need for universities to serve democratic interests within a nation as a whole, and has criticized efforts to price the value of education in micro-economic terms. The response from some institutions has been to make some pricing mechanisms more expansive – say, by including outputs not captured by conventional metrics, such as public impact and engagement. But for humanities programmes, some scholars have advanced broader arguments for the value contained in producing the 'personnel necessary for maintaining certain cultural and ethical levels in the population at large' (Hunter, 1989, p. 446). From this perspective, HDR programmes should not be evaluated through post-graduation employment rates or per capita research outputs, but through a more holistic analysis of the wider social benefits gained from the maintenance of collective understanding around culture, ethics, social conduct and so on. As Ian Hunter has argued, there are risks in romanticizing disinterested learning, rather than identifying specific spheres – policy development, secondary education, public health – to which humanities graduates may make significant contributions (pp. 446–447). Nevertheless, the marketization of higher education does frequently punish those programmes that cannot point towards tangible vocational outcomes, and in Marxist terms, prioritizes the interests of capital investment over the quality of living for those who labour.

Finally, technologies of quantification have been criticized for their alienating effects. The experience of being measured can produce stress, exhaustion and frustration, even when no direct penalty is attached to outcomes (see Thompson & Harbaugh, 2013). Metric cultures alienate academics from their own intellectual labour by producing an 'endlessly self-monitoring, planning, prioritising "responsibilised" subject' (Gill & Pratt, 2008, p. 4). Stephen Ball (2015, p. 259) describes 'neoliberal affects' in terms of 'ontological insecurity' involving 'both a loss of a sense of meaning in what we do and of what is important in what we do'. Measurement practices can also transform social relationships within institutions, insofar as metrics come to function as impersonal and bureaucratic technologies. Burrows (2012, p. 363) argues that a regime of trust has shifted to a regime of accountability, and describes favourably an earlier era where 'collegiate discussion, the occasional argument and a few rough calculations by someone in authority was normally all that was involved in working out "who did what"'. The neo-liberalization of the academy shifts agency away from communities of practitioners towards professional managers, often working at some considerable distance from classroom spaces or research projects. Sarah Ahmed (2012, p. 117) argues that the managerial goal of achieving measurable diversity 'outputs' can often supersede any consideration of the hierarchical social structures that keep racism, sexism and other forms of exclusion in place. Numbers can therefore come to 'stand in' or substitute for the absence of concrete social and political transformations.

These four critiques foreground social values and relationships within universities that cannot easily be measured, and that may be threatened by metric cultures. Commensuration threatens the singularity of ideas and disciplines; competitive incentivization threatens workplace solidarity; corporatization threatens the social benefits attending humanities education; and metric cultures alienate individuals from their own intellectual labour and from institutional decision-making. In each instance, 'strong theories' of neo-liberalism have indicted metricization as a harm to be eradicated, and in several of the works considered so far – most notably, Gill (2016), Burrows (2012) and Giroux (2011) – neo-liberalism becomes the primary battle-ground over which a range of institutional skirmishes take place. For scholars interested in doctoral education, the corresponding question could become: how can we defend the PhD from neo-liberalism, or from neo-liberal techniques of measurement?

We are broadly sympathetic to the critiques of commensuration, incentivization, corporatization and alienation. However, these critiques raise a central sociological problem: critiques of neo-liberalism in higher education are largely devoid of neo-liberals. Neo-liberalism is understood as something that happens *to* people in institutions rather than something that happens *through* people in institutions. As indicated above, this tension may be partially reconciled by accounts of 'subject formation', wherein institutional forces are understood to compose individual dispositions through particular ways of being and doing (see Foucault, 1977). Universities are not necessarily overpopulated by individuals committed to neo-liberalism ('neo-liberals'), but they do mould individual habits and orientations to be more compliant with the marketized turbulences of academic life. However, while certain situations bring forth dispositions that conform to an economic rationality, this only happens to a certain *degree*. Strong theories of neo-liberalism need to be coupled with what Sedgwick – again, following Tomkins – calls 'weak' theories (2003, pp. 134–135). Strong theories begin with a universalizing ideology that is then addressed according to its own universalizing register: in all times and all places, is neo-liberalism good or bad? By contrast, a weak theory rejects universals and compiles its account of neo-liberalism by way of disparate and heterogeneous practices. These practices may have been *captured* by institutions shaped by neo-liberalism, but they do not necessarily originate with them. Weak theories might distinguish between measurement as an effect of latent causes (neo-liberalism, capitalism, corporatization), and measurement as a practice that enters into the life-worlds of those charged with measuring others, even as they themselves are measured.

To understand neo-liberal measurement from the viewpoint of practices, we want to distinguish between what Dutch philosopher Baruch Spinoza (1996) calls 'passive affects' and 'active affects'. Institutional practices imposed from the outside can be experienced as passive affects, because we are affected by them without having any recourse to affect these practices in turn. The experience of being measured through KPIs, for example, makes the individual passive in relation to the metrics used. For Spinoza, passive affects may be transformed into active affects when the self is experienced as a cause. Critiques of neo-liberalism focus on the passive affects of being measured, and promote forms of resistance that may be understood as *active* critique. In this way, the agency of individuals in neo-liberal settings is defined in positive, humanistic terms – the individual seeks to protect personal values and well-being against neo-liberal incursions.

However, for neo-liberal metrics to become effective, individuals must be sensitized to market (or market-like) signals (see Foucault, 2008, p. 269). In their capacities as tutors, coordinators and higher degree supervisors, academics are entrusted with the task of sensitizing others to various grades, quantities and rankings. Individuals' latent capacities to measure, evaluate, judge, advocate, deliberate and critique are constantly mobilized by techniques of neo-liberal government. As a research supervisor, the academic conveys ideas about appropriate rates of progress, journal rankings, the relative merits of various projects and so on. The experience of being measured implicitly involves training to become one who measures and who can train others to be measured. Certain scholars may even regard themselves with disdain as active causes of neo-liberal affects.

Academics do not critique neo-liberalism from an external vantage point, but rather from the situation of one whose competencies actively contribute to the markets they may seek to resist. This situation conforms to aspects of Marx's conception of alienation from the commodity form. Academic researchers *as individuals* contribute to a world of objects that disempower academics *as a collective*, insofar as present benchmarks for research performance are based on the 'dead' labour of past research (see Marx, 1974, pp. 61–63). But the situation also has immediately social and subjective elements. In HDR spaces, academics are charged with teaching others to inhabit the neo-liberal academy and its metric cultures. Furthermore, such obligations may even be met with enthusiasm. Pressures to conform to metric cultures may feel compelling because individuals are already compelled by other commitments. These may involve a love of reading and writing, a sense of fulfilment in the classroom, a pleasure in mentoring future academics, a desire for social status or simply the habitual comforts of working in a familiar and supportive social environment. Here, we follow John Clarke's argument that

> [whether] we treat neo-liberalism from the standpoint of capitalist regimes of accumulation, or as a version of liberal governmentality, most of its political work involves practices of de-

and re-articulation: reorganizing principles, policies, practices, and discourses into new configurations, assemblages, or constellations. (2008, pp. 138–139)

The desire to participate in university life and to have stable employment is not exclusively a neo-liberal one, but such desires can be re-articulated within a neo-liberal context. What Spinoza might call the 'joyful' affects of being an academic are intermingled with, rather than merely opposed to, the various measurements that shape everyday institutional labour.

In the following section, we focus directly on HDR in Australian universities. HDR, and in particular the PhD, provides an important interface between two polarized tendencies within contemporary higher education: the collective desire to develop original research that furthers disciplinary knowledge, and the pressure to produce measurable outputs that make HDR programmes sustainable within a neo-liberal organizational context.

HDR in Australian universities

Massification, marketization and internationalization have underpinned significant changes in Western universities since the Second World War, and in Australia, significantly intensified in the 1980s (Barcan, 2013, p. 6). In 1980, 330,000 students were enrolled in Australian higher education, increasing to 1,221,008 by 2011 (Barcan, 2013, p. 32). The Group of Eight (2013)[2] reported in 2013 that between 2000 and 2010, doctoral enrolments at Australian universities grew from 27,966 to 47,066 (68%), and PhD completions increased from 3793 to 6053 per year. For Ruth Barcan, 'The creation of a large and variegated [Post-War tertiary] sector … put in place all the elements required for a more prominent role for the market: diversity, competition and an emphasis on consumer rights' (2013, p. 39). The demand that universities be accountable for public funding has intensified pressures on HDR Masters and doctoral completions, which are now understood primarily as institutional 'outputs'. Students are increasingly held accountable for timely completion through regular reporting, review panels, work-in-progress seminars and informal contracts. Correspondingly, the tendency towards what Pam Green and Robin Usher (2003, p. 44) call 'fast' supervision is formalized through mandatory training modules and university registers, with a focus on the frequency of meetings, length of time for feedback on work, and progress planning and annual reviews. Christine Halse and Peter Bansel characterize the outcomes-oriented model of supervision as 'reductive' because it 'construes doctoral students, supervisors, and supervision as [simply] an aggregation of identifiable, universal factors that can be reduced to quantifiable metrics' (Halse & Bansel, 2012, p. 381).

There may be three distinct benefits to embedded measurement practices within HDR candidatures. Firstly, they can help to overcome the still widespread discourse on intelligence and giftedness. When one speaks of a 'good' project, one simply refers to the potential for 'good' future outcomes for the student. This pragmatic attitude places accreditation hurdles within their proper institutional context, rather than allowing PhD and Master's projects to become inflated symbols for intellectual genius. Secondly, metrics in HDR spaces can provide important forms of leverage when seeking to secure better provisions around research training and student support (Halse & Bansel, 2012, p. 381). With a touch of irony, the measurement of learning spaces can be identified both with increasing pressures on performance and outputs, and with the development of more holistic measurements for students' experiences of anxiety, depression and so on. Thirdly, rates of non-completion are significantly reduced through continuous measurement, which is often used to identify 'at risk' projects. The event of submission is stretched backwards across the entire candidature, so that for the contemporary HDR candidate, preparedness to submit becomes an active variable from the first day of enrolment. Correspondingly, students become sensitized to a range of positive and negative indicators about their activities, from coursework to annual reviews, to peer reviews and teaching evaluations, to publication track records and the H-Index. In this context, an 'at risk' student becomes one less sensitized to institutional indicators than their peers, or who is receiving indicators from a narrower range of sources.

However, describing measurement in this way atomizes the individual, and obscures the social processes that endow institutional signs with social meanings. Postgraduate enculturation, like academic communities in general, is organized by gossip, as a source of useful information, as a means of consolidating social relationships and as tacit training in the verification of competing truth-claims (Grealy, 2016; Grealy & Laurie, in press). PhD candidates will gossip about measurements ranging from progress and annual reviews, journal article acceptances and rejections, views on an online profile, appropriate numbers of publications or teaching appointments on an academic CV, and the ranking of institutions. Such conversations are one means by which students and their supervisors come to learn which metrics have serious consequences, and which merely operate as organizational shorthands, even if constantly called into question or debunked. The metrics that matter are also likely to change across the course of a student's candidature, from revised disciplinary definitions of 'research excellence' to national funding changes, such as the Australian federal government's proposal that university funding be partially delinked from research output (see Department of Education and Training, 2016). In this context, future research on measurement in HDR programmes might consider the social worlds developed by students in relation to institutional expectations. For the remainder of this discussion, however, we want to consider some of the issues raised by measurement in relation to doctoral education *tout court*.

The proliferation of measurement practices within doctoral programmes has met with resistance. Andrew Riemer is often quoted for recollections of an era when academics regarded students with disdain, and where interventionist supervision 'would have seemed a breach of good manners – or intolerable intrusion' (quoted in Cribb & Gewirtz, 2006, p. 225; see also Barcan, 2013, p. 14). Such nostalgic criticisms can be countered by examples of students who suffer from a lack of institutional support or coherent professionalization, and who become isolated and discontinue their study. This is not about framing students as 'consumers', but about recognizing inherent organizational flaws to any trust-based regime. More compelling criticisms can be made of the unanticipated impacts of measurement practices on research cultures. We noted above that in selection processes for HDR candidates in Australian universities, it is assumed that students will have already produced signals of excellence through performance in undergraduate and Honours programmes. This early screening of students may produce unexpected harms. A survey of scientists in Britain's Royal Society, for example, showed that 46 per cent had not received a 'first' as undergraduates (see Grove, 2016). There may be potentially adverse effects of removing from the postgraduate pool students who have not reached 'peak' performance as undergraduates. Furthermore, once a HDR programme has commenced, continuous measurement may reward projects that produce immediate results in order to satisfy institutional hurdles in early candidature. Whether enforced directly by a supervisor, or indirectly normalized through a wider institutional environment, highly measured environments provide incentives towards conservatism in topics and research design.

These issues are not unique to doctoral programmes, and many have already been raised by the four critiques of neo-liberalism surveyed above. Nevertheless, doctoral research projects do have singular qualities. Singularities cannot be broken into smaller component pieces without fundamentally changing their character. For example, the three-year Doctor of Philosophy is not a research activity that merely combines six semesters into a single accreditation hurdle. For many students, the desire to complete a PhD, and to adopt an identity as a PhD student, is not experienced merely as an aggregate of networks and outputs. Candidates recognize an important and profound difference between completing and not completing, and this difference is never equivalent to the 'amount' learnt. The doctorate therefore has a special kind of temporality, or what French philosopher Henri Bergson might call a singular *duration* (1920, p. 238). Many of the benefits frequently linked to PhD candidature require a minimal passing of time: disciplinary mastery, professional know-how, experience as a teacher, the building of social and institutional relationships and so on. Doctoral candidates are therefore not encouraged to shop around for supervisors from semester to semester, and a certain modicum of instability and confusion is still tolerated in doctoral programmes for much longer than most other tertiary programmes.

Most importantly, the extended duration of doctoral education provides a space for failure. For some students, the traces of learning are strewn across a series of disappointments, misfirings and desertions. As queer theorist J. Jack Halberstam (2011) notes, the most ambitious and transformative collective projects may be experienced by individual agents as failures. Hazardous leaps towards genuinely new research may easily be disregarded as simply bad research, even by researchers themselves. Over time, failures may be recuperated as germinal moments in successful intellectual or political endeavours, but this 'over time' provides no guarantees. Society does not transform itself by realizing the goals that it sets for itself, but by creating spaces where new goals can emerge, however much they might violate existing utilitarian calculations. Failing and abandoned research projects can do important transformative work in testing the capacities and limits of a discipline. However, recognizing the productive dimensions of failure should not amount to a reckless disregard of pastoral care. Intellectual and professional failure can be highly damaging to students, and the well-being of PhD candidates is certainly linked to the personal perception of producing 'successful', 'valuable' and 'important' work. But these terms acquire an entirely different meaning – and, we want to suggest, a much less desirable meaning – in learning environments where failure is perceived in purely negative terms. A doctoral candidate should be able to make decisions in a context where failure is understood to be a productive part of disciplinary growth, and not a sign of intellectual weakness.

Conclusion

It is difficult to write about the immeasurable worth of education without a certain degree of implicit elitism. The presence of instrumentalization, professionalization and fiscal accountability does not always mean a moral failing on the part of universities. Critiques of neo-liberalism have to recognize that collective attachments to numbers may reflect real tensions in the shifting purposes of higher education. While numbers do not necessarily produce well-formed ideas about education, there are many ideas about education that can only be promoted through the institutional force of measurement practices. Furthermore, given that neo-liberal economic thought is regularly criticized for being monolithic and reductive, it is important that 'anti-neo-liberalism' does not become equally monolithic. The institutional and political projects that conflict with neo-liberalism may themselves be extremely diverse. For this reason, scholarship on higher education is not always served well by the adoption of 'pro' or 'anti' stances in relation to metrics. The issue concerns the manner by which numbers come to take effect in organizational settings, and the extent to which effective numbers sediment as unassailable social facts. It is one thing to say that a given economic structure requires the minimal diffusion of a particular practical rationality. It is another thing to infer that a structure *optimizes* this rationality, as if each individual must repeat actions in the same way, to the same degree and to the same effect. We must therefore separate the concept of neo-liberal subjectivity, a position that may not necessarily be occupied by any single individual, from the dispositions adopted by those entrusted to comply with and administer neo-liberal metrics.

This article has made no firm prescriptions concerning the desirability of measurement practices per se. The elongated data chain of measurements in education significantly exceeds the purview of any particular individual programme, school or university, and certain metrics perceived as socially deleterious (e.g., quantified research outputs) often coexist with metrics intended to produce better social outcomes (e.g., rates for participation along lines of gender, ethnicity, ability and so on). There is an inescapable gap between the numbers that carry instrumental value in the phenomenological life-worlds of practitioners, and numbers that seem to float away into the bureaucratic abyss, only to return – sometimes without warning – in annual reports, strategic planning days or grant application processes. Whatever their manner of arrival, the forces that allow new metrics to be instituted cannot be changed simply through denunciations of neo-liberalism. The introduction of bad numbers cannot be countered by an argument for no numbers unless strong alternative visions for organizational processes or educational purposes are offered. In this context, we have made some initial steps towards an engagement with the specific constraints that attend local measurements, and argued for a thicker account of organizational practices than global commentaries on the neo-liberal university would currently allow.

Notes

1. See the Special Issue of the *Journal of Education Policy* on measurement (volume 30, number 3, 2015).
2. Australian National University, Monash University and the Universities of Adelaide, Melbourne, New South Wales, Queensland, Sydney and Western Australia.

Disclosure statement

No potential conflict of interest was reported by the authors.

References

Ahmed, S. (2012). *On being included: Racism and diversity in institutional life*. Durham, NC: Duke University Press.
Anderson, G. (2006). Assuring quality/resisting quality assurance: Academics' responses to 'quality' in some Australian universities. *Quality in Higher Education, 12*(2), 161–173.
Ball, S. J. (2015). Living the neo-liberal university. *European Journal of Education, 50*(3), 258–261.
Barcan, R. (2013). *Academic life and labour in the new university: Hope and other choices*. London: Ashgate.
Bergson, H. (1920). *Creative evolution*. (A. Mitchell, Trans.). London: Macmillan.
Bowman, N. A., & Bastedo, M. N. (2011). Anchoring effects in world university rankings: Exploring biases in reputation scores. *Higher Education, 61*(4), 431–444.
Burrows, R. (2012). Living with the H-index? Metric assemblages in the contemporary academy. *The Sociological Review, 60*(2), 355–372.
Clarke, J. (2008). Living with/in and without neo-liberalism. *Focaal, 51*, 135–147.
Costas, R., & Bordons, M. (2007). The H-index: Advantages, limitations and its relation with other bibliometric indicators at the micro level. *Journal of Informetrics, 1*(3), 193–203.
Cribb, A., & Gewirtz, S. (2006). Doctoral student supervision in a managerial climate. *International Studies in Sociology of Education, 16*(3), 223–236.
The Department of Education and Training. (2016). *New research funding arrangements for universities*. The Australian Government. Retrieved from http://www.innovation.gov.au/page/new-research-funding-arrangements-universities
Donzelot, J. (2008). Michel Foucault and liberal intelligence. *Economy and Society, 37*(1), 115–134.
Flew, T. (2014). Six theories of neoliberalism. *Thesis Eleven, 122*(1), 49–71.
Foucault, M. (1977). *Discipline and punish: The birth of the prison*. London: Penguin.
Foucault, M. (2008). *The birth of biopolitics: Lectures at the Collège de France, 1978-1979*. (G. Burchell, Trans.). Basingstoke: Palgrave Macmillan.
Gill, R. (2016). Breaking the silence: The hidden injuries of neo-liberal academia. *Feministische Studien, 34*(1), 39–55.
Gill, R., & Pratt, A. C. (2008). In the social factory? Immaterial labour, precariousness and cultural work. *Theory Culture Society, 25*(7/8), 1–30.
Giroux, H. A. (2011). Neoliberal politics as failed sociality: Youth and the crisis of higher education. *Logos: A Journal of Modern Society & Culture, 10*(2), n.p.
Grealy, L. (2016). Cliché, gossip, and anecdote as supervision training. *The Review of Education, Pedagogy, and Cultural Studies, 38*(4), 341–359.
Grealy, L., & Laurie, T. (in press). The ethics of postgraduate supervision: A view from cultural studies. In J. Aksikas, S. Johnson, & D. Hedrick (Eds.), *Cultural studies in the classroom and beyond: Critical pedagogies and classroom strategies*.
Green, P., & Usher, R. (2003). Fast supervision: Changing supervisory practice in changing times. *Studies in Continuing Education, 25*(1), 37–50.
Group of Eight. (2013, March). *The changing PhD. Discussion paper*.
Grove, J. (2016, February 16). Many top scientists did not have a first, says study. *The Times Higher Education Supplement*.
Halberstam, J. J. (2011). *The queer art of failure*. Durham, NC: Duke University Press.
Halse, C., & Bansel, P. (2012). The learning alliance: Ethics in doctoral supervision. *Oxford Review of Education, 38*(4), 377–392.
Harvey, D. (2007). *A brief history of neoliberalism*. Oxford: Oxford University Press.
Hunter, I. (1989). Accounting for the humanities. *Meanjin, 48*(3), 438–448.
Kamuf, P. (2007). Accountability. *Textual Practice, 21*(2), 251–266.
Marx, K. (1974). *Economic and philosophic manuscripts of 1844*. Moscow: Progress.

Mayhew, M. (2014). Marginal inquiries. In A. Wardrop & D. Withers (Eds.), *The para-academic handbook: A toolkit for making, learning, creating, acting* (pp. 263–290). Bristol: HammerOn Press.

Redden, G. (2008). From RAE to ERA: Research evaluation at work in the corporate university. *Australian Humanities Review, 45,* n.p.

Redden, G. (2015). Culture, value and commensuration: The knowledge politics of indicators. In L. MacDowall, M. Badham, E. Blomkamp, & K. Dunphy (Eds.), *Making culture count: The politics of cultural measurement* (pp. 27–41). London: Palgrave Macmillan.

Redden, G., & Low, R. (2012). My school, education, and cultures of rating and ranking. *Review of Education, Pedagogy, and Cultural Studies, 34*(1–2), 35–48.

RMIT University. (2011). *2011 scholarships and Rts ranking: Model to determine merit-based selection*. Retrieved from http://mams.rmit.edu.au/hflhfepzk96l1.pdf

Roberts-Holmes, G. (2015). The 'datafication' of early years pedagogy: 'If the teaching is good, the data should be good and if there's bad teaching, there is bad data'. *Journal of Education Policy, 30*(3), 302–315.

Sedgwick, E. K. (2003). *Touching feeling: Affect, pedagogy, performativity*. Durham, NC: Duke University Press.

Shachter, R. D. (1988). Probabilistic inference and influence diagrams. *Operations Research, 36*(4), 589–604.

Shahjahan, R. A. (2015). Being 'lazy' and slowing down: Toward decolonizing time, our body, and pedagogy. *Educational Philosophy and Theory, 47*(5), 488–501.

Spinoza, B. de. (1996). *Ethics*. (E. Curley, Trans.). London: Penguin.

Stevenson, N. (2010). Education, neoliberalism and cultural citizenship: Living in 'X factor' Britain. *European Journal of Cultural Studies, 13*(3), 341–358.

Thompson, G., & Harbaugh, A. G. (2013). A preliminary analysis of teacher perceptions of the effects of NAPLAN on pedagogy and curriculum. *The Australian Education Researcher, 40*(3), 299–314.

The paradox of collaboration: a moral continuum

Bruce Macfarlane

ABSTRACT
Collaboration is a modern mantra of the neoliberal university and part of a discourse allied to research performativity quantitatively measured via co-authorship. Yet, beyond the metrics and the positive rhetoric collaboration is a complex and paradoxical concept. Academic staff are exhorted to collaborate, particularly in respect to research activities, but their career and promotion prospects depend on evaluations of their individual achievements in developing an independent body of work and in obtaining research funding. This central paradox, among others, is explored through analysing collaboration as a moral continuum. At one end of this continuum are other-regarding interpretations of collaboration involving the free sharing of ideas for the common good of scientific advance (*collaboration-as-intellectual generosity*), nurturing the development of less experienced colleagues (*collaboration-as-mentoring*) and disseminating knowledge claims via a range of scholarly platforms (*collaboration-as-communication*). However, other forms of collaboration are essentially self-regarding illustrating the pressures of performativity via increased research output (*collaboration-as-performativity*), through practices that reinforce the power of established networks (*collaboration-as-cronyism*) and the exploitation of junior researchers by those in positions of power and seniority (*collaboration-as-parasitism*). Whilst collaboration has always been at the heart of academic labour its paradoxes illustrate how individual and collective goals can come into conflict through the measurement of academic performance and the way in which such audits have perverted the meaning of collaboration.

Introduction

In global higher education the word 'collaboration' has become a modern mantra. It is symbolic of the positive benefits of working with others for the advancement of science through the pooling of resources and expertise. Collaboration is widely regarded as the key to innovation in a mass participation society (Leadbetter, 2009). The benefits of collaboration include sharing new perspectives across national and disciplinary boundaries, pooling scarce resources and as a means of mentoring inexperienced academics or research students. Reflecting this discourse, universities, funding agencies, industry and policy-making bodies invoke collaboration as an essential component of modern academic life. In response to this discourse research collaboration among academics worldwide has increased significantly allied with performance measures directed at increasing rates of publication output (Postiglione, 2013). Structures have been put in place to support research collaboration, usually across national boundaries, through the development of research networks and centres of excellence promoted by national funding agencies and the European Commission (Abramo, D'Angelo, & Di Costa, 2009; Griffin, Hamberg, & Lundgren, 2013). These initiatives are viewed as doubly beneficial in building cross-national critical capacity to tackle big research problems and provide economies of scale that promote administrative efficiency.

An added virtue of collaboration here is the way in which it is seen as a socially responsible means of bringing together academics to address research areas that are regarded as critical to the future of global society, such as climate change (Parker, Vermeulen, & Penders, 2010). This is the ideal of disinterestedness, as identified by Merton (1973b), where scientists come together in pursuit of discoveries that benefit mankind rather than personal glory. University-wide research initiatives and strategies seek to bring together resources in niche areas or address institutional research themes such as the four 'grand challenges' of global health, sustainable cities, intercultural interaction and human wellbeing identified by University College London (2016).

At the faculty or departmental level, collaboration between academics is encouraged via the creation of research centres or 'clusters' directed, in part, at encouraging the growth of research cultures and mentoring practices (Lucas, 2009). University–industry partnerships are seen as a further way of increasing competitiveness and wealth creation (Barnes, Pashby, & Gibbons, 2002) whilst others see collaboration as a democratic and inclusive concept enabling academics, students and practitioners to become 'co-producers' of knowledge in a partnership model of working (Healey, Marquis, & Vajoczki, 2013; McCulloch, 2009). In short, collaboration is generally assumed to be 'a good thing' that warrants encouragement (Katz & Martin, 1997). The unproblematic nature of collaboration is conveyed by Chrislip and Larson's (1994, p. 5) widely cited definition in which they refer to a 'mutually beneficial relationship between two or more parties who work together toward common goals by sharing knowledge, learning, responsibility, authority and accountability for achieving results'.

Yet, collaboration is a paradoxical and potentially more problematic concept than received wisdom might suggest. The Oxford English Dictionary provides two contrasting definitions of the word 'collaboration'. The first is the one that is probably in most common usage and refers to 'the action of working with someone to produce something'. The second definition is less benign and refers to 'traitorous cooperation with an enemy' (OED, 2016, online). Hence, the word collaboration is a contronym inasmuch as it can have opposite or contradictory meanings depending on the context in which it is used. Symbolic of this tension is the way that the word collaboration is sometimes juxtaposed with that of competition (Van Den Besselaar, Hemlin, & Van Der Weijden, 2012). In a higher education context this tension is played out in the way in which academic staff are exhorted to collaborate, particularly in respect to research activities, yet their career and promotion prospects depend increasingly on evaluations of their individual achievements as authors and in obtaining research funding. Academic careers and reputations are built on the number of papers that academic staff have to their name (Van Den Besselaar et al., 2012). Although collaboration might play a significant role in publication and research projects, being a first named author (typically first named in humanities and social science, and last named in natural sciences) or project principal investigator continues to be judged as a critical measure of a successful academic career.

These contradictions or paradoxes are evident in the manner in which the word 'collaboration' is used as part of the sacred vocabulary of the measured university. This vocabulary includes other under-examined yet widely asserted mantras such as collegiality that have also attracted critical scrutiny in this journal (Kligyte & Barrie, 2014). The complex nature of academic collaboration requires a similar level of interrogation. Subsequent analysis will identify six forms of collaboration comprising a continuum of moral permissibility stretching from *collaboration-as-intellectual generosity* to *collaboration-as-parasitism*. Constructing a moral continuum is a feature in evaluating a spectrum of ethical positions in representing controversial social issues where polar opposites exist, such as warism and pacifism (Cady, 1990) or in arguments concerning the moral merit of biotechnology projects (Fiester, 2007). Here, it is deployed as a means of illuminating the moral complexities of collaboration beyond the manner in which it is represented as an unproblematic concept in the 'measured' university. This phrase may be understood as about the increasing use of data as a mechanism for judging quality in higher education at the micro, meso and macro level.

Problematising collaboration

There are numerous forms of collaboration referred to in the literature involving university academics working with a range of different partners including their colleagues, students and research assistants (Subramanyam, 1983), with international colleagues (Postiglione, 2013), and in partnership with those from private industry (Barnes et al., 2002; Godin & Gingras, 2000). Collaboration can involve the sharing of facilities, such as equipment and laboratories, vital for experimental science; research data; socialisation of researchers across national boundaries and co-operation between institutions on the basis of spatial proximity (Rambur, 2009). Most published studies concerning collaboration are focused on analysing its prevalence in 'scientific research' (e.g., Subramanyam, 1983). This phrase is normally used as a short hand for 'physical and natural scientists as well as engineers' (Lee & Bozeman, 2005, p. 695). Hence, studies on collaboration in the biomedical sciences (e.g., Bordons, Gomez, Fernandez, Zulueta, & Mendez, 1996) are much more commonly reported in the literature than collaborative work in the social sciences. It follows that these papers are normally published in journals associated with the physical and natural sciences as well as those devoted to the quantitative analysis of 'scientific research', such as *Scientometrics* and *Social Studies of Science*. As a result, most published papers about collaboration use a quantitative method for measuring academic collaboration based on multiple or co-authorship where two or more persons publish as authors together (Smith, 1958). International collaboration is normally defined as occurring where at least one author contributing to a publication is based in a different country to a co-author, although more sophisticated measurements have also been suggested (Katz & Martin, 1997).

Whilst using bibliometric evidence of co-authorship as a proxy for collaboration is a neat and consistent means by which to carry out quantitative analysis it sheds little light on the complex social and political dynamics underlying this phenomenon.

Moreover, reliance on co-authorship data as a proxy for collaboration excludes those who may have played a role in a collaboration but may have been excluded from the list of published authors of an academic paper. Hence, whereas quantitative methods are used as a way of measuring collaboration, however crudely, few studies problematise the nature, meaning or effects of collaboration between academic researchers. A small number of qualitative studies, often based on interviews, have been carried out though (e.g., Carr, Pololi, Knight, & Conrad, 2009) and have helped to enhance understanding of the micro-politics of collaboration. The literature consists of papers concerned with the *measurement* of collaboration via the use of quantitative methods and other studies focused on analysing the *effects* of collaboration mainly via qualitative methods (Abramo et al., 2009, p. 156).

Collaboration as multiple or co-authorship is the dominant definition. However, other understandings are apparent within the broader literature. Collaboration may also be interpreted more broadly as the use of prior (published) knowledge (Subramanyam, 1983) enabling others within the wider community of scholarship to build on the understandings of others. A more active, or intellectually robust, definition of collaboration is provided by Popper who describes it as 'friendly hostile co-operation' in an academic context (Popper, 1994, p. 7). He argues that criticism is about competition between academics as well as about testing out knowledge claims rigorously in everyone's interest. Popper used the phrase 'inter-personal criticism' within a community of 'science', referring in the European sense to all academic disciplines, as a means of advancing the development of intellectual ideas and in seeking out the truth as a shared pursuit. This argument for the beneficial effects of collaboration has much in common with Merton's identification of norms aimed at the maintenance of the moral infrastructure of academic life (Merton, 1973b).

There are comparatively few papers that consider the emotional and social politics of collaboration, partly due to the focus of most of the literature on the quantitative measurement of publication via co-authorship. This may be because there is a long tradition of presenting scientific enquiry as personally dis- or uninvested practice rather than one charged with human emotion involving 'relations of power, of dependency, of loyalty, of employment, of friendship, of enmity – and a host of other factors that are rarely discussed in the context of research collaboration … ' (Griffin et al., 2013, p. 1). The realpolitik of collaboration suggests that academics need to be thought of as what may be termed 'socio-emotional entities' (2013, p. 1) rather than disinterested scientists.

This realpolitik is revealed in a number of papers where power relations between collaborators are frequently the source of discussion. Inequality between collaborators in terms of power and status lie at the heart of this literature. Collaborative research can be seen as increasing competition between researchers (e.g., Van Den Besselaar et al., 2012), as reinforcing gender inequality especially in international collaboration (Uhly, Visser, & Zippel, 2015) and hiding conflicting research priorities between researchers (Garrett-Jones, Turpin, Burns, & Diment, 2005). Early career researchers can experience collaboration as *loss* of authorship, either in respect to giving up authorship entirely to other more senior colleagues or ceding authorship credit in some form (Müller, 2012). The other side of the coin is represented in research by Lee and Bozeman (2005). This reveals that where collaboration with inexperienced or newer academics occurs it can reduce the productivity of senior investigators. Here, the mentoring relationship is described in terms of a 'tithe' (or tax) on experienced researchers that can act like a 'drag on the productivity of more experienced researchers' (Lee & Bozeman, 2005, p. 674).

This brief review of the literature on academic collaboration gives an insight into the complexities of collaboration. Broader work on collaboration processes in organisational life show that conflict, as opposed to collaboration, is a staple feature of working relationships and excessive emphasis on the maintenance of harmony in groups can be the cause of harmful effects, such as 'groupthink' (Janis, 1971). This occurs when there is an excessive emphasis on achieving consensus in groups isolating members from other perspectives. Indeed, it should not be assumed that conflict is always 'bad' whilst collaboration is 'good'; creative conflict, it has been argued, can result ultimately in better decision-making (Lishman, 1983). Naïve assumptions commonly made about collaboration include altruism on the part of those taking part and rationality in the process of collaboration itself (Booth, 1983).

Collaboration as a moral continuum

It is clear that collaboration is a slippery and ill-defined concept representing a range of behaviours and assumptions. The *effects* of collaboration are multiple and complex and need to be understood as involving moral acts, to do good by seeking to selflessly support others in the creation and development of knowledge, and disseminating empirical and conceptual ideas widely, as well as to do harm to others through behaviours involving the abuse of power and authorship theft. This section of the paper will explore six forms of collaboration in academic life represented by a continuum of moral permissibility based on the distinction between self-regarding and other-regarding behaviour (Table 1). Self-regarding (or self-oriented) behaviour refers in this context to the personal and career benefits that can be derived from collaboration that, at extreme, can result in abuses of power and position. Other-regarding (or other-oriented) behaviour is focused on the way in which collaboration is understood principally as about the exercise of academic duty and friendship in academic life to advance the interests of less experienced researchers and the wider pursuit of knowledge as a common goal for the benefit of society. In practice, scholars are often engaged in several forms of collaboration across the continuum at the same time responding to performative pressures to get involved in multiple forms of collaboration. This might include publishing more with others, advising inexperienced colleagues who are making research funding bids or producing research reports or academic papers based partly or largely on work carried out by research assistants.

Collaboration-as-intellectual generosity

Academic life is now institutionalised inasmuch as researchers belong, very largely, to higher educational establishments, usually universities. In the nineteenth century there were few universities and, thus, correspondingly small numbers of university academics. The commitment of such institutions was principally to teaching rather than research in most contexts. As a result those who undertook serious scientific research were rarely affiliated to a university. A transformation has taken place subsequently through the exponential growth in the number of universities and in their roles as research as well as teaching institutions. This means that intellectual and academic friendship is no

Table 1. Collaboration as a moral continuum.

Collaboration-as	Definition	Examples
Intellectual generosity	Sharing ideas freely with others for the advancement of science as a common good	Free exchange of unpublished ideas and data
Mentorship	Working with less experienced colleagues to encourage and support their development	Giving feedback on work-in-progress
Communication	Disseminating knowledge claims via a range of scholarly platforms	Presenting work-in-progress at a conference
Performativity	Working with others in order to increase research output or research bidding success and meet performance targets	Co-authorship
Cronyism	Practices that reinforce the power of established networks and close academic communities to new entrants involving expectations of reciprocal gifts and favours	Citation rings Unbalanced reviews Inaccurate references
Parasitism	Exploitation of junior researchers by senior academics abusing their power and hierarchical authority	Gift authorship

longer free from institutional loyalties, complicating the competitive forces of such affiliations (Emmeche, 2015).

The nature of academic friendship in the nineteenth century may be illustrated by reference to Charles Darwin's huge correspondence with many fellow botanists and other correspondents, from around the world, estimated to number around 2000. These included significant intellectual colleagues such as Joseph Dalton Hooker, Asa Grey and William Bernhard Tegetmeier. This is a high-profile illustration of collaboration undertaken well before the vast majority of academics or scientific researchers inhabited universities. It is also an example of *collaboration-as-intellectual generosity*, the free sharing of unpublished ideas between close academic colleagues in a spirit of good will and the common pursuit of truth in science.

This is perhaps the most idealistic version of the purpose of collaboration and is underscored by Merton (1973b) in his formulation of the acronym C.U.D.O.S. to represent the norms or values of research science. The first of these norms – C for communism – refers to the free sharing of intellectual property among researchers for the common good. Merton saw communism as a moral imperative along with the need for organised scepticism in subjecting all knowledge claims to the critical scrutiny of peers. This value shares much in common with Popper's stance on the importance of 'friendly hostile co-operation' (Popper, 1994, p. 7).

It is important to stress the potentially self-sacrificing nature of *collaboration-as-intellectual generosity* as it implies that free sharing of ideas is a critical moral imperative and overrides considerations of personal glory that can come when individuals are associated with discoveries or advances in knowledge. The instinct of many, especially given competitive forces, is, as reported by Rambur (2009) on the basis of interview data for scientists, to 'want to protect their ideas and their data … it is our capital' (respondent quoted in Rambur, 2009, p. 86). However, at this other-regarding end of the moral continuum the duty of the academic researcher is to work in collaboration with others, wherever they might be, in seeking answers to questions that could provide important benefits to wider society. Who receives the credit for such advances is beside the point. This is a point underscored by Weber (1973, p. 61) who offers a sobering reality check for those academics that regard research as an egotistic pursuit by arguing that every individual accomplishment is likely to be rapidly outdated or surpassed by others. This, according to Weber, is something that academics need to accept, and perhaps even celebrate, as part of a vision of collaboration based on the need to 'serve science' (Weber, 1973, p. 61).

Yet, even though collaboration-as-intellectual generosity is the idealised behavioural norm by which science advances, disputes about who deserves credit and allegations with regard to the lack of acknowledgement of others are legion in academic life with many high-profile examples such as the discovery of the structure of DNA, attributed to Watson and Crick but without, some argue, adequate recognition of the contribution of Rosalind Franklin's data (Sayre, 1975).

Collaboration-as-mentorship

A large number of authors link the purposes of collaboration to mentoring in some form (e.g., Lucas, 2009; Tierney, 2008) often implying or formally stating that such an activity is an academic duty or an inter-generational responsibility (e.g., Macfarlane, 2007; Rambur, 2009). Hence, mentoring is usually represented as an other-regarding act in terms of the moral continuum. There are a range of approaches to mentoring, including coaching, sponsorship and role modelling, represented within the literature. Even though the mentor is conventionally thought of as a senior colleague they may equally be a junior or a peer or a support group consisting of individuals occupying a range of roles and offering a wide range of expertise.

Mentoring is widely regarded as highly beneficial for doctoral students and other more junior faculty especially where this leads to publication (e.g., Long & McGinnis, 1981). Bozeman and Corley (2004, p. 609) directly identify the beneficial role of collaboration-as-mentoring as traditionally understood when they state that 'senior colleagues working with graduate students, post-docs and junior untenured colleagues is likely to pay dividends for whole scientific fields as new generations of scientists are socialized, develop skills and develop network ties'. Collaboration-as-mentoring may be further linked to a growing literature around supporting women, and other historically disadvantaged groups within higher education, in forging their academic identity and aiding their career advancement (e.g., Driscoll, Parkes, Tilley-Lubbs, Brill, & Pitts Bannister, 2009; Wasburn, 2007).

There is a tendency though for much of the literature in this area to either remain silent or ignore the problematic nature of unequal power relationships between senior faculty and more junior academics or research students (see collaboration-as-parasitism section). Being generous in sharing or ceding authorship credit to others is sometimes seen as a positive virtue of collaborative relationships but it may also be interpreted, less positively, as a gifting behaviour that fails to accurately represent relative levels of authorial contributions (Macfarlane, 2015).

Collaboration-as-communication

Academics in the normal course of their practice seek to share, publicise and disseminate their research activities in a variety of ways through the traditional medium of journal articles, books, chapters, reports, artefacts and conference papers and more contemporary forms of communication associated with the worldwide web and social media outlets. In a sense, academics are collaborating simply by seeking to share and communicate ideas bringing them to the attention of others including fellow scholars. At its most fundamental, all academic research relies, to a greater or lesser extent, on 'standing on the shoulder of giants'. This phrase, used by Issac Newton in a letter to an academic rival in 1676, is an oft-quoted metaphor for expressing the debt owed by current generations of academics to those who have attempted to answer questions and tackle problems before them. In many respects the whole edifice of academic research is based on a collaborative ethos that requires the acknowledgement of intellectual debts to others as a feature of the virtue of humility (Macfarlane, 2009).

The act of publication can in itself be classified as an unselfish act inasmuch as it may result in the sharing of data and ideas that can enable others to resolve problems or find answers to research problems, in turn.

Collaboration-as-communication is also about an opening up of research to critical interrogation by others. To some extent this demands courage to share doubts, preliminary findings and methodological problems with others at an early stage in research work, often at academic conferences, rather than withhold information that might be of benefit to other scholars within the same field.

Collaboration-as-performativity

The pressure on academics to increase their productivity is directly related in an Australasian and UK context to the introduction of research evaluation. Institutions use a variety of interventions in an attempt to increase rates of publication (McGrail, Rickard, & Jones, 2006). In the UK, the Research Assessment Exercise, dating from the mid-1980s, is widely regarded as a watershed directly attributable to increasing expectations in respect to the quantity of academic output. Similar audits of research quality have been instituted in other international contexts such as Australia, New Zealand and Hong Kong and are widely perceived as a manifestation of neoliberal policies in respect to higher education. The emergence of performance management in universities in recent years is part of a wider trend across the public sector designed to maximise efficiency and encourage entrepreneurial freedom based on free market principles (Marginson & Considine, 2000). Whereas scholars in the humanities and social sciences might have formerly produced around four or five major works in the course of an academic career, the pressure of research assessment means that their productivity has now become 'more or less persistent' leading to the attendant growth of new journals (Barnett, 2003, p. 113).

Collaboration is seen as one of the primary means by which academics can meet the demands to meet much higher levels of research output. A 20-year study of publishing patterns among university academics across a wide range of subjects concluded that the scientific article in international journals is now the dominant form of output, the number of publications per academic staff member has increased and co-authorship has become more common with levels in the social sciences starting to resemble patterns in the natural sciences (Kyvik, 2003). Other studies have concluded that academics see collaboration as leading directly to increased productivity (Carr et al., 2009). One of the other purposes of collaboration is to increase opportunities for joint research bidding particularly for funds that may require a critical capacity of academics from several different contributing disciplines (Lucas, 2009).

Tensions can arise within collaborations though due to the need for tangible outputs, often in the form of a publication of some type. Here the collectivist nature of collaboration and the individual nature of advancement within an academic career can come into conflict. It is widely acknowledged that gaining promotion requires 'an independent body of work' (Carr et al., 2009, p. 1447). This is perhaps the central paradox of collaboration as academics navigate the twin demands of collaboration and the 'insistent individualism' of the measured university (Bennett, 2008, p. 142). Despite the rhetorical strength of collaboration as a modern mantra of higher education it remains true that 'the more papers a scientist can put his/her name on, the better this is for ones' reputation and career' (Van Den Besselaar et al., 2012, p. 263). Being the first named author, at least in many humanities and social science disciplines, is a key symbol of prestige. Bourdieu (1988, p. 79) referred to it as an example of the 'symbolic capital of renown'. Determining who should be named as the first author can become a hotly disputed issue between collaborators. Even though guidelines for authorship order do exist on an international basis, there is little evidence that academics are aware of them or use them in practice (Macfarlane, 2015).

Whilst collaboration can be seen simply as a positive boom for rates of publication attitudes can vary according to the career stage of the individual academic. In their study of collaboration in academic medicine, Carr et al. (2009) found that early career researchers regarded the pressure to develop an independent body of work necessary for individualistic achievement in academic life as a 'deterrent to collaboration' (p. 1447). When early career or academics with less renown publish with more experienced or renowned colleagues the so-called Matthew effect may come into play. This means that well-known researchers tend to get more credit than less well-known authors in multi-authored publications regardless of their actual level of contribution (Merton, 1973a). It has also been suggested that certain types of highly time-consuming collaboration can have a negative effect on productivity rates, at least in the short term. Rambur (2009) argues that academic faculty involved in large-scale international collaborative projects will tend to have lower levels of research output due to the intensive demands in successfully initiating and completing such tasks.

Collaboration-as-cronyism

Cronyism is a word associated with giving benefits to friends and other close associates without regard to the claims of merit judged by qualifications, experience and talent. Relationships involving cronyism are based on gifts and favours within networks to trade privileges and opportunities without regard to merit. In an academic context, it might imply gaining a professorship, for example, on the basis of a friendship connection rather than the principles of fair hiring and a suitable judgement of relevant achievements (Emmeche, 2015). The provision of an inaccurately flattering reference may also establish a relationship based on indebtedness. In the engineering field, Tang (2000) identifies a number of examples of academic cronyism including racism and sexism in the recruitment process; unbalanced reviews of research funding proposals; unfairness in tenure and promotion processes; and gaining awards, honours and research fellowships on the basis of favouritism. Perhaps unsurprising though there is very limited literature on cronyism in academic life which Emmeche (2015, p. 44) puts down to it being '… invisible and too difficult to investigate, or simply a taboo'.

Cronyism is closely associated with the (unwarranted) benefits derived from being a member of a particular network and therefore directly related to a form of collaboration. Informally, co-citation is an indicator of close links, in terms of research topic and/or methodology, between authors and it is recognised that self-citation practices and cronyism can inflate citation statistics (Tight, 2009). Cronyism via co-citation is most common among researchers who are former co-authors or where close personal relationships exist between academic colleagues (Gipp, 2013). So-called cognitive cronyism refers to researchers acting favourably towards members of a school of thought to which they belong themselves (Emmeche, 2015). This can also occur within other types of network. Moed (2005) observed that academics in the US excessively cite the work of fellow members of the US academic community compared with scholars from other nations. Citation 'rings' or 'cartels' represent a more formal form of cronyism. This involves a deliberate conspiracy on the part of academic researchers to cite the work of other cronies within a ring or cartel each time they publish, thereby boosting their individual citation rates (Garfield & Welljams-Dorof, 1992). Other forms of cronyism connected with collaboration include review rings where members of the same academic network provide favourable reports in respect to research bids or academic papers submitted to journals.

Collaboration-as-parasitism

Popular understandings of the nature of authorship misconduct tend to be mainly about plagiarism and data fraud. However, whilst these lapses in academic integrity grab the headlines other forms of misbehaviour often connected with research collaboration lie close to the surface in academic life. Collaboration is not necessarily a partnership of equals placing more senior academics and principal investigators in powerful positions with respect to the treatment of junior colleagues. The unbalanced nature of these relationships can play out in respect to gaining authorship credit and in decisions about authorship order. It has long been known that whilst it is common for academics to publish with research students they frequently do not regard them as 'collaborators' (Hagstrom, 1965).

In discussing the virtues of academic life, Nixon identifies the way in which the lack of acknowledgement of significant contributions to the research process by early career researchers, often employed on short-term or insecure research contracts, such as doctoral and post-doctoral students, research fellows and junior academics, represents a shameful stain on the academic profession and is 'a failure of magnanimity' as a virtue (Nixon, 2008, p. 107). Sometimes the lack of acknowledgement accorded to early career and insecure research contract workers is exacerbated by publication timelines. Projects may well have concluded in terms of funding before major publication occurs off the back of the data collected and research contract workers are no longer employed by academic institutions to stake their claim to inclusion within the list of authors or even aware that publication has taken place. The position of junior academics wishing to stake a claim to authorship may be further weakened by needing to rely on a senior colleague to write a letter of recommendation to support the development of their academic career thereby establishing a continuing dependency relationship and sense of indebtedness which may diminish the extent to which they feel able to argue for a co-authorship credit. Parasitical behaviour associated with the conduct of senior academics is reported by Kwok

(2005) who labels it as the 'White bull effect', a phrase meant to convey the pressure or coercion that senior researchers use to get unmerited authorship credit. It is common practice, particularly among educational researchers in parts of East Asia, such as Hong Kong, to determine authorship order on the basis of hierarchy, by placing the senior person first, rather than intellectual contribution (Macfarlane, 2015). It is also widely accepted that supervisors should be gifted authorship by their research students when they publish on the basis of their doctoral thesis (Macfarlane, 2015). Hence, for some junior academics, in particular, collaboration can lead directly to a *loss* of authorship and can threaten the development of their own careers (Müller, 2012).

Conclusion

The emphasis on collaboration in academic life in the neoliberal university is about increasing the efficiency, performance and international impact of academic staff as well as promoting the institution as a good global citizen. However, this performative agenda has started to make some of the other-regarding forms of collaboration, such as collaboration-as-intellectual generosity and collaboration-as-mentoring, appear out-of-step, or even naïve in the measured university. Reward and recognition systems take little account of such forms of collaboration because they are hard to measure in terms of individual output even though they are essential to the nurturing of early career researchers and the advance of science as a common goal for the benefit of wider society. The stress on *measurement* in evaluating academic performance reifies individual achievement over the achievement of collective goals. Crude measurement of collaboration via co-authorship hollows out this concept and leads to greater competition between academics which, in turn, can have perverse consequences for the pace of scientific discovery (Anderson, Ronning, De Vries, & Martinson, 2007).

The moral continuum presented in this paper illustrates the complexities of collaboration in academic life as a self-regarding and an other-regarding activity. Some forms of collaboration are clearly other-regarding in intent whilst some forms are essentially self-regarding and serve to demonstrate the highly competitive nature of academic life. Collaboration-as-performativity, cronyism and parasitism are practices that symbolise the instrumentality and 'insistent individualism' (Bennett, 2008, p. 142) of the measured university. Collaboration is a paradox inasmuch as it is associated with deleterious effects, connected with the social and emotional politics and (un)ethical practices of academic life, as well as potential benefits, such as the free sharing of ideas, increased intellectual capacity and reduced administrative costs.

Whilst collaboration has always been at the heart of academic labour its paradoxes illustrate how individual and collective dispositions can come into conflict (see Jawitz, 2009) through the measurement of academic performance (or collaboration-as-performativity) and the way in which such audits have extended and have, to some extent, perverted the meaning of collaboration. What is measured (e.g., research output and impact), what counts for the most (e.g., papers in leading international journals or high status research grants) as opposed to what is left unmeasured (e.g., service activities) is indicative of the way in which only some forms of collaboration have a direct 'pay-off'. In academic life the burgeoning demands for collaboration within research groupings and in accordance with institutional or nationally determined 'themes' may further potentially conflict with one of the historic privileges of academic freedom – to individually determine the purpose and direction of research enquiry as an independent, rather than necessarily collaborative, activity.

Disclosure statement

No potential conflict of interest was reported by the author.

References

Abramo, C., D'Angelo, C. A., & Di Costa, F. (2009). Research collaboration and productivity: Is there correlation? *Higher Education, 57*, 155–171.
Anderson, M. S., Ronning, E. A., De Vries, R., & Martinson, B. C. (2007). The perverse effects of competition on scientists' work and relationships. *Science and Engineering Ethics, 13*, 437–461.
Barnes, T., Pashby, I., & Gibbons, A. (2002). Effective university–industry interaction: A multi-case evaluation of collaborative R&D projects. *European Management Journal, 20*(3), 272–285.
Barnett, R. (2003). Academics as intellectuals. *Critical Review of International Social and Political Philosophy, 6*(4), 108–122.
Bennett, J. B. (2008). *Academic life: Hospitality, ethics and spirituality*. Eugene, OR: Ankler Publishing.
Booth, T. (1983). Collaboration and the social division of planning. In J. Lishman (Ed.), *Collaboration and conflict: Working with others* (pp. 10–32). Aberdeen: University of Aberdeen.
Bordons, M., Gomez, I., Fernandez, M. T., Zulueta, M. A., & Mendez, A. (1996). Local, domestic and international scientific collaboration in biomedical research. *Scientometrics, 37*(2), 279–295.
Bourdieu, P. (1988). *Homo academicus*. Cambridge: Polity Press.
Bozeman, B., & Corley, C. (2004). Scientists' collaboration strategies: Implications for scientific and technical human captial. *Research Policy, 33*, 599–616.
Cady, D. L. (1990). *From war to pacifism: A moral continuum*. Philadelphia, PA: Temple University Press.
Carr, P. L., Pololi, L., Knight, S., & Conrad, P. (2009). Collaboration in academic medicine: Reflections on gender and advancement. *Academic Medicine, 84*(10), 1447–1453.
Chrislip, D. D., & Larson, C. E. (1994). *Collaborative leadership: How citizens and civic leadership can make a difference*. San Francisco, CA: Jossey Bass.
Driscoll, L. G., Parkes, K. A., Tilley-Lubbs, G. A., Brill, J. M., & Pitts Bannister, V. R. (2009). Navigating the lonely sea: Peer mentoring and collaboration among aspiring women scholars. *Mentoring & Tutoring: Partnership in Learning, 17*(1), 5–21.
Emmeche, C. (2015). The borderology of friendship in academia. *AMITY: The Journal of Friendship Studies, 3*(1), 40–59.
Fiester, A. (2007). Casuistry and the moral continuum: Evaluating animal biotechnology. *Politics and the Life Sciences, 25*(1–2), 15–22.
Garfield, E., & Welljams-Dorof, A. (1992). Citation data: Their use as quantitative indicators for science and technology evaluation and policy-making. *Science and Public Policy, 19*(5), 321–327.
Garrett-Jones, S., Turpin, T., Burns, P., & Diment, K. (2005). Common purpose and divided loyalties: The risks and rewards of cross-sector collaboration for academic and government researchers. *R and D Management, 35*(5), 535–544.
Gipp, B. (2013). *Citation-based plagiarism detection: Detecting disguised and cross-language plagiarism using citation pattern analysis*. Magdeburg: Springer.
Godin, B., & Gingras, Y. (2000). Impact of collaborative research on academic science. *Science and Public Policy, 27*(1), 65–73.
Griffin, G., Hamberg, K., & Lundgren, B. (Eds.). (2013). *The social politics of research collaboration*. New York, NY: Routledge.
Hagstrom, W. O. (1965). *The scientific community*. New York, NY: Basic Books.

Healey, M., Marquis, B., & Vajoczki, S. (2013). Exploring SoTL through international collaborative writing groups. *Teaching and Learning Inquiry: The ISSOTL Journal, 1*(2), 3–8.
Janis, I. L. (1971, November). Groupthink. *Psychology Today*, pp. 43–46.
Jawitz, J. (2009). Learning in the academic workplace: The harmonization of the collective and the individual habitus. *Studies in Higher Education, 34*(6), 601–614.
Katz, J. S., & Martin, B. R. (1997). What is research collaboration? *Research Policy, 26*, 1–18.
Kligyte, G., & Barrie, S. (2014). Collegiality: Leading us into fantasy – The paradoxical resilience of collegiality in academic leadership. *Higher Education Research & Development, 33*(1), 157–169.
Kwok, L. S. (2005). The white bull effect: Abusive co-authorship and publication parasitism. *Journal of Medical Ethics, 31*, 554–556.
Kyvik, S. (2003). Changing trends in publishing behaviour among university faculty, 1980–2000. *Scientometrics, 58*(1), 35–48.
Leadbetter, C. (2009). *We think: Mass innovation, not mass production*. London: Profile Books.
Lee, S., & Bozeman, B. (2005). The impact of research collaboration on scientific productivity. *Social Studies of Science, 35*(5), 673–702.
Lishman, J. (1983). Editorial. In J. Lishman (Ed.), *Collaboration and conflict: Working with others* (pp. 7–9). Aberdeen: University of Aberdeen.
Long, J. S., & McGinnis, R. (1981). Organizational context and scientific productivity. *American Sociological Review, 46*, 422–442.
Lucas, L. (2009). Research management and research cultures: Power and productivity. In A. Brew & L. Lucas (Eds.), *Academic research and researchers* (pp. 66–79). Maidenhead: Society for Research into Higher Education/Open University Press.
Macfarlane, B. (2007). *The academic citizen: The virtue of service in university life*. Abingdon: Routledge.
Macfarlane, B. (2009). *Researching with integrity: The ethics of academic enquiry*. New York, NY: Routledge.
Macfarlane, B. (2015). The ethics of multiple authorship: Power, performativity and the gift economy. *Studies in Higher Education*. doi:10.1080/03075079.2015.1085009
Marginson, S., & Considine, M. (2000). *The enterprise university: Power, governance and reinvention in Australia*. Cambridge: Cambridge University Press.
McCulloch, A. (2009). The student as co-producer: Learning from public administration about the student–university relationship. *Studies in Higher Education, 34*(2), 171–83.
McGrail, M. R., Rickard, C. M., & Jones, R. (2006). Publish or perish: A systematic review of interventions to increase academic publication rates. *Higher Education Research & Development, 25*(1), 19–35.
Merton, R. K. (1973a). The Matthew effect in science (originally published in 1968). In N. W. Storer (Ed.), *The sociology of science: Theoretical and empirical investigations* (pp. 439–459). Chicago, IL: University of Chicago Press.
Merton, R. K. (1973b). The normative structure of science (originally published in 1968). In N. Storer (Ed.), *The sociology of science: Theoretical and empirical investigations* (pp. 267–278). Chicago, IL: The University of Chicago Press.
Moed, H. F. (2005). *Citation analysis in research evaluation*. Dordrecht: Springer.
Müller, R. (2012). Collaborating in Life Science Research Groups: The question of authorship. *Higher Education Policy, 25*(3), 289–311.
Nixon, J. (2008). *Towards the virtuous university: The moral bases of academic practice*. London: Routledge.
Oxford English Dictionary (OED). (2016). *Definition of collaboration in English*. http://www.oxforddictionaries.com/definition/english/collaboration. Retrieved July 15, 2016, from https://www.ucl.ac.uk/grand-challenges
Parker, J. N., Vermeulen, N., & Penders, B. (Eds.). (2010). *Collaboration in the New Life Sciences*. Farnham: Ashgate.
Popper, K. R. (1994). *The myth of the framework: In defense of science and rationality*. (M. A. Notturno, Ed.). New York, NY: Routledge.

Postiglione, G. A. (2013). Anchoring globalization in Hong Kong's research universities: Network agents, institutional arrangements, and brain circulation. *Studies in Higher Education*, *38*(3), 345–366.

Rambur, B. (2009). Creating collaboration: An exploration of multinational research partnerships. In A. Brew & L. Lucas (Eds.), *Academic research and researchers* (pp. 80–95). Maidenhead: Society for Research into Higher Education/Open University Press.

Sayre, A. (1975). *Rosalind Franklin and DNA*. New York, NY: Norton and Company.

Smith, M. (1958). The trend toward multiple authorship in psychology. *American Psychologist*, *13*, 596–599.

Subramanyam, K. (1983). Bibliometric studies of research collaboration: A review. *Journal of Information Science*, *6*, 33–38.

Tang, J. (2000). *Doing engineering: The career attainment and mobility of Caucasian, Black, and Asian-American engineers*. Lanham, MD: Rowman & Littlefield Publishers, Inc.

Tierney, W. G. (2008). Trust and organizational culture in higher education. In J. Valimaa & O. Yylijoki (Eds.), *Cultural perspectives on higher education* (pp. 27–41). New York, NY: Springer.

Tight, M. (2009). The structure of academic research: What can citation studies tell us? In A. Brew & L. Lucas (Eds.), *Academic research and researchers* (pp. 54–65). Maidenhead: Society for Research into Higher Education/Open University Press.

Uhly, K. M., Visser, L. M., & Zippel, K. S. (2015). Gendered patterns in international research collaborations in academia. *Studies in Higher Education*. doi:10.1080/03075079.2015.1072151

University College London. (2016). *UCL grand challenges*. Retrieved July 19, 2016, from https://www.ucl.ac.uk/grand-challenges

Van Den Besselaar, P., Hemlin, S., & Van Der Weijden, I. (2012). Collaboration and competition in research. *Higher Education Policy*, *25*, 263–266.

Wasburn, M. H. (2007). Mentoring women faculty: An instrumental case study of strategic collaboration. *Mentoring & Tutoring: Partnership in Learning*, *15*(1), 57–72.

Weber, M. (1973). Science as a vocation (originally published in 1919). In E. Shils (Ed. and trans.), *Max Weber on universities: The power of the state and the dignity of the academic calling in imperial Germany* (pp. 54–62). Chicago, IL: The University of Chicago Press.

Measures of success: cruel optimism and the paradox of academic women's participation in Australian higher education

Briony Lipton

ABSTRACT
This paper examines the reworking of gender in the measured university and the impact this has on gender equality in academia. Neoliberal market rationalities and measurements embedded in academic publishing, funding and promotion have transformed Australian higher education and impacts upon the careers of academic women in ways that are gendered. Based on a series of in-depth qualitative interviews with female academics, this paper focuses on the performative and discursive decisions women make in regards to their academic careers, and argues that the mainstreaming of gender equity in Australian universities seeks to render gender inequality invisible. It employs 'cruel optimism' to highlight how our optimistic attachment to gender equity and diversity policies as tools for improving the representation of women may be detrimental to academic women's career progression and the realisation of gender equality in academia.

Introduction

The challenges facing women in academia in Australia as well as overseas are well documented, and the need to be seen to be creating change and promoting equity fits within the neoliberal doxa of the individualised and performative university. The transformation of higher education into a (quasi)market, packaged with increased measurement and shifting values, has a significant impact upon the careers of academic women. The increased representation of female academics in many ways obscures the fact that women's participation continues to be measured and evaluated in relation to male norms, participation, and achievements and women remain largely invisible as academic leaders and respected knowledge producers. Increased measurement in the neoliberal university reveals a paradox in the participation of academic women in Australian higher education. To maintain the fiction that gender plays no role in academic career progression or ability to succeed in the higher education market ignores the material and affective inequalities experienced by academic women in the neoliberal university.

This article argues that the mainstreaming of gender equity in Australian universities seeks to render gender inequality invisible. Paradoxically, the structure and discourse of gender equity and diversity prohibit sustainable and lasting change. Universities have attempted to redress the overwhelming male dominance in the professoriate and in university leadership, framing the change as economically imperative and guided by performance and merit. Yet, women's contributions continue to go mis- or un-recognised, judged against male norms and practices (Blackmore, 2014; Morley, 2011; Thornton, 2013), making it difficult for women to gain promotion to senior academic and leadership positions. In this way, gender equality in higher education and the improved representation of women in leadership become what cultural theorist Lauren Berlant (2011, p. 1) defines as a form of 'cruel optimism', a relational dynamic between individuals and a desired object that is harmful and an 'obstacle to your flourishing'. This article employs 'cruel optimism' to highlight how our optimistic attachment to gender equity and diversity policies as tools for improving the representation of women may be detrimental to achieving gender equality in academia. When the underrepresentation of women is recognised as a result of access and participation, and institutions thus push for an increased female presence, there is a correlative concern over the value of academic scholarship in fields with a critical mass of women (Leathwood & Read, 2009; Morley, 2011). The increasing number of women 'obscures the gender imperative associated with managerialism' (Thornton, 2014, p. 13). The 'hard' sciences are considered more 'productive' disciplines and 'prestigious' since it is these masculinised fields where university leaders tend to be selected from. In comparison, the humanities and the social sciences disciplines are often most at risk of downsizing, which is also where women predominate (Blackmore, 2014, pp. 185–187; Leathwood & Read, 2009). Women's inclusion in academia brings to light their previous exclusion, and their very presence instigates a moment of change and a disturbance of the status quo (Puwar, 2004). As a result, the hyper-visibility of academic women, alongside the increased individualisation of academic labour inherent in neoliberal new managerialism presents them as threatening and liable for their own success or failure.

While there are already significant bodies of literature on gender and contemporary academic careers (Bagihole & White, 2013; Blackmore & Sachs, 2007), gender inequalities in higher education (Blackmore, 2014; Crimmins, 2016; Dobele, Rundle-Thiele, & Kopanidis, 2014; Feteris, 2012) and university leadership (Blackmore, 2013; Fitzgerald, 2014; Fitzgerald & Wilkinson, 2010), little has changed in terms of gender norms, values and assumptions that underpin Australian higher education. This paper draws upon in-depth qualitative interviews with seven female academics: Alison, Amy, Dana, Kate, Lucy, Noni and Wendy to demonstrate the performative and discursive decisions women make in regards to their academic careers. Three of the women included in this paper were in continuing full-time positions and four on full- and part-time sessional contracts. These women were located in humanities, social science, and science and technologies disciplines, and were from a variety of Australian institutions, including research-intensive and teaching-focused universities. They had all worked for multiple institutions before taking up their current positions. Verran (2010) observes that numbers can be used to maintain or develop a market. Just as the focus on the numerical representation of women in higher education places a distinct political and gendered value on their participation, a preoccupation with the number of interviews in this paper also places a constructed value on this research when every experience has meaning and worth. In the measured university, in-depth narrative style qualitative interviews highlight the complex entanglements of neoliberal and gender equity discourses. While these women's reflections are constructed and can only ever be considered as partial accounts, their stories nevertheless demonstrate the 'cruel optimism' of our investment in gender equity policies and measures, revealing the discursive paradox in academic women's participation.

The 'cruel optimism' of the measured university

Berlant describes 'cruel optimism' as a relation that exists 'when something you desire is actually an obstacle to your flourishing'. Not all optimistic relations are inherently cruel but 'they become cruel only when the object that draws your attachment actively impedes the aim that brought you to it initially' (2011, p. 1). Berlant's research explores the fantasy of 'the good life' and its perseverance in neoliberal times, and she uses this object of 'the good life'; that of upward mobility, economic security, political and social equality to illustrate why people remain attached to such fragile fantasies. This notion of 'the good life' shares some striking similarities with the contemporary academic enterprise. Our desires to be deemed proficient in the work that we do, to have our work published, to be promoted, to receive praise and recognition in teaching and in our service to our communities, are a form of 'cruel optimism', in that not all types of bodies, academic activities and knowledges are considered meritorious in the measured university. This collective aspiration for the '*academic* good life' influences our subjectivities as academics. It determines how we position ourselves as scholars, which journals we read, where we submit our research for publication, which books we review and which we buy, which conferences we choose to attend, and where we form collaborations. In our pursuit of the academic good life, Julie White observes that as academics 'we author ourselves in different ways' (2010, p. 1) and even the not-so-objective measures of achievement, that of our academic biographies, and of course our CVs, influence the types of organisational cultures we create and embed us, even unwittingly, in this fantasy of the academic good life. A belief in the future realisation and attainment of equity and diversity allows academics to experience their work as bearable. For Berlant, optimism is a formal structural feeling (2011, p. 13). It allows day-to-day life to be liveable.

In *Cruel optimism* (2011), Berlant is concerned with the state of the present moment and so too this paper focuses specifically on academic women's current experiences in order to highlight the 'cruel optimism' inherent in the promotion of academic women. Berlant's focus on the present is a mediated affect that allows us to understand the 'crisis of ordinariness', or the state by which we live, which thus enables a deconstruction of our cruel attachments. How do certain gender equity measures in the neoliberal university turn everyday academic practices into an ongoing 'crisis of ordinariness' and how do these conditions exert pressure on academics in different ways? While this paper does not adopt Berlant's methodological approach of reading patterns of adjustment to aesthetic and social contexts or apply her theorisation of a collective historicity of the present, this paper does take on her overall argument of cruel optimism as its methodological moorings. In focusing on the present, this paper uses in-depth interview material including narrative anecdotes as a method for capturing the affective dimensions of the cruel optimism inherent in the promotion paradox.

Berlant's focus on the ordinariness of the present links with my use of anecdotes as method because it allows us to think about how ordinary affects and experiences can become impasses to change (Berlant, 2011, p. 11). Anecdote captures aspects of interviews that are often neglected from analysis and can offer unique insight and affective elements of women's encounters in the measured university. Anecdotes are self-reflective narratives broadly situated within the fields of auto/ethnographies. They capture the mundane of everyday life as well as documenting something out of the ordinary and unusual. They enact both difference and sameness and allow us to interrogate that which is traditionally taken for granted (Gallop, 2002). Mike Michaels observes that 'such narratives become anecdotes by virtue of their telling', and that it is through performativity in these prior events that comes to 'enact the storyteller' (2012, pp. 25-26). The stories in this paper incite critical reflection and reorientation that make them full of significance to research on gender in higher education. Such a focus on ordinariness redirects attention away from the trauma of everyday academic life, such as the absence of women in leadership, the gender pay gap, sexual harassment and racial discrimination, and towards the mundane as a means of explaining how such a crisis is embedded in the everyday. In this way, this paper's methodological innovation is in the way it empowers the voices within it rather than to constitute academic women as victims and exploit their negative experiences.

The paradox of academic women's participation

Institutions play host to a suite of academic and workplace practices; whether they be ethics reviews, codes of conduct or sexual harassment policies, these measures have sought to improve quality and equality in the workplace. In the case of gender equity policies, such as equal opportunity, and work and family responsibilities, these have been brought about by much lobbying on the part of the women's movement. These policies can be thought of as a major step forward in that they are intended to prevent the abuse of power. They may also be used as statistical tools used to track and quantify gender equality. These measures are also operational tools for neoliberalising higher education, in that they 'assure' quality and accountability increasing competition and production (Ball, 2015; Lorenz, 2012; Naidoo, 2003). Enhancing transparency and accountability is a fundamental aspect of achieving gender equality in academic recruitment and promotion (van den Brink, Benschop, & Jansen, 2010). However, the measurement of full and equitable participation in academia is neither neutral in construction or outcomes. Such measures play an integral role in the creation of value and the social construction of our reality (Adkins & Lury, 2012; Blackmore, 2014) and they have enduring consequences. Increased participation rates do not necessarily indicate broader structural change to gendered power relations in Australian higher education. An incessant focus on gender representation, compounded by the increased monitoring and individualisation of academic labour, makes women hyper visible and thus responsible for their own success or failure. This presents a paradox in women's inclusion and subsequent progression and promotional opportunities in academia, and reveals the 'cruel optimism' of our continued investment in gender equity policies.

Lawrence Berg (2002, p. 253) refers to gender equity policies as 'empty referents', undermined by understandings of merit constructed around 'masculine norms of academic behaviour and "productivity"'. Merit is intrinsic to the narrative of contemporary academic careers. It is understood as an 'objective' requirement measured on the basis of ability, skill and achievements. However, what is made apparent through the works of feminist scholars such as Jenkins (2013), Thornton (2013), and others (Burton, 1987; Fitzgerald & Wilkinson, 2010) is that recruitment and promotion are not based purely on objective measures devoid of what Nirmal Puwar describes as the 'messiness of culture and power' (2004, p. 120). Rather, they are a complex assemblage of personal and professional patronage, of close fraternities as well as peer-review and performance indicators. Moreover, such gender measures continue to situate women's achievements in relation to the persistent masculine representation of the ideal academic. The 'academic good life' can be understood as a fantasy discourse where the world becomes 'what is wanted, regular, ordered, controllable' (Walkerdine, 1988, p. 188). The optimism that we have in the 'academic good life' is distinctively cruel because it does not disband the gender binary, but rather maintains it. Despite equal opportunity policies, institutional policy discourse privileges the ideal academic as white, male, able bodied, middle class and heterosexual as normative (Hey & Morley, 2011; Thornton, 2013). Thus, women in academia are positioned not only failing to enter certain 'prestigious' disciplines and senior leadership roles but also posing a threat to the values of the neoliberal patriarchal academy (Blackmore, 2014; Hey, 2011; Hey & Morley, 2011). Academic women's success, their scholarly achievements and promotion also breeds a feared exposure of those underperforming academics. Louise Morley describes this as an 'equity paradox', which has over time, morphed into a 'crisis discourse of feminisation' (2011, p. 227), a 'misogynistic impulse', or nostalgia for patriarchal patterns of participation and exclusion (Morley, 2011, p. 223).

The following sections present direct quotations as well as narrative anecdotes from interviews with academics: Alison, Amy, Dana, Kate, Lucy, Noni and Wendy. They explore their present disenchantment with certain purportedly objective forms of measurement and valuation in the neoliberal university, or what Berlant might refer to as 'optimistic objects', such as research output, and grant funding, and the impact these have upon their career progression.

'Twenty shitty papers'

Fantasies of the academic 'good life' are increasingly bound up in publishing practices and academics trust in the outmoded linear academic career trajectory from assistant lecturer, to professor and then senior executive (Bagihole & White, 2013; Grummell, Devine, & Lynch, 2009; Morley, 2014). Measurements of research output, a valued commodity on the international higher education economic market, are used to gauge productivity and performance. An increased focus on the outcomes of quality assurance reporting is altering the ways in which research 'quality' is measured and subsequently valued by those inside and outside of the academy. Moreover, quality of research becomes not just a matter of whether academics publish their research, but about what they publish, where they publish it and how often it is cited. I have suggested elsewhere (Lipton, 2015) that since the first full round of the Excellence in Research for Australia (ERA) reporting occurred in 2010, there has been limited critical discussion on the ways in which ERA perpetuates gender inequality in Australian universities. This is because to do so requires a radical disentanglement of the presumed purposes and values of academic work from the interests of neoliberalism.

The measured university with its rankings and performance appraisals places unprecedented pressure on academics, particularly those early in their careers that Amy finds to be at odds with the management of her more senior male colleagues. As Amy shares:

> Yeah, given they don't do anything, oh my god, they seriously don't. Not all of them, obviously some of them work extremely hard, but some of them published a paper in 1982 and haven't done anything since, except consume oxygen. Which is also kind of upsetting, like I expect to work really hard and I don't expect to have an excellent job handed to me. But we're being evaluated by these measures that just would have broken successful researchers, who have established themselves now. But if they were being judged by what I'm being judged, they wouldn't have made it.

Amy both adopts and resists the logic of measurement in that she contrasts her own productivity and diligence with that of the professor who has not published anything since 1982, therefore invoking the notion of merit. In the moment of telling this story, there is what Jennifer Charteris, Susanne Gannon, Eve Mayes, Adele Nye, and Lauren Stephenson (2016, p. 35) describe as a loosening of the academic subject's sense of self, both alert to and complicit in the ways in which the measured university accords value to certain bodies and forms of knowledge. As Carole Leathwood and Barbara Read (2009), and Morley (2011) assert, feminisation discourses situate women's achievements in relation to men's punitive under performance.

Women's research outputs are less than those of men (Baker, 2010; Bentley, 2012; Feteris, 2012; Fitzgerald & Wilkinson, 2010; Wilson, 2012); this is in part due to the fact that academic women continue to take on greater responsibilities for teaching, administration and pastoral care which are accorded less weight than research, entrepreneurialism and leadership (Thornton, 2013, p. 128). Metrification of research output becomes an obstacle to quality, innovative research. This risk averseness was not what Amy was expecting and it wore away at her academic drive:

> She sat outside in the sunshine tilting her coffee cup on its saucer and looking down into the depths of her half finished flat white. A black dog sat behind her. It followed her wherever she went. It started turning up after she'd been pinched on the bottom on a fieldwork trip, when she walked the corridors of her building to a cacophony of men whistling from their offices, their backs facing open office doors. It was there when colleagues made sexist, homophobic, and racist comments right in front of her, and it was there when she had to deal with the aftermath of a student-teacher relationship that had resulted in her mediating a sexual harassment allegation. She was angry and disappointed. So much had happened to her in the few short years she had been at her university that her sense of her academic identity had irrevocably changed, and she had begun to doubt her ability as a research academic. These experiences were making her bitter. She found that quite upsetting, to realise that academia wasn't what she had first thought it would be when she started in her new position. Her department didn't support her in her research, except when of course she won an award. 'It's all just so incredibly low risk', she thought to herself. 'Why would you take a chance on something being interesting or useful, when you could just do something that you know will work okay. You'll get a shitty paper out and then you can have more shitty papers, and then everyone will think you're good because you have twenty shitty papers.'

When these gendered experiences of being in the academy become the norm, and there is such a preoccupation with output, everyday academic life becomes an ongoing 'crisis of ordinariness'. When I asked Amy about where the pressure to publish is coming from, particularly in light of recent reportage that academics feel compelled to produce positive results at the expense of research quality (Sarewitz, 2016), I was struck by the way she individualised many external, structural pressures into her reasoning:

> I think we've put it on ourselves, I think we're just really lazy about evaluating people. We'd rather just reduce people to a number. I think we've done that, I understand there's these different expectations and benchmarking and all of that, compared to when my supervisors were ECRs [Early Career Researchers]. But I really do think that we've decided this is a good way to evaluate ourselves and we're going to go with that. Instead of actually thinking about [it in] a more complicated way.

This is how neoliberalism internalises the logic of capital, whereby we internalise and individualise our collective or institutional failings to push us to achieve and accumulate more capital (Lorenz, 2012; Skeggs, 2014). By way of thinking in 'a more complicated way', Amy is referring to the need to reflect on the purpose of academic research, on the impact of quality assurance measures on individuals and groups of academics.

Publication lists and academic CVs are 'a shrine to the notion of linear career development' (Klocker & Drozdzewski, 2012). These records and measures become key instruments of neoliberal governance within the university sector (Ball, 2015; Crang, 2007). Individuals' feelings of anxiety around academic publishing and the sector's intent on the measurement and ranking of research output create the ideal conditions for universities to justify exerting increased pressure on academics in different ways. Kate tells me how research output and her publication record were intrinsically linked to her job security. When her faculty announced, 'they were going to cut from every discipline and that everyone had to pretty much apply for their positions' in order to 'not lose them'. The restructure 'pitted people against each other'. Kate states that until this point:

> We had a really good, quite collegiate atmosphere...and so that made everyone really stressed and tense. This dragged on with all sorts of inappropriate meetings where all sorts of inappropriate things were being said at the team meetings. Then eventually I, being part-time, wasn't in the best head space, I hadn't published much for a while. I'd been on maternity leave; I'd [just] come back. Also I was only working part-time. So in [re]applying for my job, compared to the other staff in my small area, I just couldn't compete. So I got told that I was being made redundant which was one of the most horrible things I've experienced. Especially coming back part-time. They ticked the box saying they take into account that I was on maternity leave, but they don't say how or why or whatever.

Natascha Klocker and Danielle Drozdzewski (2012) ask 'how many papers is a baby worth?' While Klocker and Drozdzewski's provocation is somewhat of a hypothetical one, in the United Kingdom, under the Research Excellence Framework, each period of maternity leave equates to a reduced output expectation equivalent to one paper (out of a minimum of four) across each four-year period (Donald, 2011). Although Klocker and Drozdzewski recognise that you cannot adequately quantify research quality and output in this way, 'for those who offered up a number, the average impact of parenting a young child (for the primary carer) was estimated at around three papers per year'.

After the stress and uncertainty of her faculty's restructure and her acceptance of a redundancy, Kate since found out that many of the academics she was up against in the re-application of her position had less publications than she had and that she 'would have compared more favourably against' them if she had re-applied. For Kate, this 'was a really interesting and horrible experience'. One in which she still tries to see the positive outcomes of such an incident in a way that highlights just how embedded the fantasy of the academic good life is in the psyches of many academics; that 'maybe something good will come out of it'. She reflects that, 'I managed to get some [sessional] teaching at [another] university which was good just to see another university and meet other people and get that experience.'

'Relative to opportunity'

Competitive grants, awards and fellowship applications often include a section on 'research opportunity and performance evidence'. This allows applicants to outline any extenuating circumstances relevant to their application. This might include career interruptions, their date of PhD completion, periods spent in non-academic employment and other factors that have impacted on career progression (Klocker & Drozdzewski, 2012). Such extenuating circumstances also termed as 'relative to opportunity' in the Australian Research Council competitive grant criteria seek to provide 'positive acknowledgement of what can be or has been achieved given the opportunities available', but are not about providing '"special consideration" or expecting lesser standards of performance' (Rafferty et al., 2010, p. 5, qtd. in Klocker & Drozdzewski, 2012). Such measures are also considered to improve the gender representation of women by recognising the career interruptions and circumstances that disproportionately affect female applicants. Ideally, a focus on achievement relative to opportunity provides scope to challenge the 'existence of a singular norm' against which all academic careers are measured (Dalton, 2011, p. 5; Thornton, 2013). It implies that all candidates are thus on a level playing field, but as Amy witnesses when sitting on an appointment panel, it merely enables certain recruiters to 'put a stranglehold on candidates into accepting unreasonable or unfair working conditions'. Klocker and Drozdzewski (2012) find that 'the application of "relative to opportunity" fails to live up to its potential' and similarly Lucy does too:

> She enters the meeting room and sits down at the large oak table. The room smells of furniture polish and the oil paintings of male chancellors that cover the walls and stare down at her from all sides of the tiered conference room. The school had expressed a direct desire to focus on selecting a potential female candidate for their early career award and Lucy had been invited to sit on the panel. As the only female in attendance, her male colleagues disclose to Lucy that she had been invited to join the selection committee because they thought, 'we should make sure we have a woman on the panel'. Then, in the next breath the chair of the committee adds, 'oh, and Lucy, do you mind taking the minutes [for the meeting].' This comes in the form of a statement rather than a question. When Lucy tells me this she rolls her eyes and hangs her head in utter exasperation. 'They all looked very smug,' she said, 'feeling very good about themselves' when they added this 'special clause' to the award. Sure enough, Lucy tells me, plenty of female academics applied, dispelling the overarching gendered trend that fewer women apply for awards and grants and hence are less competitive than their male counterparts, and yet when the committee reconvened to nominate a candidate all of the women were discredited because of the gaps in their careers. This was in spite of the posed aim of the award, which was to acquire and support female early career academics. The panel, without Lucy's consensus, settled on three men. 'They all felt really satisfied that they had done gender equity' Lucy tells me. Their rationale was that 'in a couple of years' time these women would be ready for an early career award' and that 'it was too early in their careers; they hadn't done their time' Lucy said in frustration.

These men had 'talked themselves out of choosing a woman' and hence 'felt good without doing anything' all the while looking at Lucy as if for approval: Approval that they had in fact already granted themselves. 'Their focus on doing the right thing didn't go beyond talk' and inevitably the award and its funds went to a male applicant. As we talked, Lucy and I discussed the irony that in a few years' time these women will most likely be considered ineligible for an early career award, as they will be too far advanced into their academic careers. Their focus on doing the right thing doesn't go beyond the talk at the table.

This is where the act of having a policy document, or a guideline for actions required becomes what Ahmed (2012) describes as brick wall. She uses this metaphor to expose how the language of diversity prohibits change. The broadness is scope or the 'hollowness' of such language, while it 'get[s] people to the table' (2012, p. 67); such policies lack clearly defined commitments to equity, equality and social justice. Such ideals become co-opted. While 'concepts of equity and equal opportunities imply an underlying concept of social justice ... diversity invokes the existence of difference and variety without any necessary commitment to action or redistributive justice' (Deem & Ozga, qtd. in Ahmed, 2006, p. 745). The difficulty of equality as a politics is that, in legislating for equality, 'it can be assumed that equality is achieved in the act' (Ahmed, 2012, p. 11). Such policies become part of the paradox, in that they become a substitute for action and change, and yet action and change are integral to such policies.

The mainstreaming of equality and diversity is synonymous with the advent of new managerialism and the rhetoric of 'good governance' (Hunter, 2008, p. 510). Despite the presence of these policies and procedures, the discussion, as Lucy observes, is limited to only what is directly referenced in such policy clauses. There is, as Shona Hunter reveals, overdependence in the words of policy documents, and a constant return to the document can be a way of blocking conversations. She notes that there is a crucial difference between 'documenting diversity and the transformation of diversity into a document' (2008, p. 516). When universities do confront sexism, racism or indeed when their equality failings are exposed, their response is invariably a reiteration of conservative institutional values. Such language allows for the 'feel good factor' Lucy witnesses without any lasting change to the status quo.

Amy is also fed up with being the token woman on selection panels and committees 'that no one wants to serve on'. She sarcastically imitates:

> We'll have a woman on the selection panel and then there won't be any bias. We'll have a woman here and everything will be equitable. It's like no, I don't want to do that shitty job that's going to take up my time and we're going to hire a man anyway. Why don't you just think about what you're doing, and behave like a human and then it's not my job to make you accountable. Can't you just do that yourself?

She highlights that it is not women's job to domesticate the workplace or administer equity and diversity policies. Instead, academic women are needed because:

> They're equally qualified and they have something to bring, we're missing out on a lot by not having them. I think my School especially doesn't understand that that's actually part of the problem.

Puwar notes, 'the language of diversity is today embraced as a holy mantra across different sites. We are told that diversity is good for us. It makes for an enriched multicultural society' (2004, p. 1). Such gender policies separate out masculinities and femininities making women's participation whether it be at the application or administrative end of funding and grant opportunities the gender that is out of place. Amy and Lucy realise the 'cruel optimism' in academic institutions' investment in such equity policies and clauses. While they aim to level the playing field in terms of merit, they make gendered disadvantage more visible, locating women's difference as the issue.

Conclusion

Why have academics been so compliant with and for the most part, uncritical of these measures in public discourse? What further complicates a critique of this paradox in contemporary Australian higher education is that collective interests have been replaced with competitive relations (Ball, 2015, p. 259). Neoliberalism has individualised and internalised the norms of the metricised university, making the individual culpable for their own success or failure (Blackmore, 2014; Blackmore & Sachs, 2007; Davies & Petersen, 2005; Gill, 2010). Fiona Jenkins (2014, p. 49) asserts that 'what lacks market value also lacks the right to exist' and thus in order to survive, academics must uphold the fiction of the 'academic good life' by cooperating in various forms of academic measurement and valuation. Vered Amit (2000, p. 217) argues that the university 'is being remade into a panopticon in which university professors censor, police, audit and market themselves while institutional administrations strive ever harder to limit their own liability'. In academia, the value of subjects is their ability to produce particular kinds of products and research findings within the specified timescales and parameters. They learn to perform to external audits and enact a form of self-governance lest they be rendered exchangeable and dispensable (Davies & Petersen, 2005, p. 5).

Increased measurement and focus on women's representation in the neoliberal university reveal a paradox in the participation of academic women in Australian higher education. In many ways, the 'optimistic objects' that are mainstream equity and diversity policies can both improve and impede gender equality objectives. Gendered practices are imbued in gender equality measures. The development of gender equity policies and procedures, their interpretations and implementation continue to be measured and evaluated in relation to male norms of the ideal academic and understandings of participation, and achievement. Gender equality in higher education becomes a form of 'cruel optimism'. Failing a complete and collective indictment of the measured university system more broadly, there must be a move away from masculine, individualised notions of merit and academic achievement, which places the impetus back onto institutions to implement policies, practices and cultures that create sustainable gender change.

Disclosure statement

No potential conflict of interest was reported by the author.

References

Adkins, L., & Lury, C. (Eds.). (2012). *Measure and value*. Malden, MA: Wiley-Blackwell.
Ahmed, S. (2006). Doing diversity work in higher education in Australia. *Educational Philosophy and Theory, 38*(6), 745–768.

Ahmed, S. (2012). *On being included: Racism and diversity in institutional life*. Durham, NC: Duke.

Amit, V. (2000). The university as panopticon: Moral claims and attacks on academic freedom. In M. Strathern (Ed.), *Audit cultures: Anthropological studies in accountability, ethics and the academy* (pp. 215–235). London: Routledge.

Bagihole, B., & White, K. (Eds.). (2013). *Gender and generation in academia*. New York, NY: Palgrave Macmillan.

Baker, M. (2010). Career confidence and gendered expectations of academic promotion. *Journal of Sociology, 46*(3), 317–334.

Ball, S. (2015). Living the neoliberal university. *European Journal of Education, 50*(3), 258–261.

Berg L. (2002). Gender equity as 'boundary object': Or the same old sex and power in geography all over again? *Canadian Geographer 46*(3) 248–254.

Bentley, P. (2012). Gender differences and factors affecting publication productivity among Australian university academics. *Journal of Sociology, 48*(1), 85–103.

Berlant, L. (2011). *Cruel optimism*. Durham, NC: Duke University Press.

Blackmore, J. (2013). A feminist critical perspective on educational leadership. *International Journal of Leadership in Education, 16*(2), 139–154.

Blackmore, J. (2014). Disciplining academic women: Gender restructuring and the labour of research in entrepreneurial universities. In M. Thornton (Ed.), *Through a glass darkly: The social sciences look at the neoliberal university* (pp. 179–194). Canberra, ACT: Australian National University Press.

Blackmore, J., & Sachs, J. (2007). *Performing and reforming leaders: Gender, educational restructuring, and organizational change*. Albany: State University of New York.

van den Brink, M., Benschop, Y., & Jansen, W. (2010). Transparency in academic recruitment: A problematic tool for gender equality? *Organization Studies, 31*(11), 1459–1483.

Burton, C. (1987). Merit and gender: Organisations and the mobilisation of masculine bias. *Australian Journal of Social Issues, 22*(2), 424–435.

Charteris, J., Gannon, S., Mayes, E., Nye, A., & Stephenson, L. (2016). The emotional knots of academicity: A collective biography of academic subjectivities and spaces. *Higher Education Research & Development, 35*(1), 31–44.

Crang, M. (2007). Flexible and fixed times working in the academy. *Environment and Planning A, 39*(3), 509–514.

Crimmins, G. (2016). The spaces and places that women casual academics (often fail to) inhabit. *Higher Education Research & Development, 35*(1), 45–57.

Dalton, B. (2011). *Assessing achievement relative to opportunity: Evaluating and rewarding academic performance fairly* (Discussion paper, Equity and Diversity Centre). Australia: Monash University.

Davies, B., & Petersen, E. (2005). Neo-liberal discourse in the academy: The forestalling of (collective) resistance. *LATISS: Learning and Teaching in the Social Sciences, 2*(2), 77–98.

Dobele, A. R., Rundle-Thiele, S., & Kopanidis, F. (2014). The cracked glass ceiling: Equal work but unequal status. *Higher Education Research & Development, 33*(3), 456–468.

Donald, A. (2011, November 7). Levelling the playing field: Maternity leave, paternity leave and the REF. Retrieved July 11, 2016, from http://blogs.lse.ac.uk/impactofsocialsciences/2011/11/07/levelling-the-playing-field/

Feteris, S. (2012). *The role of women academics in Australian universities*. Paper presented at the Australian Institute of Physics Conference, Sydney.

Fitzgerald, T. (2014). *Women leaders in higher education: Shattering myths*. Oxon: Routledge.

Fitzgerald, T., & Wilkinson, J. (2010). *Travelling towards a mirage? Gender, leadership and higher education*. Mt Gravatt: Post Pressed.

Gallop, J. (2002). *Anecdotal theory*. Durham, NC: Duke UP.

Gill, R. (2010). Breaking the silence: The hidden injuries of the neoliberal university. In R. Ryan-Flood & R. Gill (Eds.), *Secrecy and silence in the research process: Feminist reflections* (pp. 228–244). Oxon: Routledge.

Grummell, B., Devine, D., & Lynch, K. (2009). The care-less manager: Gender, care and new managerialism in higher education. *Gender and Education, 21*(2), 191–208.

Hey, V. (2011). Affective asymmetries: Academics, austerity and the mis/recognition of emotion. *Contemporary Social Science, 6*(2), 207–222.

Hey, V., & Morley, L. (2011). Imagining the university of the future: Eyes wide open? Expanding the imaginary through critical and feminist ruminations in and on the university. *Contemporary Social Science, 611*(2), 165–174.

Hunter, S. (2008). Living documents: A feminist psychosocial approach to the relational politics of policy documentation. *Critical Social Policy, 28*(4), 506–528.

Jenkins, F. (2013). Singing the post-discrimination blues: Notes for a critique of academic meritocracy. In K. Hutchinson & F. Jenkins (Eds.), *Women in philosophy: What needs to change?* (pp. 81–102). New York, NY: Oxford.

Jenkins, F. (2014). Gendered hierarchies of knowledge and the prestige factor: How philosophy survives market rationality. In M. Thornton (Ed.), *Through a glass darkly: The social sciences look at the neoliberal university* (pp. 49–64). Canberra, ACT: Australian National University Press.

Klocker, N., & Drozdzewski, D. (2012). Commentary: Career progress relative to opportunity: How many papers is a baby 'worth'? *Environment And Planning A, 44*(6), 1271–1277.

Leathwood, C., & Read, B. (2009). *Gender and the changing face of higher education: A feminized future?* Maidenhead, Berkshire: Open University Press.

Lipton, B. (2015). A new 'ERA' of women and leadership: The gendered impact of quality assurance in Australian higher education. *Australian Universities' Review, 52*(2), 60–70.

Lorenz, C. (2012). If you're so smart, why are you under surveillance? Universities, neoliberalism, and new public management. *Critical Inquiry, 38*, 599–629.

Michaels, M. (2012). Anecdote. In C. Lury & N. Wakeford (Eds.), *Inventive methods: The happening of the social* (pp. 25–35). Abingdon, Oxon: Routledge.

Morley, L. (2011). Misogyny posing as measurement: Disrupting the feminisation crisis discourse. *Contemporary Social Science: Journal of the Academy of Social Science, 6*(2), 223–235.

Morley, L. (2014). Lost leaders: Women in the global academy. *Higher Education Research & Development, 33*(1), 114–128.

Naidoo, R. (2003). Repositioning higher education as a global commodity: Opportunities and challenges for future sociology of education work. *British Journal of Sociology of Education, 24*(2), 249–259.

Puwar, N. (2004). *Space invaders: Race, gender and bodies out of place.* Oxford: Berg.

Sarewitz, D. (2016). The pressure to publish pushes down quality. *Nature, 533*, 147.

Skeggs, B. (2014). Values beyond value? Is anything beyond the logic of capital? *The British Journal of Sociology, 65*(1), 1–20.

Thornton, M. (2013). The mirage of merit: Reconstituting the 'ideal academic'. *Australian Feminist Studies, 28*(76), 127–143.

Thornton, M. (2014). Introduction: The retreat from the critical. In M. Thornton (Ed.), *Through a glass darkly: The social sciences look at The Neoliberal University* (pp. 1–15). Canberra, ACT: Australian National University Press.

Verran, H. (2010). Number as an inventive frontier in knowing and working Australia's water resources. *Anthropological Theory, 10*(1–2), 171–178.

Walkerdine, V. (1988). *The mastery of reason: Cognitive development and the production of rationality.* London: Routledge.

White, J. (2010). Speaking 'over' performativity. *Journal of Educational Administration and History, 42*(3), 275–294.

Wilson, R. (2012). Scholarly publishing's gender gap: Women cluster in certain fields, according to a study of millions of journal articles, while men get more credit. *The Chronicle of Higher Education.* Retrieved from http://chronicle.com/article/The-Hard-Numbers-Behind/135236/?cid=wb&utm_source=wb&utm_medium=en

Counting on demographic equity to transform institutional cultures at historically white South African universities?

Masixole Booi, Louise Vincent and Sabrina Liccardo

ABSTRACT
The post-apartheid higher education transformation project is faced with the challenge of recruiting and retaining black academics and other senior staff. But when we shift the focus from participation rates to equality–inequality within historically white universities (HWUs), then the discourse changes from demographic equity and redress to institutional culture and diversity. HWUs invoke the need to maintain their position as leading higher education institutions globally, and notions of 'quality' and 'excellence' have emerged as discursive practices, which serve to perpetuate exclusion. The question then arises as to which forms of capital comprise the Gold Standard at HWUs? Several South African universities have responded to the challenge of recruiting and retaining black academics by initiating programmes for the 'accelerated development' of these candidates. The Accelerated Development Programme (ADP) on which this investigation is based was located at one HWU. The paper draws on interviews with 18 black lecturers who entered the academic workforce through the university's ADP. Employing a theoretical framework of social and cultural reproduction, we examine how racialised, classed and gendered assumptions remain deeply entrenched in the values, norms and practices of historically white measured universities in South Africa. The findings suggest that it is difficult for even the most conscious and personally invested agents to interrupt the naturalised norms and values that form part of the existing institutional culture. Agents struggle to interrupt normalised practices because of the highly valued currency of capital possessed by dominant actors in the form of white-middle-class habitus, disguised as academic experience and 'excellence'.

Introduction

Transformation of higher education has been conceptualised as encompassing equity and redress, diversity, social cohesion and social inclusion, institutional culture, curriculum and research, teaching and learning, and community engagement (Department of Education, 1997). But in the context of neoliberalism, globalisation and financialisation, universities are concerned with measuring the progress of change to predict when transformation of higher education will be achieved so as to increase their reputation and stakeholder valuation. The contested 'Equity Index', for instance, devised by Govinder, Zondo, and Makgoba (2013), seeks to measure equity against research productivity to determine 'the pace of transformation' in South African universities (p. 1). Govinder et al. (2013, 2014) conclude that while historically white universities (HWUs)[1] are high-level knowledge producers but have poor equity indices, historically black universities (HBUs) produce less research but have a good equity profile. It is clear, however, that Govinder et al. (2013) have equated transformation in higher education with racially orientated equity targets:

> [R]egardless of the different components and qualitative measures for transformation, the ultimate (and most important) indicator is that of *demographics* (racial and gender statistics) ... Our Equity Index (EI) measures the distance all institutions and organisations have to travel to arrive at the constitutional imperative of a non-racial, non-sexist and democratic society. (pp. 1–2; emphasis in original)

The 'Equity Index' has been criticised for its many flaws, some of which include the use of 'transformation as a code word for race', the separation of equity from development and educational performance from socio-economic class (Cloete, 2014, p. 1), in addition to its lack of reliability and validity (Moultrie & Dorrington, 2014). The 'Equity Index' is an example of the prevailing illusion that transformation can be reduced to the measurement of race and gender equity, which implies that diversity and institutional culture are not 'as important' in the process of working towards transformation.

Several South African universities have responded to the challenge of recruiting and retaining black[2] academics by initiating programmes for their 'accelerated development'. The recruitment and retention of black academics and senior staff members have been cited as some of the main challenges facing HWUs in South Africa, which continue, even two decades into democracy, to have academic staff profiles that do not reflect the demographics of South Africa. While these programmes do make a contribution to changing the demographic composition of the academic workforce, in this paper, we suggest that what is also needed is a radical change of institutional cultures and practices inherited from the colonial and apartheid past and exacerbated by neoliberal economic forces. We need to interrogate the experiences of covert discrimination and the practices at play in the micro-social day-to-day experiences within institutions that continue to resist transformation at a primary level.

In thinking about the special issue of this journal, 'Academic life in the measured university: Pleasures, paradoxes and politics' we consider the rhetoric of transformation within HWUs in South Africa. This paper interrogates the 'paradox' or apparent discrepancy between the measured increase in participation rates of black individuals into academia through ADPs and the reproduction of dominant white-middle-class institutional cultures through micro-social day-to-day lived experiences. Put differently, counting on demographic equity will not give HWUs the 'pleasure' of proving that their institutional cultures are being transformed so as to increase their reputation and stakeholder valuation. This 'paradox' of commitment, to equity in the measured university but not to diversity as central to academic life, is maintained by a politics of 'quality' and 'excellence' which have emerged as discursive practices, invoked by HWUs, to reproduce social class differences and maintain their position as leading higher education institutions globally. The contention concerns how equity, academic excellence and diversity could not only coexist within the university but also be co-requirements of one another.

Higher education is increasingly recognised as a key generator of new knowledge for economic and social development. The cultivation of 'ecologies of knowledges' (Santos, 2007) is dependent on equity and diversity as the cornerstones of transformation and innovation. However, the developmental potential of higher education is not easily attainable due to the racialised, classed and gendered assumptions that remain deeply entrenched in institutional practices. The current fallist student movement[3] for free education and decolonisation of the university in Africa is a turning point in history (Heffernan & Nieftagodieen, 2016). It is a critical moment of confrontation with what W. E. B. Du Bois has called 'the problem of the color-line'.[4] In other words, it is a stark reminder that whiteness comprises the Gold Standard of the 'colour-line' as evident in the widening gap between the rhetoric of transformation and the experiences of black students and academics at South African universities. The reproduction of existing patterns of power and privilege in education through normalised practices and sedimented traditions of knowledge is a moral and epistemic injustice. However, questions of social justice in higher education, transformation of institutional cultures and the politics of knowledge production are seldom raised in the global ranking industry (Amsler & Bolsmann, 2012). It is thus crucial for researchers in the field of higher education to interrogate how racialised, classed and gendered assumptions remain deeply entrenched in the values, norms and practices of historically white measured universities in South Africa, and with what consequences.

Theoretical framework

We draw on Pierre Bourdieu's understanding of social and cultural reproduction to investigate how dominant values, norms and practices in higher education come to be reproduced through naturalised cultural processes. The global ranking industry locks higher education into a competing field in which differently positioned institutions and agents compete in a constant struggle to realise their interests (Bourdieu, 1998). Discourses of 'quality' and 'excellence' are thus underpinned by 'performance measures, output-based funding, measures of economic value, tests of relevance and impact, and relations with funding agencies based on contracts, accountability and audit' (Marginson, 2009, p. 587).

Brown (2016) contends that the future value of a measured university is dependent on speculation about its ability to attract future investors, which in turn is dependent on the perceived 'quality' and 'excellence' of an entity as determined by its position in the global ranking game. Speculation about the 'quality' of a measured university implies a value judgement about whether or not an entity or person inherently possesses characteristics or dispositions considered to be excellent in relation to others (Strike, 1985). Naidoo (2004) has noted that, in South Africa, academic excellence is evaluated against the 'intrinsic' dispositions of those 'typical' students from the white schooling system (i.e., those individuals who attended private schools and former Model C schools).[5] Soudien (2010) adds: 'Exclusion in the higher education system in [South Africa] continues to be characterised, perhaps no longer formally, by racism [but] it can be rendered also in class terms' (p. 883). The structural nature of the South African higher education system continues to conflate race, class and academic ability (Botsis, Dominguez-Whitehead, & Liccardo, 2013). The HWUs in South Africa often present themselves as being associated with a tradition of academic excellence and prestige. For example, when the HWU study site celebrated its centenary, the theme was one of celebrating a history of 'excellence':

[Our HWU] has a history that has made us proud. The achievements of old [alumni] bear testimony to what we strive for: – the pursuit of excellence in all areas... Your support will see [our HWU] into its second centenary of excellence.

This claim to excellence can act as a bulwark against change. If something is 'excellent', the argument for changing it is rendered moot. Similarly, if excellence is associated with the characteristics of individuals from private schools and former Model C schools, then discriminatory practices that reproduce patterns of privilege and exacerbate economic injustice are also rendered moot. While some agents are in a position to strategically negotiate the field's possibilities to realise their own drives, others are forced to adapt to the structuring principles by sublimating themselves. Field and habitus thus account for both the potential for change and resistance to transformation. Cultural hegemony within the field is reproduced by silencing and excluding different ways of being that do not reflect the dominant, approved of, cultural dispositions (Bourdieu, 1997). Thus, the global ranking industry fosters inequitable practices, as historically and socially situated agents are not in an equal position to strategically compete for a notion of academic 'excellence' that is evaluated against white middle-class habitus in South Africa.

We will now discuss how the components of social and cultural reproduction are to be viewed through the interrelationship between economic, cultural and social forms of capital (Bourdieu, 1973, 1986). Whereas cultural capital can exist in the 'embodied state', 'objectified state' and the 'institutionalised state'; social capital is the acquisition of resources and benefits linked to institutionalised networks of mutual familiarity and recognition (Bourdieu, 1986). Bourdieu (1986) argues that cultural and social capital are 'disguised forms of economic capital [which is] at the root of their effects' (p. 24). The practices of 'new managerialism' (Clarke & Newman, 1997) in the global ranking industry are directed towards economic revenues and stakeholder valuation, without much regard to the political and social values that underpin teaching and community engagement. University rankings could thus be viewed as an indicator of consumer product ratings or 'corporate social capital' (Amsler & Bolsmann, 2012, p. 285), which provides entry into 'profits of position or of rank' (Bourdieu et al., 1999, pp. 127–128).

It is likely that agents with cultural capital entering the academic field would already have established networks from which they could make capital withdrawals. Social capital derives its durable currency from networks of connections that agents have mobilised from socially instituted formations and associations such as one's family name, class, type of school and tribe (Bourdieu, 1986). Agents utilise networks of connections as an investment strategy aimed at maintaining social relationships that can produce profits in the short or long term (Bourdieu, 1986). The volume of social capital accrued by agents, particularly in the academic field, is determined by the size of their classed networks and volume of economic and cultural capital.

Durable networks that foster relationships of mutual familiarity and trust enable agents to strategically position themselves within the field of play. Trust is 'a particular level of the subjective probability with which an agent assesses that another agent or group of agents will perform a particular action [that maintains the identity of a network]' (Gambetta, 1988, p. 217). Bourdieu (1986) posits that networks of relationships are maintained through exchange processes (of words, scarce information, favours, etc.) that reproduce mutual familiarity and recognition. In contrast, it is a 'social risk' to form networks with people outside that class because they are perceived to be untrustworthy or unlikely to perform particular actions that would reproduce the cultures of dominant social groups.

Methods

In this paper, we examine the ways in which racialised, classed and gendered assumptions remain deeply entrenched in the values, norms and practices at the HWU study site. In-depth interviews were conducted with 18 black lecturers aimed at eliciting information about their experiences of participating in the ADP and entering the academic workforce through the ADP. The interviews were approximately one hour in duration, audio-recorded and transcribed verbatim.

Data analysis

The NVivo qualitative data analysis software facilitated the coding of the interview transcripts. Pierre Bourdieu's theoretical framework of social and cultural reproduction informed the qualitative content analysis of interview data, which unfolded in three coding cycles. First, descriptive information about each participant was recorded, pseudonyms were assigned and biographical features, which might have identified the participants, were also changed. Second, the interview data were coded and categorised according to Bourdieu's key concepts of habitus, field, cultural capital and social capital. Viewed through the lens of these theoretical constructs, the experiences of the participants were analysed in relation to the ways in which racialised, classed and gendered assumptions inform the values, norms and practices of historically white measured universities in South Africa, and with what consequences.

Findings

Drawing on Bourdieu's theoretical framework of social and cultural reproduction, the two overarching themes that emerged from the data were: (1) 'approving the right type of black academics into academia' and (2) 'rejection, exclusion and invisibility'. The first overarching theme was interpreted using the concepts of habitus and social capital, whereas the second overarching theme was interpreted using the concepts of cultural capital and the rules of the field.

Approving the 'right type' of black academics into academia: informal recruitment practices

In the extract below, Maryna maintains that one must be the 'right type' of black person to gain entry into networks of power within the university field:

> **Maryna**: You see the problem with the accelerated programme for me, is that, sometimes it depends on who do you have close ties with in your department and within the institution – some sort of informal relationships – you know what I mean? And it is not easy if you do not come from a privileged background to be part of such networks. Yes, the programme has made an impact to retain black academics in some departments but you must be a right type of black person to represent [this HWU], you know.

As the 'right type' of black people share the characteristics, values and normalised practices of a dominant group, the group identity is thus reproduced and personified through black academics who come from middle-class backgrounds.

Luyanda expresses her concern with how white senior academics, as gatekeepers, have the power to 'approve' black people's access into academia.

> **Luyanda**: In order for you as a black postgraduate student doing Masters or PhD to be retained here you must know people, particularly white senior academics and they must firstly approve you as a black person and to me that is very problematic and paternalistic. So in some departments if you are not friendly with these senior white academics then you must forget it. There is this white paternalistic supervision in the process of grooming black academics that makes me uncomfortable.

According to Luyanda, the gatekeeping role, which is preformed by white senior academics, could be viewed as a form of policing in which the identity of an academic network comes to embody the dispositions and practices of its most influential members. As these dispositions and practices have been normalised, this 'approval' is based on the condition that black people become assimilated into the white middle-class institutional culture. The university's identity is sustained through networks of connections which retain the 'right type' of black graduate students who are familiar with the rules of the field that govern a 'HWU way of doing things'. The highly valued currency of social capital possessed by dominant actors in the form of white-middle-class habitus thus comprises the Gold Standard at HWUs.

Mandla, Xolani and Brenda explain how 'approved' black candidates are recruited into academia through informal practices such as receiving 'scarce information' and 'the call'. For instance, Mandla receives 'scarce information' about the ADP academic position due to his social capital networks:

> **Mandla**: While I was still trying to settle on what to do for my PhD one of my lecturers told me to contact one of the senior lecturers in our department here at [this university] to get more information about the Accelerated Programme before applying. Since I was on my PhD proposal stage and I already knew what I wanted to do for my PhD I applied and I got the job.

Mandla's relation to his former lecturer has facilitated access to an information-rich, resourceful network from which he is able to withdraw the benefits of being informed of the ADP position and viewed as a favourable candidate by virtue of his social capital.

Similarly, Xolani is trusted as a suitable candidate for a job in academia due to his relationships with people in position of power; thus, he is 'sent the call' (i.e., offered a job at the University):

> **Xolani**: I did my Honours at [another HWU] where I also got my undergraduate degree, then after my Honours actually I worked a little bit in Pretoria and it was during that year that I was working that I was sent the call for this job and so I took it. I don't think I was deliberately going to become an academic. I think I just wanted to do my Masters and this was being offered and I thought that would be nice because I enjoy teaching so that's how I got here.

It is clear that social capital networks provide a critical resource for accessing profits in the form of scarce information and job opportunities. Bourdieu (1986) shows that 'profits' accrue from one's membership in a group but membership is not automatic; rather, it is often based on the commonalities among agents (e.g., based on class, family name or prior schooling).

Brenda also notes the influence of established social relationships in the facilitation of black lecturers' entry into the university field:

> **Brenda**: In 2006 I worked a lot because I was a research assistant in the department and I was very involved with not just the tutoring. I just went above and beyond that year [...] So when I was applying for my Masters I needed the funding [but] I didn't think I would keep teaching. So what happened is that my HOD spoke to me [because] he wanted me to stick around and he told me about the ADP and asked me if I would be interested in teaching and that he had seen all the department tutoring [I had done] since 2006. So they all thought it will be a good idea for me to stay and teach.

Brenda has gained trust and recognition from agents who are powerful in the field through her investment in departmental tutoring. She concludes that the Head of Department (HOD) offered her a job because 'he had seen her departmental tutoring'. In addition to gaining recognition from powerful agents through her strong work ethic, Brenda might also be trusted as an insider who is more likely to 'fit in' and safeguard the reproduction of dominant cultural dispositions. What we are suggesting is that these kinds of informal recruitment practices may have the (unintended) consequence of unfairness towards external candidates who have not had the opportunity to develop the trust and confidence of those who have the authority and standing in the university to make opportunities available. If external candidates struggle to gain entry into existing networks and to be viewed as trustworthy candidates by powerful agents in those networks, then the likelihood is that such recruitment practices will serve to perpetuate the dominant institutional culture. External candidates are 'unknown quantities' who face an uphill battle when their race, class and gender are very different from that of those whose trust they must win.

Rejection, exclusion and invisibility

The 'right kind' of black candidates are carefully identified by their familiarity with the university's existing 'way of doing things' and whether their embodied dispositions reflect the dominant white middle-class institutional cultures. These individuals are recognised or approved by white senior academics as legitimate candidates for their inclusion into academia. Conversely, Sibahle notes that those individuals who do not possess these characteristics or do not want to be the 'right kind' of black candidates are alienated by the institutional culture:

> **Sibahle**: Some little things just demonstrate what [this university] is all about, [for instance] I am not that right sort of black person and so that institutional culture is very alienating. I am not that sort of right person for them and I don't want to be.

However, the findings suggest the 'approved' candidates who embody the dominant dispositions are also made to feel excluded, rejected and invisible when they attempt to interrupt the dominant institutional culture of the university. Sinazo's department, for instance, could be viewed as a field in which agents, who hold differing amounts of capital, struggle to preserve or transform the existing values, orientations and institutional practices.

In the extract below, Sinazo explains how alienating an institutional culture can be for newcomers whose suggestions about changing existing practices are rejected:

> **Sinazo**: I came into a department that was a little bit divided, as there was a very conservative force on the one hand that wanted things to stay the same, and there was a group of academics who wanted things to change. I came in with the assumption that I was brought in to help change [but] I really got the impression that the older established academics didn't want that. So my very presence and experience from elsewhere to them was very annoying so we fought a bit. For example our department is teaching intensive and I made the point which I thought was very obvious [that] no other university in the country [has so many tutorials]. There are other ways that universities have operated and this has been a major point of contention: that the 'university's way of doing things' is based on the tutorial system. But I immediately stepped on the wrong feet. I thought we're not helping ourselves and we're not helping our students but it is just an old way of thinking that doesn't gel with the reality of this institution right now.

As 'older established academics' operate according to existing norms or the 'HWU way of doing things', they are able to use insider knowledge to their own advantage while simultaneously devaluing outside expertise and rendering newcomers in a subordinate position. It is evident that not all agents in a field compete on equal terms because 'older established academics' possess large volumes of capital, which enable them to defend the 'HWU way of doing things', and preserve old existing normalised traditional practices in a field. Sinazo is viewed as a guest whose 'presence is annoying' rather than a legitimate member of the academic community. This is what Yuval-Davis (2011, p. 10) has referred to as the politics of belonging which entails a 'specific political project aimed at constructing belonging to particular collectivity/ies which are themselves being constructed in these projects in very specific ways and in very specific boundaries'. In other words, the 'older established academics' play a central role in 'the binding and marking of symbolic boundaries' (Hall, 1996, p. 17) by constructing belonging (or the rules of the game) to a particular collectivity that embodies white, masculine, middle-class dispositions with the aim of reproducing the university's 'old way of thinking' and the identity of the normative group.

Similarly, Xolani notes that the large amounts of capital possessed by dominant actors enable them to exclude newcomers from decision-making processes and thus reproduce existing curriculum development practices:

> **Xolani**: If we look at institutional culture there are two parts; we change the representation of the staff but we need to also change how we view and understand knowledge in the context in which we are creating this diversity. [In a course within my department] there was an option between this [book], which is by people in Oxford University, and then we had a South African book about what happens in South Africa and how we apply this Global North knowledge in our context. But the decision was made by staff to use this book that was created at Oxford University. But how can we acknowledge, understand and push for transformation when we base our knowledge production on the Global North? So there is a discrepancy [between] what we believe and what our principles are and how we are implementing these [principles] or our understanding of what transformation is.

In this extract, Xolani expresses his feelings of alienation from the decision-making process of curriculum change, which has the potential to disrupt and transform privileged forms of knowledge production activities. The unequal power relations make it difficult for new agents entering the field to influence decision-making processes on issues of transformation. While Xolani and Sinazo, as black lecturers, do not have a deciding voice on curriculum development, established academics use the rules of the field to reproduce the old way of doing things in the form of 'knowledge production [based] on the Global North'.

While one of the assumptions behind ADPs is that they will have the effect of providing a pool of black lecturers to serve on committees, faculties and other decision-making bodies, some participants spoke of their deliberate decision to limit their sphere of influence and interaction in the field as a more long-term strategy to improve on their position in the field. In the extract below, Lesego explains that he has 'remained quite invisible' to the decision-making processes within his department due to his decision to obtain institutionalised capital:

> **Lesego**: One of the things I decided to do was to remain quite invisible you know what I mean. Do my teaching and do my research and not get involved in too many committees and things like that or things that will involve me in the wider institution. I did that for all the pragmatic reasons because I thought if I can be involved in that stuff I will never finish my work. The first few years I didn't do any committee work really and I didn't go to many faculty meetings.

Whereas Lesego made a conscious choice to 'remain quite invisible to finish his work', Athini's lack of involvement in institutional activities is attributed to feelings of disempowerment:

> **Athini**: I was never really involved in institutional things, especially at the faculty or those types of meetings and things because it felt like I am still just that person. So in the faculty it is more of I am just there to hear what is happening. I had little understanding of what goes on because I have been reserved and was stuck in the department getting my work done.

Similarly, Luyanda 'shrinks back' from such involvement because she experiences these forums to be unwelcoming towards young ('inexperienced') black women:

> **Luyanda**: There is an intersection of age, inexperience, blackness and womanness. The first time I would really be, like, I didn't know how to present myself in any space so you kind of shrink back.

The involvement in faculty and committee activities would enable individuals to situate themselves in positions of influence over the decision-making processes within the institution. However, the ADP lecturers' strategic position taking in maximising access to institutionalised future capital has meant that established values, norms and the existing 'ways of doing things' remain unscathed.

As Athini suggests, the structure reproduces itself through individuals who 'tend to adjust, manage and cope' with the 'HWU way of doing things':

> **Athini**: As an individual, I think I just adjust to these things. If you are experiencing it a lot you tend to adjust, manage and cope with these things. I don't know whether it has changed or whether I have changed but I hope my approach and understanding in things has changed.

Morrow and Torres (1995) argue that in the process of reproduction, 'some fundamental features must be preserved [through adjusting, managing and coping] as the basis of the identity of the system' (p. 8). Although black lecturers, recruited by the ADP, slowly deracialise the academic staff representation, the existing (white, middle-class, masculinist) identity of the university is retained and replicated as a result of this imperative 'to adjust, manage and cope' with the existing (inherited) institutional practices. The ideological naturalisation of ranking reproduce systems of 'networking power' (Castells, 2009) that serves to not only exclude and invisibilise but also render agents socially non-existent (Amsler & Bolsmann, 2012).

Conclusion

Our findings suggest that senior white academics possess the means of cultural reproduction within the university structure because of their power to approve the 'right type' of black lecturers into academia who share the characteristics, values and normalised practices of the dominant group. The familiarity with white-middle-class culture is seen as a dispositional feature necessary to reproduce the institutional image and the university's existing 'way of doing things' or the only way of maintaining academic 'excellence'. Social capital, in the field where this study took place, takes the form of white-middle-class habitus, where those who went to private schools and former Model C schools are seen as safe options to safeguard the institutional culture. Thus, social capital is an instrument employed by dominant actors to sustain and reproduce an institutional identity that is founded on racialised and classed assumptions.

This is not to say that dominant actors collude with one another to exclude outsiders and maintain their positions of power; instead, the field of higher education in a global competitive environment acts as a mirror to a social space 'that permits the realization of social classification in guises that allow it to be accomplished invisibly. In this way, universities contribute to the "misrecognition" and therefore "naturalization" of structures of domination' (Naidoo, 2004, p. 460). When the naturalisation and inevitability of rankings are viewed as matters of fact rather than political positions, it perpetuates 'the belief that the dominant are endowed with the properties of nature that legitimate them to rule' (Wacquant, 1993, p. 28). The normalisation and legitimisation of rankings, which serves the interests of dominant actors, are represented as equal opportunity for all thus reproducing inequitable practices due to the fact that agents do not compete on a level playing field (Amsler & Bolsmann, 2012).

The institution reproduces itself in its own image reflected by the most influential members in its network who have the power to decide who will and will not be hailed into those networks. The recognition of potential network members is likely to be shaped by the values and predispositions of dominant actors. These social relationships work to include as well as exclude particular people from academic representation. What we have suggested is that the insiders who benefit from these networks possess the dispositions that are aligned with the dominant institutional values and norms. When people in positions of influence in these networks are predominantly white, male and middle class, then the dispositions that are normalised by these networks will be white, masculine and middle class. Outsiders often fail to be included into social networks because they are viewed as lacking dominant cultural dispositions, which are constructed as a prerequisite for academic representation, or as a risk.

Most of the ADP academics were former students of their respective departments and informally recruited by their lecturers. These academics had effectively been socialised into the university's culture. However, while these academics may possess the institutionalised and embodied cultural capital that is recognised and valued by those in positions of influence in the university, this does not immunise them from cultural alienation and self-doubt in decision-making which limits their agency to effect transformation and interrupt the dominant practices. This finding alerts us to the fact that dominant–subordinate positions are dependent on one's volume of capital that shape and maintain specific rules of the field. Agents use the rules of the field, consciously or unconsciously, to transform or preserve university practices. The possession of or access to privileged networks of social capital is a powerful resource for realising these aims. Bourdieu (in Wacquant, 1993) posits that while power is reproduced culturally, it is socially grounded in the material world. Drawing on the work of Bourdieu (in Wacquant, 1993), Amsler and Bolsmann (2012) argue that the global ranking industry strategically reproduces social inequality by obscuring 'struggles of unequal power as struggles for meritocratic recognition' (p. 294).

Our findings suggest that the consequences of such normalised practices result in black academics feeling excluded, rejected and invisible and that their ability to interrupt the fundamental features of dominant raced, classed and gendered institutional practices and cultures is limited. Existing unequal structural power relations, disguised as neutral and objective values of academic experience and 'excellence', are used by players in the field to sustain their own privileged position and to reproduce the institution in their own image. In this way, the ability of the ADP academics to interrupt prevailing institutional cultures is blunted, as they tend to 'adjust, manage and cope', thus reproducing the dominant institutional values and norms which serve to perpetuate alienation, marginalisation and exclusion. In Lyotardian terms, the field becomes a game of performativity in which performance is measured as an end in itself, with little regard to teaching and community engagement. As noted by Marginson (2009), '[a]ll universities have stronger incentives to put performance ahead of social access [in] a rankings-based *reputational race*' (p. 595, emphasis added).

For instance, the contested 'Equity Index' arranges universities according to their equity profiles in relation to research status, thus constructing a reputational hierarchy in which HWUs are not represented as high-level knowledge producers but as leading universities (Marginson, 2009). As a result, the divisions between HWUs and HBUs gain legitimacy through reputational rankings that evaluate the quality of qualifications from privileged HWUs in comparison to historically disadvantaged black universities. Global university ranking systems thus reproduce prestige, privilege and power through the naturalisation of the 'principles that make [ranking] possible: elitism, hierarchy, inequality and competition' (Amsler & Bolsmann, 2012, p. 293).

This paper has focused on unequal power relations structured by principles of the HWU field to the exclusion of the internal structuring or content of a field; this is an acknowledged limitation of the study. As Bernstein's (1996) theory accounts for the internal structuring of knowledge in a field and the potential for change, further research could explore the ways in which the participants' disciplines have shaped their social relations in the field and how this has affected their decision-making processes on issues of transformation.

Notes

1. In the apartheid era, the differentiation of the higher education system along racial and ethnic lines not only resulted in HWUs and historically black universities (HBUs), but inequalities

were also shaped along these lines. For instance, whilst HWUs (English and Afrikaans-speaking) were located in urban areas and positioned as institutions of research, HBUs were ethnic-based institutions that were marginalised by their rural locations and limited to being institutions of teaching. Robus and Macleod (2006) propose that this urban–rural divide has created 'white space as the desirable, urban centre and black space as the undesirable, rural periphery [which] dovetails with a discourse of "white excellence/black failure"' (p. 473). Currently, HWUs remain advantaged and elitist while HBUs remain disadvantaged and under-resourced.
2. We use the apartheid-era racial categories as redress measures. 'Black' is utilised in this chapter as an overarching term for African, Coloured (mixed-race) and Indian individuals.
3. The current fallist student movement began in 2015 at South African universities under the banners of #RhodesMustFall and #FeesMustFall to protest the increase of university fees and demand for the decolonisation of institutional practices and curricula (Heffernan & Nieftagodieen, 2016).
4. The colour-line refers to race and racism in society, or as W. E. B. Du Bois has noted:

> the problem of the 20th century is the problem of the color line – the question of the relation of the advanced races of men who happened to be white to the great majority of the undeveloped or half-developed nations of mankind who happen to be yellow, brown or black. (2013, p. 119)

5. Former Model C schools are schools that were reserved for white learners in South Africa under apartheid (Roodt, 2011). After political pressure in the 1990s, Piet Clase (Minister of Education) introduced reforms to allow previously disadvantaged groups to access white schools (Hofmeyr, 2000) in a limited and conditional way. The model system was dismantled after 1994 when a single unified state was created.

Acknowledgements

The authors would like to thank the two anonymous referees for their critical input on an earlier version of this paper.

Disclosure statement

No potential conflict of interest was reported by the authors.

References

Amsler, S. S., & Bolsmann, C. (2012). University ranking as social exclusion. *British Journal of Sociology of Education, 33*(2), 283–301.
Bernstein, B. (1996). *Pedagogy, symbolic control and identity: Theory, research, critique*. London: Taylor and Francis.
Botsis, H., Dominguez-Whitehead, Y., & Liccardo, S. (2013). Conceptualising transformation and interrogating elitism: The Bale scholarship programme. *Perspectives in Education, 31*(4), 129–140.
Bourdieu, P. (1973). Cultural reproduction and social reproduction. In L. Karabel & A. H. Halsey (Eds.), *Power and ideology in education* (pp. 487–511). Oxford: Oxford University Press.
Bourdieu, P. (1986). The forms of capital. In J. G. Richardson (Ed.), *Handbook of theory and research for the sociology of education* (pp. 241–258). New York, NY: Greenwood Press.
Bourdieu, P. (1997). *Pascalian meditations* (R. Nice, Trans.). Stanford, CA: Stanford University Press.
Bourdieu, P. (1998). *The state nobility: Elite schools in the field of power*. Stanford, CA: Stanford University Press.

Bourdieu, P., Accardo, A., Balazs, G., Beaud, S., Bonvin, F., Bourdieu, E., ... Wacquant, L. (1999). *The weight of the world: Social suffering in contemporary society.* Stanford, CA: Stanford University Press.

Brown, W. (2016, June 7). *The university and its worlds: A panel discussion* [Video file]. Retrieved from https://www.youtube.com/watch?v=s07xFdD-ivQ

Castells, M. (2009). *Communication power.* Oxford: Oxford University Press.

Clarke, J., & Newman, J. (1997). *The managerial state: Power, politics and ideology in the remaking of social welfare.* London: Sage.

Cloete, N. (2014). A new look at demographic transformation: Comments on Govinder et al. (2013). *South African Journal of Science, 110*(1/2), 15–19.

Department of Education. (1997). *White paper 3 – A programme for higher education transformation white paper.* Pretoria: Government Gazette. Retrieved from http://www.che.ac.za/sites/default/files/publications/White_Paper3.pdf

Du Bois, W. E. B. (2013). *The problem of the color line at the turn of the twentieth century: The essential early essays* (N. D. Chandler, Ed.). New York, NY: Fordham University Press.

Gambetta, D. (1988). Can we trust trust? In D. Gambetta (Ed.), *Trust: Making and breaking cooperative relations* (pp. 213–237). New York, NY: Basil Blackwell.

Govinder, K. S., Zondo, N. P., & Makgoba, M. W. (2013). A new look at demographic transformation for universities in South Africa. *South African Journal of Science, 109*(11–12), 1–11.

Govinder, K. S., Zondo, N. P., & Makgoba, M. W. (2014). Taking the transformation discourse forward: A response to Cloete, Dunne and Moultrie and Dorrington. *South African Journal of Science, 110*(3–4), 1–8.

Hall, S. (1996). Who needs 'identity'? In S. Hall & P. Du Gay (Eds.), *Questions of cultural identity* (pp. 15–30). London: SAGE.

Heffernan, A., & Nieftagodieen, N. (Eds.). (2016). *Students must rise: Youth struggle in South Africa before and beyond Soweto '76.* Johannesburg: Wits University Press.

Hofmeyr, J. (2000). *The emerging school landscape in post-apartheid South Africa.* Unpublished paper for Independent Schools Association of South Africa (ISASA). Retrieved from http://stbweb01.stb.sun.ac.za/if/Taakgroepe/iptg/hofmeyr.pdf

Marginson, S. (2009). University rankings, government and social order: Managing the field of higher education according to the logic of the performative present-as-future. In M. Simons, M. Olssen, & M. Peters (Eds.), *Re-reading education policies. Studying the policy agenda of the 21st century* (pp. 584–604). Rotterdam: Sense.

Morrow, R., & Torres, C. (1995). *Social theory and education: A critique of theories of social and cultural reproduction.* Albany, NY: SUNY Press.

Moultrie, T. A., & Dorrington, R. E. (2014). Flaws in the approach and application of the equity index: Comments on Govinder et al. (2013). *South African Journal of Science, 110*(1–2), 25–30.

Naidoo, R. (2004). Fields and institutional strategy: Bourdieu on the relationship between higher education, inequality and society. *British Journal of Sociology of Education, 25*(4), 457–471.

Robus, D., & Macleod, C. (2006). 'White excellence and black failure': The reproduction of racialised higher education in everyday talk. *South African Journal of Psychology, 36*(3), 463–480.

Roodt, M. (2011). *Research and policy brief: "Model C" is the model to emulate. South African institute for race relations.* Pretoria: University of Pretoria. Retrieved from http://irr.org.za/reports-and-publications/research-policy-brief/research-and-policy-brief-model-c-is-the-model-to-emulate-1-february-2011.pdf

Santos, B. d. S. (2007). Beyond abyssal thinking: From global lines to ecologies of knowledges. *Review, XXX*(1), 45–89.

Soudien, C. (2010). Grasping the nettle? South African higher education and its transformative imperatives. *South African Journal of Higher Education, 24*(5), 881–896.

Strike, K. A. (1985). Is there a conflict between equity and excellence? *Educational Evaluation and Policy Analysis, 7*(4), 409–416.

Wacquant, L. (1993). From ruling class to field of power: Interview with Bourdieu. *Theory, Culture and Society, 10,* 19–44.

Yuval-Davis, N. (2011). *The politics of belonging: Intersectional contestations.* London: SAGE.

The mismeasure of academic labour

Angelika Papadopoulos

ABSTRACT
In quantifying and qualifying the scope of academic labour, workload models serve multiple ends. They are intended to facilitate equitable and transparent divisions of academic work, to provide academics with a sense of whether their workload is reasonable relative to their colleagues, and universities with a mechanism for rationalising the allocation of responsibilities. Existing scholarship exploring workload models examines the impact of modelling on career progress or occupational stress, or takes the form of advice from academic unions. A third body of research attempts to theorise the operational challenges and impact of workload models using small studies of their implementation. Workload models can also be seen as a 'policy technology' shaping academic identities. Priorities are signalled through the differential weighting of academic activities. In a climate of looming workforce shortages and increasing staff/student ratios, workload intensification is a managerial strategy attempting to meet institutional needs without incurring additional costs. Workload models cannot protect workers against this, but they should provide a mechanism by which thresholds of reasonableness can be defined. Analysis of workload models demonstrates that they incorporate assumptions about teaching that have been subverted by structural shifts in operating practices. Further dissonances between model assumptions and contemporary practices are illustrated through secondary analysis of responses to a survey of academic staff conducted in 2015. The unintended consequence of workload modelling's effort to regulate academic labour is a performance guided by simulacra that incorporate representations of academic work no longer reflected in contemporary conditions of practice. This performance ultimately conceals the absence of what models were supposed to achieve – transparent and reasonable allocations of work.

Today abstraction is no longer that of the map, the double, the mirror, or the concept. Simulation is no longer that of a territory, a referential being, or a substance. It is the generation by models of a real without origin or reality: a hyperreal ... present-day simulators attempt to make the real, all of the real, coincide with their models of simulation. (Baudrillard, 1988, p. 166)

This paper explores the construction of academic labour through key documents associated with workload allocation processes adopted by Australian universities. The primary materials for analysis are clauses written into enterprise agreements, principles for workload allocation and specific instances of metrics allocating academic work.

This material is complemented by secondary analyses of documents submitted to the Australian Fair Work Commission (FWC) under the review of modern awards process. For the first time in the history of Australian universities, the National Tertiary Education Union is making a claim for what is effectively the regulation of working hours, through seeking provision for payment of overtime in specific circumstances (NTEU, 2016). Working hours in academia have not previously been subject to regulation, and opponents of the union's claim point to factors such as professional autonomy and vocational dedication as inherently unamenable to regulation.

The NTEU's argument is based on surveys of academic working hours, which demonstrated that few were working 'ordinary' hours (38 hours per week), and a majority are routinely working in excess of 45 hours per week (NTEU, 2016, p. 12).

A review of modern awards is required by the *Fair Work Act 2009* every four years. The *Higher Education (Academic Staff) Award 2010* provides minimum conditions of academic labour. While universities have enterprise-level agreements that exceed the award in terms of salary entitlements, the award provides both a safety net and a standard for renegotiating enterprise agreements. Any agreement approved in the commission needs to pass the 'better-off-overall-test' in order to be considered a valid agreement.

The NTEU claim for regulation of working hours rests on the absence of limit:

> ... without a limitation in the Academic Award on the amount of hours which can be required of an academic employee, the Award does not operate as a fair and enforceable minimum safety net of terms and conditions, and cannot be a fair comparator for the better-off-overall test. (NTEU, 2016, p. 7)

This claim has prompted reactions ranging from suggestions that the sector will collapse (Smith, 2016), to fear that in an international market for academics, it will select for mediocrity (Go8, 2016). Australian universities have undergone successive cuts in their funding, while changes in policy have increased student numbers. Although this trend has been apparent since the late 1980s, it is only in the last few years that policy has shifted into a new register, with the deregulatory step of 'uncapping' funded places in 2012 meaning that universities are free to enrol as many students as they can. According to the Department of Education, between 2011 and 2013, the number of students enrolled increased by nearly 100,000 (DET, 2014). Consistent with practices in the United Kingdom and United States (Pauls, 2013; UCU, 2010), universities seeking to increase the productivity of their labour force have in workload models an opportunity to reframe expectations of academic labour. As noted by Ball (2000, 2005, 2012) and others (Fanghanel, 2011), such shifts in policy have the potential to influence not only academic practices, but also academic identity.

Models

Introduced as a mechanism to quantify and qualify the distribution of academic work, modelling is one response to accountability clauses in institutional labour contracts negotiated in the collective bargaining process. For example: '(w)orkloads will be realistic, reasonable, transparent and manageable' (RMIT, 2014) or 'academic work will be allocated in a transparent, equitable, flexible and accountable manner' (VU, 2013).

There is significant variation around a common core of practices concerning different forms of academic labour recognised by different models. While Boyd (2014) noted that inconsistency in the terminology used to describe work allocation processes hampers comparisons, terms such as 'framework', 'principles' and 'guidelines' also signal the degree of 'granularity' (Hull, 2006) or detail made explicit. Few universities include quantifications of different activities in their collective agreements, instead announcing principles of workload allocation without associated metrics.

Models quantify various dimensions of academic labour and allocate nominal amounts of time for each activity included. They refer to time, but duration is not the principle governing the allocations of work; expectations are framed in terms of either teaching requirements (contact hours or students) or outputs ('three quality publications'). While enforceable accountability statements are made at the institutional level, implementation is devolved to faculties or discipline groups, depending on institutional configuration. This is justified by variation in work practices within organisational units, and enables significant discretionary possibility in the allocation of work. Most models start from a statement of annual hours ranging from 1595 hours to 1800 hours, then through a combination of metrics derived from other policies (e.g., acknowledgement of research output or maximum teaching contact hours), apportion annual hours to the respective activities.

Consistent with traditional conceptions of academic labour, activities are categorised as teaching and related duties, research and scholarship, and service and leadership. Proportional loads vary according to model; while there was a 40:40:20 (teaching, research and service) formula, this teaching-research norm is increasingly displaced through academic profiles described as 'teaching focussed' (Probert, 2013); such appointments are typically apportioned between 60% and 90% of their annual hours in teaching and related duties (e.g., Deakin, 2013; UNISA, 2014; WSU, 2014).

Hull (2006) and Vardi (2009) explored the development of workload models, finding significant variation in composition, intent and reception by academic staff in their own institutions. For example, some models count allocated teaching hours only, while others attempt instead to apportion load across all domains of academic practice. Some allocate points to activities to signal the quantity of academic time that they are deemed to consume. A combination approach includes models focused on allocated teaching contact hours, but which incorporate adjustments to teaching allocations based on a retrospective assessment of research performance. Reception of workload models by staff varies according to the extent of involvement in the development of the model, and the extent to which it approximates the perceived reality of academic work (Hull, 2006; Pauls, 2013; Watson, King, Dekeyser, Bare, & Baldock, 2015).

Models are multifaceted fabrications (Ball, 2000); constructs that signal performance requirements while simultaneously instantiating norms of academic practice. As Ball notes (2000, p. 8) 'The fabrications that organisations (and individuals) produce are selections among various possible representations or versions of the organisation or person.' Discussing the implications of audit culture as it influences academic identity, Ball observes that ' ... tactics of transparency produce a resistance of opacity, of elusivity – an escape from the gaze ... ' (2000, p. 2). This resistance can also be found at the institutional level. Institutionally, '(t)echnologies and calculations which appear to make public sector organisations more transparent may actually result in making them more opaque, as representational artefacts are increasingly constructed with great deliberation and sophistication' (Ball, 2000, p. 10). For Ball, the key consequence of policy technologies like workload models is their privileging of the visible, with two main implications – an increase in the labour of making visible in the name of accountability, and the primacy of performance considered by reference to visible outputs, leading to a reshaping of what it is to be an academic.

These fabricated workload models are simulacra (Baudrillard, 1988). Baudrillard developed his concept of simulacra in order to understand scenarios in which direct experience of the reality of a situation is displaced by representations of that situation. Workload models are a prime example of simulacra; they are not grounded in an empirically derived approximation of the time activities take: in other words, they do not proceed from 'the real'. Tynan, Ryan, Hinton, and Lamont (2012) identified perceptions of the unreality of models in their study of the impact of online technologies on workloads, illustrated by respondent comments such as: 'It's just an arbitrary measure ... you may as well turn around and say your workload reflects how many window panes you've got in your room ... ' (p. 27). Models are built on the premise that a uniform representation of the multiple dimensions of academic labour is possible. Yet, in their implementation, they contradict this very premise.

Method and information sources

The following analysis compares workload modelling principles included in formal documentation and models with perceptions of workload model implementation reported by respondents to the *State of the Uni* survey (NTEU, 2015; 2016b). Models are not easily found in publicly accessible documents on university websites, except where incorporated into policies (e.g., ACU, 2015). Review of a range of current approaches documented in enterprise agreements, policies and examples of specific workload models provides a picture of current practice.

The picture generated is then compared with academic responses to one question in the 'State of the Uni 2015' (NTEU, 2015) survey of academics. Survey responses were made publicly accessible through their upload to the FWC website in submissions by the NTEU (2016a). This secondary analysis of 1138 responses to the question 'Do you have any comments you wish to make about working hours?' explored how models were perceived by academics whose work was organised by them.

The survey responses are significant because they express sentiments that academics tend not to express outside of an anonymous survey, the sample size is large relative to prior studies of workload modelling and because their collection postdates recent increases in student numbers associated with the demand-driven system. The methodological background and warrants of rigour of the survey are outlined in NTEU (2015, p. 21).

The survey responses are further contrasted with submissions to the FWC by representatives of universities opposed to the regulation of working hours (AHEIA, 2016; Go8, 2016). From these statements come articulations of academic identity and practices which are reflected in what Hull (2006) describes as 'first order' measures used to construct models, that is, the classification schemes that underpin the model's categories.

Together, these three sources of information (formal documents, survey responses and witness statements) illustrate tensions between a dominant conceptualisation of academic practice and reports of the experiences and perceptions of academics.

Caveats

Two epistemological caveats attend this analysis, caveats of consequence for any general claims about academic work. They are: there is no one university (Forsyth, 2014) and there is no one manager (Kinman & Jones, 2003).

The first caveat acknowledges the shaping of the Australian university system into a quasi-market composed of universities established through, and benefiting from, a century of public funding; of universities constructed in the expansions of the 1960s and 1970s; and of universities created by the 'Dawkins revolution' (Croucher, Marginson, Norton, & Wells, 2013), which forced amalgamations between teaching institutes and colleges of advanced education in the development of the unified national system in the early 1990s. Constituted according to different imperatives and with different degrees of public investment in infrastructure, the Australian university system has not been built on a level playing field. In the last two decades, universities have attempted to further differentiate themselves as marketisation has led them into relations of competition, while other universities with perceived affinities have formed cross-institutional alliances to advance their interests. As a consequence, universities are stratified both internally and across the sector. Barcan (2013) argued that the confluence of mass expansion, marketisation and economic constraint re-constitutes universities as palimpsests of three institutional forms – bureaucracy, corporation and scholarly institution, each with its own logic. Tensions in strategy and practice can be understood as conflicts between bureaucratic, corporate and scholarly logics.

Fanghanel (2011) describes a range of styles of academic management, highlighting the temporary nature of many of these roles, and the existence of managers for whom academics are merely human resources to be allocated in a maximally efficient manner. While managerialism in the academy has been the object of sustained critique (Forsyth, 2014; Fredman & Doughney, 2012; Sharrock, 2012), issues related to workload modelling are not solely attributable to managerialism. It is, however, important to note evidence of differences between procedures as formally documented and as they are interpreted and implemented, signalling the importance of managerial practice as a variable (e.g., Kenny, Fluck, & Jetson, 2012; Lyons & Ingersoll, 2010; NTEU, 2016c) and the need for analysis informed by experience.

Current practices

Teaching and teaching-related activities represent the bottom line in a sector that derives more than half of its income from student fees via commonwealth grants (DET, 2014). Table 1 shows aspects of a selection of models, illustrating variability in the equation of contact hours and proportions of time, and contingency of research time allocations for two academic profiles, teaching and research academics, and teaching-focused academics.

Differences between and within institutions in quantifying recognition of common activities are significant, signalling that universities either value the same activities differently, or are operating on divergent assumptions as to what constitutes a competent professional standard. They also have significance for understanding the plural identities that are subsumed by the word 'academic'.

One constant across universities appears to be the practice of assessing research performance by retrospectively averaging outputs over a three- to five-year period. Within

Table 1. Academic workload model variations.

University	Annual hours	Teaching contact hours: teaching and research academic	Teaching contact hours/parameters: teaching focused	Marking	Research allocations and output expectations	Block research time
Australian Catholic University (ACU, 2015)	1595	Capped at 336/annum, max 30 weeks	'Normally' not exceeding 480 hours	1 hour/student	20%**–50% (max) ERA benchmarked. Possibility of 0%	Implied 22 weeks
Central Queensland University (CQU, 2013)	1650	40:40:20 – capped at 32 EFTSL (i.e., up to 256 students)	70:10:20 – capped at 32 EFTSL	Included in teaching %	10–70% depending on profile. Benchmarked by discipline ERA	'Normally' one teaching free day/week
Edith Cowan University (ECU, 2013, 2014)	1695	40% (260 hours)–60% (364 hours)	75% (468 hours)	Included in teaching %	20–40% Minimum 5 outputs/5 years, based on assumption of 50:30:20.	4 weeks
Flinders University (Flinders, 2010)	1725	Norm 30% (518 hours – includes preparation) up to 50%, not less than 20%	N/A	Up to 100 hours/annum.	30–50%, not less than 20%	N/A
James Cook University (JCU, 2015)	1638	Up to 50% capped at 300 hours	Up to 70% capped at 500 contact hours	Included in teaching %	20–60%. Minimum five outputs over five years	12 weeks without timetabled classes
Macquarie University (Macquarie, 2010, 2014)	1575	40:40:20, but can be up to 60% of workload	Up to 80%	Included in teaching %	Contingent on minimum five outputs over five years	N/A
University of Southern Queensland (USQ, 2015)	1702.5	Max 70% of workload	Max 70% (1191.75 hours)	'Normally' 65 minutes/student	10–40%, (30% is contingent on performance)	N/A
University of Western Australia (UWA, 2016)	1725	60% teaching contingent on research output 40% research	90% teaching	Included in teaching block	20–80% Varying according to outputs over five years benchmarked to Go8 discipline codes	N/A
Western Sydney University (WSU, 2014)	1610	Up to 13 hours/week, capped at 50 EFTSL	17 hours/week capped at 65 EFTSL	Capped at 135/semester	Assessed over three years	12 weeks

Notes: 'N/A' = not apparent/available, ** 'normally' = not necessarily, ERA = excellence in research Australia. Most of the models considered are reviewed annually; therefore, practices attributed to a university may quickly become dated.

this practice, however, different universities make use of different benchmarks. While there is invariance in the assessment of research activity as falling into one of three categories (publications, research income and higher degree by research completions), some models set the quantity of output expected in terms of ERA-defined averages, while others factor in disciplinary variations measured as part of that reporting exercise (CQU, 2013). Some allocate 'full points' for a multi-authored book (Macquarie, 2010), others apply a scaling factor in the event of multiple authors. Sector-derived benchmarks disregard institutional variations, with the research performance of academics with high teaching loads compared with academics without a similar load. Supervision of research students is variously counted as teaching (CQU, 2013; JCU, 2015; Macquarie, 2014), or research (ACU, 2015; UWA, 2016). Some provide for exceptions to be negotiated where staff members have had personal or parental leave (JCU, 2015). There are also provisions to adjust workload that do not require the staff member's agreement; these apply in the event that a staff member is deemed not to have met expectations, and are invariably adjustments that increase teaching load (e.g., UNISA, 2014). While Coates and Goedegebuure (2012, p. 884) cautioned that adaptation to the pressures of the contemporary environment through role customisation should not be '… in order to penalise staff because they haven't met unrealistic targets … to ensure that underperformance is wiped out, [or] … to "squeeze the lemon dry"', reallocation of workload or academic profile contingent on performance suggests that functional specialisation or 'unbundling' (Macfarlane, 2010) of academic labour is proceeding through workload allocation processes.

Conceptualisations of academic labour

The tension across these workload allocation documents is between a dominant characterisation of academia as vocation and counter discourses that invoke vocational commitment, but which question whether that commitment is being directed towards other ends. The AHEIA (2016) describes academics as 'autonomous professionals' enjoying considerable flexibility in how they manage their work. The Group of Eight elaborates:

> Academic staff perform a significant proportion of their work as self-determined and self-directed work at hours and at locations that they themselves determine. They generally pursue their particular discipline or research as a vocation and a life-long passion, both to innovate, discover and create new knowledge and in doing so to advance their own domestic and international standing and their careers. (Go8, 2016, pp. 14–15)

In submissions to the Fair Work Commission, six distinguished professors endorsed this perspective. The curricula vitae accompanying their statements emphasise research publication, income and leadership achievements. The most recent dates of classroom teaching roles noted for this group range from the mid-1990s to 2009. The picture presented of the academic year is of stability in teaching, and substantial non-teaching research periods:

> Academic work, particularly teaching-related activities, is cyclical across the year and is predominantly undertaken during the two 13 week semesters throughout the year. There are therefore 26 weeks of the year where the majority of academic staff generally do not have any allocated teaching hours but may undertake some teaching-related activities such as marking assessments. (Biggs, 2016)

The statements emphasise the requirement for autonomy and flexibility for academic work to attain the standards of excellence that their curricula vitae display:

> The individual academic has, and values, a high level of individual control over the balance of the work that he or she does and when and how that work is done. (Freshwater, 2016)

> Fundamental to the nature of academic work are concepts such as autonomy, freedom, flexibility and self-direction. Outside of timetabled student teaching and academic committee work, staff enjoy the flexibility to arrange their work as they see fit to maximise outcomes … (Biggs, 2016)

The discourse is of academia as a realm of professional autonomy, peopled by vocationally driven, committed scholars. Perspectives running counter to this discourse (reported below) identify and are shaped by structural adjustments to conditions of academic work reflecting the broader context of resource constraints, maximisation of revenue from teaching through multiple session offerings, increased class sizes and online delivery.

Of the responses to the *State of the Uni* survey, 792 respondents (69.6%) were critical of current practice, 39 respondents (3.43%) were positive and 307 (26.98%) offered clarifying statements. Clarifications related either to the inadequacy of the survey question to current role because the bulk of their work was research student supervision or work-integrated learning coordination, both of which run throughout the year, or their teaching was intensive mode which sat outside the weekly frame of the preceding questions. A second group of clarifications were ambiguous, for example:

> don't get as much done as i used to be able to

> I was putting in longer days a decade or more ago when I was young and idealistic concerning my research prospects …

A third category of clarifications signalled a theme recurring in critical responses; that the boundary between teaching and non-teaching time was blurred:

> teaching weeks vs research weeks are a misnomer; assignment marking, for example, is done in non teaching weeks

> Teaching weeks also need to include preparation particular with on line development and administrative input marking and student engagement this changes the figure to 40 weeks

The reasonableness of norms of academic practice depends on the structural environment of practice. The multiple requirements of the academic role were previously accommodated through division of the academic year into teaching and non-teaching phases. Formerly, two teaching semesters were punctuated by sessions during which academics expected to have time for research activities – this expectation continues to appear in collective agreement requirements to have uninterrupted research time (e.g., JCU, 2015). Consequent to marketisation, many universities offer multiple teaching sessions – whether through the addition of summer, spring and winter semesters to the standard two or whether through adoption of a 'trimester' system – and these non-standard modes of teaching have become standard. Respondents reported that non-standard sessions in concert with different offerings for different levels of study ultimately eradicated the idea of 'non-teaching weeks':

> I seem to be flat out all the time – doing 2 semesters for undergrad plus 3 trimesters for post grad it seems like I'm on a treadmill with no break

Changes in the modes of teaching delivery, which also included 'off-shore' and online teaching left many respondents reporting that they were teaching all the time, with any research they were able to do of necessity conducted on their own time. Disruptions to teaching practice as an orderly activity interspersed with non-teaching periods also came from 'new' modes of delivery which have been employed for some time, but which require constant updating due to technological developments. Frequent decisions to change digital platforms generate more work:

> Reduced admin. support and constant changes to systems means that a lot of time is spent on learning new things and systems. It takes a lot of time to gain proficiency in new systems work

> ... increased dramatically within the last 5 years. Both research and teaching have suffered. They could reduce the amount of admin with teaching by not changing the forms every year or two, or changing the web teaching system. I have worked with 5 different web teaching systems in 9 years

Perceptions of models

While survey respondents were asked a specific question about their hours of work, many reflected on perceived conflicts between models and their 'actual' workload. This was a dominant theme, along with comments about the impacts of structural and operational change.

Of 88 respondents making explicit reference to models, over half noted examples of inaccuracies in the ways in which workloads were calculated, signalling their belief that there is (or should be) an objective reference point for such calculations. For these responses, the implementation level is significant – a level which remains opaque in aggregated data presented to meet transparency requirements. Yet others were unable to ascertain how their workloads had been calculated, with several commenting that it remained unknown. These themes are presented below with reference to the principles of transparency, reasonableness and equity that authorise the use of models in enterprise agreements.

Models simulate measurement

Respondents frequently commented on underestimation of the time required to perform teaching responsibilities to a high standard, due to many of their regular activities not being 'counted' by their institutional models:

> Our university only considers 'teaching weeks' to include the time students are on campus. It does not include preparation prior to the start of semester, mid-semester breaks or end of semester. The real number of teaching weeks in a year are more likely to be about 34

> No time is allocated for preparing tutorials

> ... Supervision of research and honours students does not receive workload points that are commensurate with the task and time involved

While there is evidence of benchmarking of research output requirements, there is little evidence to suggest that universities benchmark teaching practice. For some respondents, the inaccuracy of the time allocation was an inherent concern, while for others, its implications for their quality of teaching were paramount. Perceptions that teaching is not valued by the respondent's institution were frequent. While not a new development, modelling seems to have entrenched the devaluation of teaching practice:

> Academic workloads at my university drastically undervalue the amount of real work that goes on behind the scenes especially with respect to subject coordination, online teaching, and delivery of first year undergrad subjects

> I accept that teaching is an important part of my role and I generally love teaching the students. The university does not value teaching and yet are happy to burden us with excessive teaching loads. This is getting worse. All the workload tools I have seen are inconsistent when measuring teaching load

> Teaching-related activity such as admin, compliance, reporting, catering for flexible delivery (materials and recorded lectures for distance/offcampus students) has increased time required for teaching by at least five-fold in last 10 yrs ... As a result everything else is getting the squeeze, but expectations of output for all facets continue to increase

There was recurring reference to the unrealistic nature of models, with no sense that there was any way of changing the situation, an observation also reported in Tynan et al. (2012). Their interviews with academics across four universities found '... a high proportion of all participants [86%] perceived that their allocated work hours do not adequately reflect the actual time that it takes to engage in various teaching tasks' (Tynan et al., 2012, p. 25). Models are being reified, while failing to capture the realities of contemporary academic practice:

> The calculation of workloads are fantasy based, not based on real investment of hours in each task, especially in relation to teaching

> ... My workload does not reflect the reality, it is a fairytale document

> The loads are not calculated in 'real hours', so they require much more than is allotted

Several respondents commented that even with documented 'overloads', there was no adjustment of their commitments:

> My workload was recently doubled by the university measurement system. It was previously excessive – I am now burning out...

> Management has introduced a workload allocation model and consistently I am over committed by 150% and nothing has been done about this, rather workload has been added

Models simulate equity

Some respondents expressed the perception that the process was being used to the detriment of specific groups, highlighting Hornibrook's (2012) observation that modelling in itself does not prevent the perception of inequity in practice:

> The workplace load formula does not work fairly. Some staff are allocated a lot to research and the rest of us have to pick up their teaching and admin to cover them, and our research time suffers because of it. Then we get flagged for not doing enough research, and they don't care about our teaching or admin loads

> ... in my discipline in the physical sciences, female academics always seem to be given classes with large numbers of students (and therefore higher real workload in marking, coordination duties), in workload models that take into account only face to face hours

> Many people have been promoted to higher levels for doing nothing that I can see and who do not have substantial research records

These responses add to Ball's discussion of performativity as 'making visible' in pointing out the corollary practices of 'making invisible' pastoral and educational activities that support delivery.

Others were of the view that the use of modelling was an expression of managerial maleficence, affirming the view in Lyons and Ingersoll (2010) and Kenny et al. (2012) that managerial prerogative remains a determining factor:

> we are expected to do too much and it is never enough. everything is calculated down, so that the managers look good. the real time it takes to do tasks is not accounted for

> Current workload model at our institution is being pushed through by those who have never or have not taught for a very long time – little respect for how long it takes to prepare quality lectures …

Models and change

A frequent observation concerned ongoing alteration in the ways workloads were calculated, or in the structural organisation of teaching delivery, leading invariably to increasing load:

> Teaching weeks are only counted by the faculty as those during semester, this is completely unrealistic. We are moving to a three semester which includes a summer semester so this structure will change again, less time for research again

> We have had many changes to systems this year which have seriously had an impact on the hours worked that are not reflected accurately in the new work allocation model

> … our research allocation has been halved, and our teaching increased, which means no time for research in reality … increasingly, admin tasks are being moved into academic workloads, e.g., entering marks into different systems, re-organising timetabled room bookings when there is a clash, organising deferred sittings of exams…

Many respondents identified changing structural conditions – for example, a reduction in administrative support leading to loss of institutional procedural knowledge, leaving academics with increased administrative responsibilities. This is paradoxical in an environment in which administrative staff numbers outweigh ongoing academic staff (DET, 2016):

> … Overworked doing admin that should be done by professional staff – but most are casual and get piecemeal contracts. No corporate knowledge

> There is no such thing as non-teaching weeks. Mandated admin and course development has gone mad, there are no times that are teaching free (including Annual Leave where we are harassed to meet unrealistic and arbitrary deadlines). None of these things improve real teaching outcomes …

Finally, the responses illustrated an absence of perceived limits to expectations, and a lack of mechanisms to protect academics from the imposition of workloads requiring them routinely to exceed their limits, whether conceived in terms of hours, physical limits (health) or limits created by responsibilities outside academia (family). Further analysis should consider a range of health and safety concerns, and impacts on life outside of work.

Models as simulacra

In evaluating whether an allocation of work is reasonable, transparency is critical. It is not clear whether universities in their current operating configurations and scale are actually capable of transparency. While information technologies give the impression of panoptic scope, data collection still proceeds according to pre-determined fields. Beneath the spreadsheets are layers of interpretation that cloud transparency (Hull, 2006; Poster, 1990) and require caution in interpretation.

Many models agglomerate preparation, assessment and student administration into 'teaching and related duties', counted as a percentage allocation of annualised hours. While some models cap teaching contact hours, bundling of core elements of academic practice facilitating student learning transfers responsibility to the academic, with time in excess of the nominal allocation spent on these activities 'costing' time allocated to research. The allocation of research time contingent on retrospective achievement of pre-ordained performance requirements rationalises increasing teaching loads for academics deemed research-underperforming, formalising the idea of teaching and research as in competition. A new typology of 'under- and over-loaded' attends discussions about work-load allocation and performance.

A component of the salary of teaching-research academics is intended to fund research activity, but heavy teaching loads and non-standard delivery modes structurally inhibit academics from completing the activities they are funded to undertake. While Norton (2015) argued that universities were using their teaching income to fund research, this suggestion is challenged by survey respondents, who univocally expressed the view that their research time was eroded by the teaching–administration nexus.

Modelling has now provided a mechanism for the simulation of measurement rather than basing workload allocation on a measured reality. The variability of models obviates the very idea of a 'model' understood as a common measure or basis for comparison, with survey respondents' comments about models highlighting individual consequences of this contradiction for perceptions of transparency and fairness. With the model preceding the reality it models, it is increasingly difficult to argue that teaching loads have become unreasonable, for reference to the model displaces negotiation. Following Barcan (2013), while models utilise bureaucratic logic in framing fairness as procedurally secured by the presence of a model, their imprecision (or flexibility), in concert with funding austerity and structural change, makes them susceptible to colonisation by corporate logic, at the expense of scholarly logic. Consequently, norms of educational practice that are expedient for purposes of economy displace conversations concerning how educational quality can be enhanced in mass higher educational contexts. Perhaps most significantly, models provide a virtual site wherein major changes to educational practices can be introduced through alterations to models, rather than by consultation and consideration of impact upon academic workers.

In *The Mismeasure of Man*, Stephen Jay Gould targets biological determinism premised upon

... the abstraction of intelligence as a single entity, its location within the brain, its quantification as one number for each individual, and the use of these numbers to rank people in a single series of worthiness, invariably to find that oppressed and disadvantaged groups – races, classes, or sexes – are innately inferior and deserve their status. (1996, p. 21)

Academic performance and productivity are similarly unamenable to metrics that depend on reductive quantification. Workload allocation models which reduce the complexity of academic practices to a pie-chart on a spreadsheet, take past performance (construed narrowly as outputs) as indicative of future potential, and reallocate academic time according to judgements which precede consideration of aspirations or underlying constraints, constitute a mismeasure of academic labour. The unintended consequences of such an approach include the possibility that the measures contradict their stated aims: transparency, equity and reasonableness.

Disclosure statement

No potential conflict of interest was reported by the author.

References

ACU. (2015). *Academic workload policy approved 27 April 2015*. Retrieved from https://www.acu.edu.au/policies/169055

AHEIA. (2016). *AM 2015/6 submission in reply and witness statements*. Australian Higher Education Industry Association. Retrieved from https://www.fwc.gov.au/documents/sites/awardsmodernfouryr/am2014224andors-sub-aheia-060616.pdf

Ball, S. (2000). Performativities and fabrications in the education economy: Towards the performative society? *Australian Educational Researcher, 27*(2), 1–23.

Ball, S. (2005). *Education reform as social barberism: Economism and the end of authenticity*. Paper presented at the Scottish Educational Research Association Annual Conference, Perth, Scotland. Retrieved from http://www.scotedreview.org.uk/media/scottish-educational-review/articles/251.pdf

Ball, S. (2012). Performativity, commodification and commitment: An I-Spy guide to the neoliberal university. *British Journal of Educational Studies, 60*(1), 17–28.

Barcan, R. (2013). *Academic life and labour in the New University: Hope and other choices*. Abingdon: Routledge.

Baudrillard, J. (1988). Simulacra and simulations. In M. Poster (Ed.), *Jean Baudrillard, selected writings* (pp. 166–184). Stanford, CA: Stanford University Press.

Biggs, S. (2016). Witness statement in Go8, ed. 2016. Submission and witness statements. AM2014/229 – Higher Education Industry – Academic Staff – Award 2010. Fair Work Commission. Retrieved from https://www.fwc.gov.au/awards-and-agreements/modern-award-reviews/4-yearly-review/award-stage/award-review-documents/MA000006?m=AM2014/229

Boyd, L. (2014). Exploring the utility of workload models in academe: A pilot study. *Journal of Higher Education Policy and Management, 36*(3), 315–326.

Coates, H., & Goedegebuure, L. (2012). Recasting the academic workforce: Why the attractiveness of the academic profession needs to be increased and eight possible strategies for how to go about this from an Australian perspective. *Higher Education, 64*(6), 875–889.

CQU. (2013). *Workload allocation model – academic workloads*. Central Queensland University. Retrieved from http://policy.cqu.edu.au/Policy/policy_file.do?policyid=2625

Croucher, G., Marginson, S., Norton, A., & Wells, J. (2013). *The Dawkins revolution: 25 years on*. Carlton: Melbourne University.

Deakin. (2013). *Deakin University Enterprise Agreement 2013*. Deakin University. Retrieved from https://policy.deakin.edu.au/download.php?id=5

DET. (2014). *Higher education report 2011–2013.* Canberra: Commonwealth Department of Education and Training. Retrieved from https://docs.education.gov.au/node/37869

DET. (2016). *2015 Staff numbers.* Canberra: Commonwealth Department of Education and Training. Retrieved from https://docs.education.gov.au/node/38385

ECU. (2013). *Academic and professional staff union collective agreement 2013.* Edith Cowan University. Retrieved from http://intranet.ecu.edu.au/__data/assets/pdf_file/0017/521153/ECU-Academic-and-Professional-Staff-Union-Collective-Agreement-2013.pdf

ECU. (2014). *Academic staff performance expectations and outcomes framework.* Edith Cowan University. Retrieved from http://secure.ecu.edu.au/GPPS/policies_db/tmp/hr175.pdf

Fanghanel, J. (2011). *Being an academic: The realities of practice in a changing world.* London: Routledge.

Flinders. (2010). *Academic workload distribution policy School of Medicine.* Flinders University of South Australia. Retrieved from http://www.flinders.edu.au/medicine/fms/staff/documents/Board20of20Education/Academic20Workload20Distribution%20Policy.pdf

Forsyth, H. (2014). *A history of the modern Australian university.* Sydney: New South Publishing.

Fredman, N., & Doughney, J. (2012). Academic dissatisfaction, managerial change and neo-liberalism. *Higher Education, 64*(1), 41–58.

Freshwater, D. (2016). Witness statement. In Go8 (Ed.), *Submission and witness statements. AM2014/229 – Higher Education Industry – Academic Staff – Award 2010.* Fair Work Commission. Retrieved from https://www.fwc.gov.au/awards-and-agreements/modern-award-reviews/4-yearly-review/award-stage/award-review-documents/MA000006?m=AM2014/229

Gould, S. J. (1996). *The mismeasure of man (revised and expanded).* New York, NY: W.W. Norton and Company.

Go8. (Ed.). (2016). *Group of eight submission and witness statements. AM2014/229 – Higher Education Industry – Academic Staff – Award 2010.* Fair Work Commission. Retrieved from https://www.fwc.gov.au/awards-and-agreements/modern-award-reviews/4-yearly-review/award-stage/award-review-documents/MA000006?m=AM2014/229

Hornibrook, S. (2012). Policy implementation and academic workload planning in the managerial university: Understanding unintended consequences. *Journal of Higher Education Policy and Management, 34*(1), 29–38.

Hull, R. (2006). Workload allocation models and 'collegiality' in academic departments. *Journal of Organizational Change Management, 19*(1), 38–53.

JCU. (2015). *James Cook University academic workload guidelines.* James Cook University. Retrieved from https://www.jcu.edu.au/__data/assets/pdf_file/0009/123849/jcu_132293.pdf

Kenny, J., Fluck, A., & Jetson, T. (2012). Placing a value on academic work: The development and implementation of a time-based academic workload model. *The Australian Universities' Review, 54*(2), 50–60.

Kinman, G., & Jones, F. (2003). 'Running up the down escalator': Stressors and strains in UK academics. *Quality in Higher Education, 9*(1), 21–38.

Lyons, M., & Ingersoll, L. (2010). Regulated autonomy or autonomous regulation? Collective bargaining and academic workloads in Australian universities. *Journal of Higher Education Policy and Management, 32*(2), 137–148.

Macfarlane, B. (2010). The unbundled academic: How academic life is being hollowed out. In M. Devlin, J. Nagy, & A. Lichtenberg (Eds.), *Research and development in higher education: Reshaping higher education* (33 Vols, pp. 463–470). Melbourne: Higher Education Research and Development Society of Australasia, Inc. Retrieved from https://herdsa.org.au/publications/conference-proceedings/research-and-development-higher-education-reshaping-higher-40

Macquarie. (2010). *Macquarie University research active definition.* Retrieved from http://www.research.mq.edu.au/current_research_staff/forms_templates_and_useful_information/useful_information/Research_active_definition.pdf

Macquarie. (2014). *Macquarie University academic staff enterprise agreement 2014.* Retrieved from http://staff.mq.edu.au/human_resources/ea/academic_staff_agreement/

Norton, A. (2015). *The cash nexus: How teaching funds research in Australian universities.* Melbourne: Grattan Institute.
NTEU. (2015). *State of Uni survey 2015, Report No. 2 Workloads, July 2015.* Melbourne: Author.
NTEU. (2016). *AM 2015/6 Outline of submissions.* National Tertiary Education Union. Retrieved from https://www.fwc.gov.au/documents/sites/awardsmodernfouryr/am20156andors-sub-nteu-110316.pdf
NTEU. (2016a). *Witness statement of Ken McAlpine, Attachment H.* National Tertiary Education Union. Retrieved from https://www.fwc.gov.au/documents/sites/awardsmodernfouryr/km-attachmenth.pdf
NTEU. (2016b). *Witness statement of Ken McAlpine Attachment F-1.* National Tertiary Education Union. Retrieved from https://www.fwc.gov.au/documents/sites/awardsmodernfouryr/km-attachmentf-1.pdf
NTEU. (2016c). *Notification of dispute – School of Health Sciences (School).* National Tertiary Education Union. Retrieved from http://www.nteu.org.au/article/Formal-dispute-notified-over-%242.8-million-cut-in-School-of-Health-Sciences-19047
Pauls, T. N. (2013). *Building an instrument for measuring academic administrator and faculty member perceptions of the workload allocation process as it applies to higher education.* Ann Arbor: West Virginia University, ProQuest Dissertations.
Poster, M. (1990). *The mode of information: Poststructuralism and social context.* Chicago: University of Chicago Press.
Probert, B. (2013). *Teaching-focused academic appointments in Australian universities: Recognition, specialisation, or stratification?* Canberra: Office of Learning and Teaching. Retrieved from http://apo.org.au/files/Resource/olt_teachingfocusedacademicappointments_jan_2013.pdf
RMIT. (2014). *RMIT University academic & professional staff enterprise agreement 2014.* Retrieved from http://mams.rmit.edu.au/7m44dtqzbmtd.pdf
Sharrock, G. (2012). Four management agendas for Australian universities. *Journal of Higher Education Policy and Management, 34*(3), 323–337.
Smith, G. (2016, May 18). OT reforms would lead to unis playing ducks and drakes. *Campus Review.* Retrieved from www.campusreview.com.au/2016/05/opinion-new-workplace-reforms-will-lead-universities-playing-ducks-and-drakes/
Tynan, B., Ryan, Y., Hinton, L., & Lamont, A. (2012). *'Out of hours': Final report of the project e-Teaching leadership: Planning and implementing a benefits-oriented costs model for technology enhanced learning.* Sydney: Australian Learning and Teaching Council.
UCU. (2010). *Workload protection: A UCU local negotiating guide.* London: Author. Retrieved from https://www.ucu.org.uk/media/3409/HE-workload-protection-A-UCU-local-negotiating-guide-revised-October-2010/pdf/HE_workload_protection_doc_rev_Oct_2010.pdf
UNISA. (2014). *University of South Australia academic workload guidelines.* Retrieved from http://w3.unisa.edu.au/hrm/industrial/academic_workload_guidelines_FINAL.pdf
USQ. (2015). *USQ academic division academic workload allocation model.* Retrieved from http://www.nteu.org.au/defendourunis/article/USQ-Academic-Division-Academic-Workload-Allocation-Model-17420
UWA. (2016). *UWA academic activity model & business school expectations for academic performance.* Retrieved from http://www.business.uwa.edu.au/__data/assets/pdf_file/0005/2566310/UWA-Business-School-Academic-Actvity-Model.pdf
Vardi, I. (2009). The impacts of different types of workload allocation models on academic satisfaction and working life. *Higher Education, 57*(4), 499–508.
VU. (2013). *Enterprise agreement 2013.* Retrieved from http://w2.vu.edu.au/HR/Employment/LIB/PDF/LIB10.PDF
Watson, R., King, R., Dekeyser, S., Bare, L. & Baldock, C. (2015, August–September). *Current practice in academic workload allocation processes in Australia.* Tertiary Education and Management Conference, Leading Locally Competing Globally, Wollongong, Australia.
WSU. (2014). *Western Sydney University enterprise agreement.* Retrieved from https://www.westernsydney.edu.au/__data/assets/pdf_file/0004/1159789/FINAL_ACADEMIC_STAFF_AGREEMENT_2_FWC_APPROVED_091214.pdf

Rendering the paradoxes and pleasures of academic life: using images, poetry and drama to speak back to the measured university

Catherine Manathunga, Mark Selkrig, Kirsten Sadler ⓘ and (Ron) Kim Keamy

ABSTRACT
Measurement of academic work has become more significant than the intellectual, pedagogical, cultural, political and social practices in which academics and students engage. This shifting emphasis creates paradoxes for academics. They experience a growing sense of disconnection between their desires to develop students into engaged, disciplined and critical citizens and the activities that appear to count in the enterprise university. As measurement discourses preclude the possibilities of human emotion and hinder intellectual labour, we embarked on an arts-informed research project that established new creative spaces for our colleagues to illustrate the pleasures and paradoxes of their academic work. In the research project, we developed critical pedagogies through art and poetry that enabled academics to speak back to university management – and each other – about how they experience their work. In this paper, we draw upon poststructural 'micro-physics' of power, the poststructuralist 'politics of reinscription', and art, poetry and drama as critical pedagogies to interrogate the potential of arts-informed research to speak back to the measured university. The key contribution of this article is to recommend arts-informed methodologies as a forum for dissent and resistance at a time when the spaces of collegiality, pleasure and democracy in the measured university are under attack.

Introduction

Contemporary university policies seek to make universities captive sites of 'cybernetic capitalism' (Peters, 2015, p. 10), producing consumable knowledge for transnational corporations and flexible, knowledge worker-entrepreneurs. Increasingly 'electronic circuits based on mathematical algorithms' that enable the production of learning analytics (Peters, 2015, p. 21) are designed to control academic work. Measurement of academic work has become more significant than the intellectual, pedagogical, cultural, political and social practices in which academics and students engage (Barcan, 2013; Peters, 2015). This creates a number of paradoxes for academics. Many academics from our own experiences report a growing sense of disconnection between their desires to develop students into engaged, disciplined and critical citizens and the activities that appear to count in the entrepreneurial university (Barcan, 2013). These activities include the endless completion of compliance-driven unit and course amendments, spreadsheets, the continuous [re]entry of existing publication data and the sweating over dashboards of student satisfaction. The automated university operates as though academics are technical functionaries employed to enter, interrogate and justify measurements of academic 'performance' (Barcan, 2013; Peters, 2015; Rolfe, 2013).

As measurement discourses 'make emotion, humour, poetry, song, a passion for a life of the intellect unthinkable' (Davies, 2005, p. 7), we embarked on an arts-informed research project to deliberately surface academics' emotions and create opportunities for collegiality (Butler-Kisber, 2010). Once we obtained approval from the University's ethics committee, we invited all of our colleagues in the College of Education at an Australian university with a reputation for its commitment to marginalised communities, to provide images and text to represent their academic work in the form of postcards. We were seeking to reconnect with 'the heartland' of academic work, its emotions, passions and poetics (Davies, 2005; Weber & Mitchell, 1996). From these postcards, we constructed poster-size collages of Teaching, Research and Community Engagement and provided these to our colleagues, the Dean and the Pro-Vice Chancellor for display in prominent locations around our college and executive buildings. These posters have provoked a number of corridor conversations about the changing nature of academic work, some of which we have been privy to and others which we have not. These conversations, both imagined and real, were fictionalised and transformed into the basis of our performance/presentation at the *2016 Academic Identities Conference*. On this occasion, we extended our arts-informed methodology further, employing these readers' theatres about reactions to the posters to prompt additional discussion and involvement. We also encouraged participants' responses through mark-making (both textual and visual) using quality art materials to interrogate this project's potential for ongoing academic dissent and micro-resistance. In the research project, we have adopted a focus on small-scale, localised struggles that draw on art, poetry and now drama as forms of critical pedagogies, to demonstrate how the use of 'visual culture and the politics of seeing and being seen' (Tavin, 2003, p. 201) empowers academics to speak back to university management about how they experience their work.

In this paper, we draw upon Foucault's (1980) notion of the 'micro-physics' of power, the poststructuralist 'politics of reinscription' (Thomas & Davies, 2005, p. 715), critical pedagogy and visual culture (Tavin, 2003) and Greene's ideas of 'teaching for openings' (1995) and 'wide-awakeness' (1978) to illustrate the potential of arts-informed research to speak back to the measured university. Drawing on the ways in which other forms of political resistance, such as the Anti-Apartheid Movement, postcolonial literature and art, and African-American and Indigenous feminists have used images and creative texts, our research seeks to trace the lived experiences and values of academics in new ways. It seeks to give 'voice' to academics' values, pleasures and pains at a time when those who determine university policies are no longer capable of, or interested in hearing us. The images and text produced by our colleagues evocatively renders the pain and uncertainty of teaching, researching and engaging community in the measured university as well as the ways in which practices of care, kindness and pleasure persist in academic work. We argue that one of the few ways left for academics to protect the spaces of collegiality, pleasure and democracy is to engage in art, poetry and drama to provide a forum for collegiality, dissent and resistance (Anderson, 2008). We draw upon Duncombe's (2002, p. 8) argument that cultural resistance involves creating 'a "free space" *ideologically* ... creat[ing] new language, meanings and visions of the future [and] *materially* ... to build community [and] networks'.

Academic work in the measured university

The extensive changes experienced in the higher education sector have been well documented in the literature on academic identities and work since the late 1990s. The capture of the university by managerial, neoliberal agendas has ensured that administration rather than content and knowledge have become its driving force (Readings, 1996; Rolfe, 2013). This results in the ruin of the Enlightenment university, with its commitment to building national culture, truth and emancipation on the one hand and paradoxically its participation in imperialism and colonisation on the other (Readings, 1996). Outputs, outcomes and spreadsheets have become the order of the day in the measured university. Academics are given individual publication and grant income targets in the same way as for a corporate sales department. While it has been common for some time to have these targets, *past* achievements are increasingly linked to *future* workload planning so that time for research becomes progressively foreclosed if these targets are not met. At our Australian university, attempts are currently underway to *change* these targets three years *after* they were accomplished, meaning that research time earned for the same outputs could, in some cases, be halved. Research assessment exercises around the globe, like the Excellence Research Australia (ERA) in Australia, the Research Excellence Framework (REF) and Teaching Excellence Framework (TEF) in the UK and the Performance Based Research Fund (PBRF) in Aotearoa/New Zealand, have academics in a stranglehold. This, for us, is not easy to write about. Our stomachs clench, our foreheads knot, our shoulders tighten. We feel sick as we struggle to sketch in what has come to count in the entrepreneurial university and lament not only what has been lost, but also the ways that our successes with students and our creation of new ideas have become reduced to numerical representations. This has been, and continues to be, our lived experience.

This is a collective, system-wide experience about which much has been written. Readings (1996) argued that the discourse of 'excellence' has replaced the development of culture as the key driving force in universities; the quality of teaching becomes measured by the efficiency with which academics push students through the system. Research then becomes 'an information machine driven by the ethos of efficiency and administration rather than intellectual craftsmanship [sic], the desire for knowledge and the building and testing of theory' (Rolfe, 2013, p. 11). The effect of these shifts is to recast students as customers, while academics begin to feel like 'the meat in the sandwich' (Emerson & Mansvelt, 2014, p. 477). Research becomes reformulated as the generation of marketable information for the knowledge economy, resulting in significant changes in researcher identities (Elizabeth & Grant, 2013), which shift towards becoming 'entrepreneurial knowledge managers' (Cannizzo, 2016).

One of the most useful recent arguments about academic work in the measured university has been made by Barcan (2013, p. 69), who describes universities as a 'fractured and palimpsestic work world'. Barcan (2013, p. 69) outlines how universities have become three different types of institutions simultaneously: 'a scholarly community, a bureaucracy and a corporation'. Each of these institutions has its own demands, expectations, values, rhythms, senses of time and purpose. Often, these beliefs and goals are diametrically opposed. Academics are creative workers and their creativity and well-being is actively stifled when the mind-numbing administrivia associated with bureaucratic and corporate institutions is accorded greater importance than the creation, discussion and dissemination of ideas. As Barcan (2013, p. 70) clearly states 'academics feel the strain of trying to be the human glue that holds it all together'. Working under these strenuous and contradictory conditions has provoked in academics what Bochner (1997, p. 431) calls '*institutional depression*, a pattern of anxiety, hopelessness, demoralization, isolation and disharmony' (emphasis in the original). Many other authors chart the high levels of stress currently experienced by academics (for instance, Billot, 2010; Ditton, 2009; Tytherleigh, Webb, Cooper, & Ricketts, 2005; Winter & Sarros, 2002). Yet, somehow, academics need to find a way to 'dwell in the ruins' of the university that moves us beyond 'an impasse between militant radicalism and cynical despair' (Readings, 1996, pp. 162, 165).

Micro-resistance

Many academics have experienced the real dangers and ultimate futility of engaging in acts of explicit, open resistance to managerial agendas. Anderson's (2008) research illustrates how, in the absence of strong collective action, public protests are often cast as individual. This results in the construction of these individuals as being 'difficult' and 'individually deviant' (Clegg, 1994, p. 291), rendering them easy targets for 'victimization and retaliation' by the university management (Anderson, 2008, p. 259). More covert, micro acts of resistance are often more effective and can be accomplished with, as Anderson (2008) illustrates, great creativity and humour. Anderson (2008, p. 262), building upon the work of Scott (1985, 1990) on the 'weapons of the weak' and 'hidden transcripts' of subordinated workers, argues that organisational resistance in higher education has increasingly become covert, symbolic and discursive. This includes 'feigned ignorance and footdragging; forgetting; avoidance; and compliance that was partial, reluctant or superficial' (Anderson, 2008, p. 254). These forms of resistance are much harder to trace and have been used in a range of non-violent political protests such as those used in Robben Island Prison during Mandela's incarceration.

Like Thomas and Davies (2008, p. 719), we draw upon Foucauldian feminist understandings of resistance that are founded on Foucault's (1980) notion of the 'micro-physics' of power (Collier, 2009). Foucault contends that power operates at the micro-level of the self and is broader than the state. As Foucault (1991, p.194) argues, 'power produces; it produces reality; it produces domains of objects and rituals of truth. The individual and the knowledge that may be gained of him [sic] belong to this production' (Foucault, 1991, p. 194). Games of truth are engaged in through language and knowledge to produce dominant discourses that become internalised by subjects as 'normal' or common sense. Managerialism and neoliberalism are some of the key regimes of truth that increasingly construct university policy discourses and seek to shape academic subjectivities. Butin (2001, p. 158) argues that resistance and agency were at the heart of Foucault's work (especially in his later writings) because 'for Foucault, resistance was inherent within relations of power ... resistance was not an isolated, quixotic event; rather Foucault saw it as a means of self-transformation through the minimisation of states of domination'.

Foucault believed that it was the particular role of the intellectual to 'make people aware of how intolerable taken-for-granted exercises of power actually are and show them that things could be different' (Ball, 2013, p. 145). Academics, as intellectual workers, have a responsibility to expose the regimes of truth which operate in their own workplaces and use this knowledge to engage in practices of resistance. A powerful form of micro-resistance used by academics occurs 'at the level of meanings and identities' (Thomas & Davies, 2005, p. 687). Given that power operates through the adoption of particular technologies of self, academics are able to decide what types of subjectivities they choose to adopt. Academics engage in 'a constant process of adaptation, subversion and reinscription of dominant discourses' where academics reflect upon the contradictions and tensions they experience and 'pervert and subtly shift meanings and understandings' (Thomas & Davies, 2005, p. 687).

As neoliberal audit approaches to academic work adopt divide-and-rule strategies deliberately designed to privilege individualism and create docile, isolated subjects (Davies, 2005), just the mere act of maintaining relationality and collegiality in the measured university constitutes a significant act of resistance. For example, Waitere, Wright, Tremaine, Brown, and Pausé (2011) describe the formation of a writing group to explore through cooperative inquiry the impact of the Aotearoa/New Zealand research assessment exercise (PBRF) as a highly effective resistance strategy. They illustrate how this writing group not only enabled them to speak back to the measured university but also to act back through the formation of community. Their academic identities were 'realised, revitalised and affirmed in community' through cooperative inquiry (Waitere et al., 2011, p. 215).

The use of creative arts in higher education research

There is an emerging trend in research in higher education settings in Australia and internationally, to employ visual and other creative methods (Cousin, 2009). Barone and Eisner (2012, p. 3) argue that

> the contribution of arts-based research is not that it leads to claims in propositional form about states of affairs but that it addresses complex and often subtle interactions and that it provides an image of those interactions in ways that make them noticeable ... arts-based research is a heuristic through which we deepen and make more complex our understanding of some aspects of the world.

King (2013) illustrates the potential of creative inquiry methods to explore aspects of academic identity, for example, through mapping, metaphoric analysis based on a selected novel and word grid analysis of emails with key themes represented through images. Loads and Collins (2016) draw upon arts-informed research practices as a form of academic professional development and identity work. Loads and Collins (2016, p. 178) engage academics in art-making sessions that explore their identities as teachers and act as spaces for 'rest and refreshment: a restorative space'. While these sessions enable academics to express ambiguity about their teaching work, Loads and Collins' research does not seem to explore the potential of these artistic forms for resistance.

Just as Loads and Collins (2016) refer to Greene's notion of 'releasing the imagination', we too see Greene's concept of 'wide-awakeness, of awareness of what it is to be in the world' (Greene, 1995, p. 35) and the need to 'transcend passivity' (Greene, 1978, p. 2) and be nurtured with our colleagues, as:

> the freedom of wide-awakeness [that] has to be expressed in intentional action of some kind. The one who drifts, who believes that nothing matters outside of his or her own self-preservation, can hardly be considered to be free. (Greene, 1978, p. 153)

Similarly, we support Greene's insistence that the arts are crucial in promoting wide-awakeness, as art can bring people in touch with themselves, permit confrontation with the world and allow us to access multiple perspectives. Art also affords an aesthetic experience 'provid[ing] a ground for the questioning that launches sense making and the understanding of what it is to exist in the world' (Greene, 1978, p. 166).

We also look to Tavin's (2003, p. 209) connections between critical pedagogy and visual culture as both are 'reactions to and counter movements against conservative formations, positivistic theories, and undemocratic institutional structures ... [equally they] challenge dominant paradigms that sustain inequalities and maintain hegemonic relations'. Benske, Cunningham, and Ellis (2016, p. 182) describe an 'arts-enriched approach', where academics outline a critical incident in their teaching using text, poetry and drawing. In their analysis, there appears to be a gesturing towards the possibilities of arts-informed approaches to capture moments of conflict with senior managers (including 'Jungian form[s] of metanoia ... [or] meltdown'), although a greater emphasis appears to be placed on the ability of these approaches to foreground emotions (Benske et al., 2016, p. 191). In a recent article from this research project, we have also explored how the use of visual arts-informed methodologies allows us to grapple with academics' thoughts, feelings and ideas about their teaching (Sadler, Selkrig, & Manathunga, 2016). However, few authors in higher education research have interrogated the potential of art, poetry and drama to speak back to the measured university. In our previous article, we hinted at the moments when images and texts vividly captured the experiences of angst about teaching generated in the neoliberal university (Sadler et al., 2016). In this article, we are seeking to extend our thinking about the ongoing subversive potential of images and creative text about academic work and to theorise this as a form of covert micro-resistance.

We also draw upon models of arts-informed resistance used by political activists in social movements. Poetry and art were used extensively during the Apartheid era to foreground inequalities in South Africa (e.g., Daymond, 2003). Indigenous, Chicana and African-American feminists have used creative works to speak back to white women (e.g., Anzaldúa, 2012; Moreton-Robinson, 2000; Walker, 1984). Some studies have sought to summarise the role of art within protest movements across time and place. Using shantytown women's protests in Pinochet's Chile as a case study, Adams (2002, pp. 22, 29) argued that art and music can be used to interpret people's conditions, galvanise protest, mobilise resources, arouse emotions, reinforce values, create solidarity and collective identity, 'break the complicity of silence' and engender hope. McCaughan (2012) explores how art in Mexican and Chicano student protest movements helps create new visual discourses.

Context and methodology of project

In this study, we applied a visual arts-informed approach to explore what it means to do academic work in the current higher education climate, from the perspective of individual academics themselves. Arts-informed approaches have been employed in diverse educational research contexts, for example, Mockler and Groundwater-Smith (2015), King et al. (2014), Ewing and Hughes (2008) and Lawrence (2008). Drawing on some visual methods outlined by Leavy (2015), 24 academics (approximately 25% of all academics) from the College of Education at an Australian university consented to becoming involved in what became known as the Postcard Project over a period of 15 weeks. They also agreed to the future dissemination of their images and texts. Participants were sent emails at predetermined time intervals with a series of prompts, namely 'Teaching is … ', 'Research is … ' and 'Community engagement is … '. In responding to the prompts, participants were invited to think of their responses as being akin to creating a postcard. They were asked to email an image or images, either by taking photos, drawing or sourcing images (online or from personal albums), and write a short text of less than 30 words. Twenty participants responded to the 'Teaching is … ' prompt, 18 responded to the 'Research is … ' prompt and 18 responded to the 'Community Engagement is … ' prompt.

Each participant's response was then formatted as an individual postcard that juxtaposed the image/s and words provided. This juxtaposition can, as Leavy (2015) suggests, generate new unanticipated meanings. Postcards were then grouped into suites related to each prompt, resulting in three posters for display and discussion.

Participants were also invited to work with us as co-researchers in collaboratively analysing the collected materials, which was the first time that each participant became aware of many of the other participants in the project. Around half of the participants attended some or all of these collaborative analysis sessions, with some others being unable to attend these sessions due to their work commitments. We sought to generate 'meaningful partnerships with the researched seeking meaningful data for social transformation' (Byrne, Canavan, & Millar, 2009, pp. 68–69).

Working across three group meetings with our participant colleagues, we began the analysis as a group with some of the visual analysis questions that Cousin (2009), Weber (2007) and Grbich (2007) propose. Questions included: which images/text: resonate with your own image/text? Are at odds with your own image/text? Disturb or surprise you? Do you have an emotional response to? We experimented with analysing our own and others' postcards, evolving Mitchell, DeLang, Molestane, Stuart, and Buthelezi's (2005) questions: what do the images mean to those who selected them? How do we balance the interpretations of the group against the interpretations of individuals? To address this, individuals then pursued deeper interpretation of their own postcards, followed by further group discussion to consider how to generate shared narratives. Participants were prepared to disclose the postcards they had produced but did display some reluctance to 'analyse' the images and texts of their colleagues. Informed by Cahill (2007), who suggests that experimentation with different combinations of research products and authors is one way to hold multiple voices in creative tension, in this article we combine three postcards from three different participants – one each from teaching, research and community engagement – representative of the pain, paradox and pleasures of academic work expressed by our participants (who are also our colleagues). In this article, there is only space to include these three representations. Other postcards and additional details about the approach, including methodology, methods and ethical considerations relating to the use of visual images, can be found in Sadler et al. (2016).

Rendering pleasure in the measured university

Across the collective set of postcards, tensions emerged between idyllic representations (pleasure) and conflicted representations (pain and paradox) of academic work. Revealing pleasure in spite of the measured university, the idyllic representations incorporated positive, generative, calm or pleasant images (such as sunsets, lush landscapes, shared feasts or rich jewels) and words (such as inspire, delight, passion, grow and joy) about teaching, research and community engagement. For example, the postcard in Figure 1 provides an image of research as a lush green maze that beckons and delights, promising an elusive yet rewarding experience in which institutional constraints are absent:

The participant who created this image and text was not available to participate in co-analysis sessions. However, our interpretation of this image suggests to us that the representation of a maze – made up of multiple pathways, with many entry and exit points as well as dead ends – along with the delights expressed in the text suggest that the participant may be conveying that research is convoluted, complex but ultimately achievable and personally rewarding irrespective of institutional rewards. The fact that the maze is also organic and growing suggests the possibility of renewal and transformation. Mazes have been linked with an awakening to, and undertaking of personal, psychological and spiritual transformation (Eversole, 2009; The Labyrinth Society, 2016), which may have potential parallels with research. This postcard (and others that reflect pleasure through abundance) seems to reveal research as regenerative for academics.

Postcards illustrating positive emotions were evident across each of the categories of teaching, research and community engagement, indicating that many academics gain a deep abiding pleasure from the core components of academic work, particularly research and community engagement. They also illustrate how much of this pleasure lies within the unanticipated, creative features of academic work that escape measurement or linear, pre-determined output models, as Barcan's (2013) research also affirms.

Rendering pain and paradox in the measured university

In stark contrast to the pleasures expressed by some, other participants revealed a range of negative emotions and conflict in their selected images and text. Revealing pain and

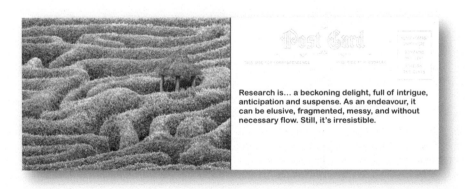

Figure 1. Colleague's image (Paul Nash/Shutterstock, used under license from Shutterstock.com) and text of pleasure.

paradox in the measured university, these postcards incorporated images of 'in trouble' figures and often sepia tones (such as witches, a girl floating across a dystopian landscape), words (such as ridiculous, frustration, dilemma, lack or unnecessary). The image of the person below (in Figure 2) reveals a character in terrible pain:

The imagery of the melting, screaming witch in Figure 2 reveals the profound level of physical anguish and frustration one academic experiences in the measured university that values administration over core academic pursuits such as 'thinking and writing' (Readings, 1996). The fact that the witch is melting suggests a fear that academics and the work they consider valuable may disappear altogether. This postcard (and several others that reflect on the challenges of teaching within the constraints of the neoliberal university) would seem to illustrate the conditions of the university in ruins (Readings, 1996; Rolfe, 2013).

Paradox was also revealed in the postcards where there was a significant disjuncture between idyllic images and conflicted words. For example, in one postcard an image of a teacher happily surrounded by students was accompanied by text about the rewards of teaching being obscured by pressures of administrative loads. Paradox also emerged in the major gaps between what is demanded by the institution compared with what is valued by the academic. For example, one postcard foregrounded the paradox between the desire to meet the needs of students or communities in stark contrast to institutional foci on market positioning, as expressed in Figure 3:

In Figure 3, the participant selects the image of the front cover of an edited collection (Blackmore, Brennan, & Zipin, 2010) that sought to problematise contemporary shifts in university governance and academic work. The book cover represents the university as a large and dominating institution. Their text illustrates a belief that the work of community engagement enables academics to counteract this present perspective through a focus on service to marginalised communities, social justice and ethics. Therefore, this research project provided academics with an opportunity to render the pain and paradox they experience as they work in the measured university where there is a sharp disjuncture between their values and those of the institution (Barcan, 2013; Readings, 1996; Rolfe, 2013). Adopting this arts-informed methodology enabled academics to engage in critique

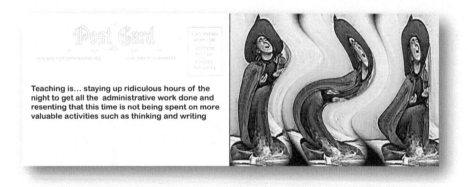

Figure 2. Colleague's image (manipulated from the original provided, with permission from the participant, to avoid copyright complications) and text of pain.

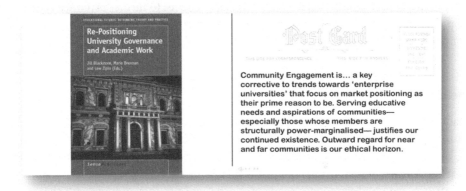

Figure 3. Colleague's image and text of paradox (sourced from original photograph by editor of book cover of their edited collection. Permission sought from publisher).

and resistance that was symbolic and creative (Anderson, 2008; Thomas & Davies, 2005, 2008). Locating the posters of these postcards in key thoroughfares and central faculty and administration buildings spreads the impact of this micro-resistance, provoking ongoing critical conversations about academic work and engendering ongoing dissent.

Engendering ongoing dissent and micro-resistance: readers' theatre and mark-making

To further explore the potential for ongoing dissent and micro-resistance created by our original images and poetry, we engaged members of the audience at the Sydney 2016 *Academic Identities Conference* in the performance of a series of readers' theatres about the posters generated from the postcards. Readers' theatre was one of the examples of performance canvassed by the conference co-convenors (Peseta & Barrie, 2016). It is a technique used in a range of educational settings where readers read from a prepared script without any need for memorisation and costuming, but with opportunities for vocal expressiveness, dramatic gesture and active learning (Teaching Heart, 2008). Norris (2000) also outlines how drama is increasingly used to collect, analyse and disseminate research findings and suggests that it has become more widely used at educational academic conferences. The inclusion of this style of conference presentation inspired us to explore options for building upon our initial arts-informed research design. Beyond the three readers' theatres we created, the opportunity to present at the conference also inspired us to experiment with mark-making during the performances to engage our audience differently and to generate additional opportunities for creativity and resistance.

Conference participants confirmed the power of adopting these arts-informed approaches. Some spoke of these approaches as enabling a 'different way of thinking and recording thoughts'. Others enjoyed producing 'a tangible representation of their thoughts to share with others'. Several emphasised the evocative and tangible experience of 'thinking as pencil slid across the page' and 'capturing symbols to represent ideas'.

We will provide a detailed account of our readers' theatre and mark-making methodology and the audiences' detailed responses and artwork in another paper. Our purpose in mentioning it here is to convey how it has been possible to build upon the initial Postcard

Project to incorporate additional arts-informed approaches to further explore and critique notions of academic identity and actively engage in subversive opportunities for ongoing dissent and micro-resistance with a wider audience of academics.

Conclusion

If academics are to continue to survive and thrive in the ruins of the university, then we need to create effective ways in which we might protect any remaining spaces of collegiality, pleasure and democracy from the forces of measurement. We have demonstrated that arts-informed research methodologies enable us to vividly and evocatively render the pleasures, pain and paradoxes academics experience as they grapple with the conflict between the bureaucratic and corporate cultures that have been superimposed upon the top of older scholarly cultures of university work (Barcan, 2013). Participants in the original research project illustrated through images and text the deep joy they found in engaging in teaching, research and community engagement that could never be captured or measured through audit mechanisms. They also demonstrated their profound level of commitment to the *vocation* of academic life and the principles of social justice, emancipation and ethics that they passionately ascribed to and believed they enacted through their engagement with students, research participants and community partnerships (Barcan, 2013). Being able to convey these emotions and values so vividly through their images and text provided a significant avenue to speak back to university administrators who do not appear to comprehend or value these commitments. Therefore, like models of political resistance using creative arts (Adams, 2002), this research provided opportunities for our colleagues to confront what many saw as deteriorating academic working conditions. Further, this activity enabled academics to protest subversively and anonymously, to arouse emotions and explore shared values.

The research approach adopted in the research project created a collegial and democratic space for colleagues to share the pleasures, challenges, tensions and uncertainties inherent in their work at a time of great turmoil and conflict within the college. In a deeply divided workforce, these research meetings enabled us to reconnect with shared values and commitments and develop renewed empathy and understanding for each other. As a result, they engendered the types of relationality and collegiality that subvert the isolation, disharmony and demoralisation created by the audit culture and dispel some of the institutional depression and stress we were experiencing (Billot, 2010; Bochner, 1997; Tytherleigh et al., 2005; Waitere et al., 2011; Winter & Sarros, 2002). This mirrors the use of art in protest movements to renew solidarity and collective identity and to engender hope (Adams, 2002).

By moving these representations into public or collective spaces initially within our college and then later within the Academic Identities Conference, where we added drama elements to our repertoire of art and poetry, there is the potential to generate an aesthetic experience that lays the foundation for critical pedagogy. Such collective spaces generate the conditions for 'wide-awakeness' and cultural resistance that Greene (1986) and Duncombe (2002) describe as essential for democracy and freedom:

> We may be able to empower people to rediscover their own memories and articulate them in the presence of others, whose space they can share. Such a project demands the capacity to

unveil and disclose. It demands the exercise of imagination, enlivened by works of art, by situations of speaking and making. (Greene, 1986, p. 441)

Encouraging colleagues to interact with each other through speaking and making in turn allows for representations to appear, be performed or exhibited through surreptitious or formal events in the public realm of the institution. By employing the conventions of art such as farce, comedy, allegory and tragedy in the work that is displayed in these events, openings appear where it is possible to disrupt the visual culture and dominant meta-narrative of institutions (Adams, 2002; McCaughan, 2012). 'It is in adopting the interrogative disposition that arts-based research (like much art) promotes a level of dislocation, disturbance, disruptiveness, disequilibrium that renders it sufficiently – even highly – useful, and therefore ... truthful' (Barone & Eisner, 2012, p. 3).

Finally, we demonstrate how the arts-informed methodologies we have deployed in this project and through its dissemination enable academics to engage in micro, covert, symbolic and discursive resistance within the measured university (Anderson, 2008; Thomas & Davies, 2005, 2008). Through the use of art and poetry in our original project and drama in our conference session, we have opened up spaces for alternative discourses about academic work to resurface and reignite. Our research has created new visual and creative discourses in ways that learn from models of artistic resistance in political movements (McCaughan, 2012). We have provided participants with opportunities to engage in a 'politics of reinscription' whereby the intolerable exercises of control enacted by the audit culture within universities are adapted, subverted and opposed (Thomas & Davies, 2005, p. 715). As a result, we argue that arts-informed methodologies provide academics with powerful aesthetic experiences through which to minimise the domination of bureaucratic and corporate ideologies within our technologies of self and to safeguard our scholarly and vocational subjectivities (Barcan, 2013).

Disclosure statement

No potential conflict of interest was reported by the authors.

ORCID

Kirsten Sadler http://orcid.org/0000-0002-0221-7399

References

Adams, J. (2002). Art in social movements: Shantytown women's protest in Pinochet's Chile. *Sociological Forum, 17*(1), 21–56.
Anderson, G. (2008). Mapping academic resistance in the managerial university. *Organization, 15*(2), 251–270.
Anzaldúa, G. (2012). *Borderlands/La Frontera: The new mestiza*. San Francisco, CA: Aunt Lute Books.
Ball, S. (2013). *Foucault, power and education*. London: Routledge.
Barcan, R. (2013). *Academic life and labour in the new university*. Farnham: Ashgate.
Barone, T., & Eisner, E. (2012). *Arts based research*. Thousand Oaks, CA: Sage.

Benske, K., Cunningham, C., & Ellis, S. (2016). The metanoia of teaching: Translating the identity of the contemporary academic. In J. Smith, J. Rattray, T. Peseta, & D. Loads (Eds.), *Identity work in the contemporary university* (pp. 181–194). Rotterdam: Sense.

Billot, J. (2010). The imagined and the real: Identifying the tensions for academic identity. *Higher Education Research & Development, 29*(6), 709–721.

Blackmore, J., Brennan, M., & Zipin, L. (Eds.). (2010). *Re-positioning university governance and academic work*. Rotterdam: Sense Publishers.

Bochner, A. (1997). It's about time: Narrative and the divided self. *Qualitative Inquiry, 3*(4), 418–438.

Butin, D. (2001). If this is resistance I would hate to see domination: Retrieving Foucault's notion of resistance within educational research. *Educational Studies, 32*(2), 157–176.

Butler-Kisber, L. (2010). *Qualitative inquiry: Thematic, narrative and arts-informed perspectives*. London: Sage.

Byrne, A., Canavan, J., & Millar, M. (2009). Participatory action research and the voice-centred relational method of data analysis: Is it worth it? *International Journal of Social Research Methodology, 12*(1), 67–77.

Cahill, C. (2007). Participatory data analysis. In S. Kindon, R. Pain, & M. Kesby (Eds.), *Participatory action research approaches and methods: Connecting people, participation and place* (pp. 1–7). Hoboken, NJ: Taylor and Francis.

Cannizzo, F. (2016). The transformation of academic ideals: An Australian analysis. *Higher Education Research & Development, 35*(5), 881–894. doi:10.1080/07294360.2016.1138454

Clegg, S. (1994). Power relations and the constitution of the resistant subject. In J. Jermier, D. Knights, & W. Nord (Eds.), *Resistance and power in organisations* (pp. 274–325). London: Routledge.

Collier, S. (2009). Topologies of power: Foucault's analysis of political government beyond 'governmentality'. *Theory, Culture and Society, 26*(6), 78–108.

Cousin, G. (2009). *Researching learning in higher education: An introduction to contemporary methods and approaches*. London: Routledge.

Davies, B. (2005). The [im]possibility of intellectual work in neoliberal regimes. *Discourse: Studies in the Cultural Politics of Education, 26*(1), 1–14.

Daymond, M. (Ed.). (2003). *Women writing Africa: The southern region*. New York, NY: Feminist Press at City University New York.

Ditton, M. (2009). How social relationships influence academic health in the 'enterprise university': An insight into productivity of knowledge workers. *Higher Education Research & Development, 28*(2), 151–164.

Duncombe, S. (2002). Introduction. In S. Duncombe (Ed.), *Cultural resistance reader* (pp. 1–16). London: Verso.

Elizabeth, V., & Grant, B. (2013). 'The spirit of research has changed': Reverberations from researcher identities in managerial times. *Higher Education Research & Development, 32*(1), 122–135.

Emerson, L., & Mansvelt, J. (2014). 'If they're the customer, I'm the meat in the sandwich': An exploration of tertiary teachers' metaphorical constructions of teaching. *Higher Education Research & Development, 33*(3), 469–482.

Eversole, F. (2009). *Art and spiritual transformation: The seven stages of death and rebirth*. Rochester, VT: Inner Traditions.

Ewing, R., & Hughes, J. (2008). Arts-informed inquiry in teacher education: Contesting the myths. *European Educational Research Journal, 7*(4), 512–522.

Foucault, M. (1980). *Power/knowledge: Selected interviews and other writings, 1972–77*. New York, NY: Pantheon.

Foucault, M. (1991). *Discipline and punish: The birth of a prison*. London: Penguin.

Grbich, C. (2007). *Qualitative data analysis: An introduction*. London: Sage.

Greene, M. (1978). *Landscapes of learning*. New York, NY: Teachers College Press.

Greene, M. (1986). In search of a critical pedagogy. *Harvard Educational Review, 56*(4), 427–441.

Greene, M. (1995). *Releasing the imagination: Essays on education, the arts, and social change*. San Francisco, CA: Jossey-Bass.

King, V. (2013). Self-portrait with mortar board: A study of academic identity using the map, the novel and the grid. *Higher Education Research & Development, 32*(1), 96–108.

King, V., Garcia-Perez, A., Graham, R., Jones, C., Tickle, A., & Wilson, L. (2014). Collaborative reflections on using island maps to express new lecturers' academic identity. *Reflective Practice, 15*(2), 252–267.

The Labyrinth Society. (2016). *Learn about labyrinths*. Retrieved from https://www.labyrinthsociety.org/about-labyrinths

Lawrence, R. (2008). Powerful feelings: Exploring the affective domain of informal and arts-based learning. *New Directions for Adult and Continuing Education, 120*(Winter), 65–77.

Leavy, P. (2015). *Method meets art: Arts-based research practice* (2nd ed.). New York, NY: The Guilford Press.

Loads, D., & Collins, B. (2016). Recognising ourselves and each other in professional recognition. In J. Smith, J. Rattray, T. Peseta, & D. Loads (Eds.), *Identity work in the contemporary university* (pp. 169–180). Rotterdam: Sense.

McCaughan, E. J. (2012). *Art and social movements: Cultural politics in Mexico and Aztlán*. Durham, NC: Duke University Press.

Mitchell, C., DeLang, N., Molestane, R., Stuart, J., & Buthelezi, T. (2005). Giving a face to HIV and AIDS: On the uses of photo-voice by teachers and community health care workers working with youth in rural South Africa. *Qualitative Research in Psychology, 2*(3), 257–270.

Mockler, N., & Groundwater-Smith, S. (2015). *Engaging with student voice in research, education and community: Beyond legitimation and guardianship*. Dordrecht: Springer.

Moreton-Robinson, A. (2000). *Talkin' up to the white woman: Indigenous women and feminism*. St Lucia: University of Queensland Press.

Norris, J. (2000). Drama as research: Realising the potential of drama in education as a research methodology. *Youth Theatre Journal, 14*(1), 40–51.

Peseta, T., & Barrie, S. (conference co-convenors) (2016). *Academic life in the measured university: Pleasures, paradoxes and politics*. 5th International academic identities conference. Retrieved from http://sydney.edu.au/education-portfolio/ei/getinvolved/aic2016/default.htm#.V5GrO7h97IU

Peters, M. (2015). The university in the digital epoch: Fast knowledge in the circuits of cybernetic capitalism. In P. Gibbs, O. H. Ylijoki, C. Guzmán-Valenzuela, & R. Barnett (Eds.), *Universities in the flux of time* (pp. 9–31). London: Routledge.

Readings, B. (1996). *The university in ruins*. Cambridge, MA: Harvard University Press.

Rolfe, G. (2013). *The university in dissent: Scholarship in the corporate university*. London: Routledge and SRHE.

Sadler, K., Selkrig, M., & Manathunga, C. (2016). Teaching is ... opening up spaces to explore academic work in fluid and volatile times. *Higher Education Research & Development, 36*(1), 171–186. doi:10.1080/07294360.2016.1171299

Scott, J. (1985). *Weapons of the weak – everyday forms of peasant resistance*. New Haven, CT: Yale University Press.

Scott, J. (1990). *Domination and the art of resistance*. New Haven, CT: Yale University Press.

Tavin, K. (2003). Wrestling with angels, searching for ghosts: Towards a critical pedagogy of visual culture. *Studies in Art Education, 44*(3), 197–213.

Teaching Heart. (2008). *Reader's theatre scripts and plays*. Retrieved from http://www.teachingheart.net/readerstheater.htm

Thomas, R., & Davies, A. (2005). What have the feminists done for us? Feminist theory and organizational resistance. *Organization, 12*(5), 711–740.

Thomas, R., & Davies, A. (2008). Theorising the micro-politics of resistance: New public management and managerial identities in the UK public services. *Organization Studies, 26*(5), 683–706.

Tytherleigh, M., Webb, C., Cooper, C., & Ricketts, C. (2005). Occupational stress in UK higher education institutions: A comparative study of all staff categories. *Higher Education Research & Development, 24*(1), 41–61.

Waitere, H., Wright, J., Tremaine, M., Brown, S., & Pausé, C. (2011). Choosing whether to resist or reinforce the new managerialism: The impact of performance-based research funding on academic identity. *Higher Education Research & Development, 30*(2), 205–217.

Walker, A. (1984). *In search of our mother's garden: Womanist prose.* London: Women's Press.

Weber, S. (2007). *Analysing visual qualitative data.* Retrieved from http://iirc.mcgill.ca/txp/?s=Methodologyandc=Visualmethodologies

Weber, S., & Mitchell, C. (1996). Drawing ourselves into teaching: Studying the images that shape and distort teacher education. *Teaching and Teacher Education, 12*(3), 303–313.

Winter, R., & Sarros, J. (2002). The academic work environment in Australia: A motivating place to work? *Higher Education Research & Development, 21*(3), 241–258.

Made to measure: early career academics in the Canadian university workplace

Sandra Acker and Michelle Webber

ABSTRACT
While Canada lacks explicit central directives towards research productivity, academics experience frequent and intense reviews of their research, teaching and service through mechanisms such as elaborate tenure and promotion procedures and annual performance reviews. Given that newer academics are sometimes thought to be especially susceptible to contemporary performativity pressures, this article considers seven early career academics (ECAs), interviewed as part of a larger qualitative study, and the nuances of their reactions to evaluative processes, especially the tenure review. On the whole, the ECAs create and deploy strategies to ensure that they meet ever-rising standards, because they love their work and believe they are 'lucky' to be on track to secure a permanent position. They hope for more freedom in 'life after tenure'. However, all have trenchant criticisms of the corporatized university and the ways in which evaluation proceeds.

Untoward impacts of neo-liberal university reform on academic practice have been comprehensively documented (e.g., Leišytė & Dee, 2012; Olssen, 2016). Critics engage with many aspects of the new university configuration: corporatization, entrepreneurialism, managerialism, marketization and others. This article reflects those concerns about the ways in which academic subjectivities are influenced by the changing academic environment, in particular how academics have been called upon not only to be more productive but also to display that productivity in measured, measurable and/or accountable forms. It focuses on early career academics (ECAs) in Ontario, Canada, that is, individuals in their first five or six years in a full-time 'tenure-track' position. They have yet to go through the tenure review process which holds out the promise of a permanent place in academe.

Efforts to incentivize university researchers towards greater research productivity imposed by governments have been termed 'audit cultures' (Shore & Wright, 2000) and denounced as 'surveillance' (Lorenz, 2012). Despite the many critiques of the metrics, methods and consequences of these exercises (e.g., Burrows, 2012; Olssen, 2016), externally driven evaluative processes continue to spread across the world (Enders, de Boer, & Leišytė, 2009; Uzuner-Smith & Englander, 2014).

While Canada is not exempt from the global tendencies towards audit cultures in higher education, it lacks the explicit central directives towards academic performativity evident elsewhere. There are no research assessment exercises or their equivalent. Nevertheless, Canadian academics experience frequent and intense reviews of their research, teaching and service through other mechanisms such as elaborate tenure, promotion and annual reviews. The purpose of this article is to investigate how a group of ECAs makes sense of a system that emphasizes measurement and performativity, and takes place within the context of an increasingly corporatized academic world, yet is not externally driven by government as is the case in so many other nations. In doing so, we contribute to the international literature by recalling the importance of 'the local' (Vidovich & Slee, 2001) in comprehending change in academe.

Context

In this section, we review some of the literature and theories that illuminate academics' identity development within the contemporary academic audit culture and describe the career structure that new academics encounter in Canada.

Making sense of the early academic career

How academic identity develops and changes has been of interest to many scholars. Notably, McAlpine, Amundsen, & Turner (2013, 2014) have created and refined the notion of an 'identity trajectory' that operates through the doctoral stage and into early career academic employment. Various writers have considered the impact of the audit culture on academic identity (Billot, 2010; Henkel, 2005), raising questions such as the extent to which a neo-liberal subjectivity has penetrated the academic mindset and what space might remain for personal responses and resistances (Archer, 2008; Clegg, 2008). It is sometimes suggested that newer academics may respond differently to audit cultures than veterans who can remember better times (Wilson & Holligan, 2014).

We reason that looking closely at the perspectives of a small number of participants who are situated in a similar position gives us important insights into academic identity construction. This focus does not mean ignoring other levels of influence; with Kreissl, Striedinger, Sauer, and Hofbauer (2015), we see these interpretations as taking place within larger contexts of changing ideas about the purpose of knowledge production (macro level) and organizational structures that promote such purposes (meso level).

Three recent studies on academic identity inform our approach. Nygaard (2015) argues that 'research productivity' reflects decision-making in multiple *sites of negotiation*. In a Norwegian research institute context where performance is measured and rewarded in an elaborate points system, she identifies four main areas where decisions had to be made and re-made: genre (what kind of output), collaboration (whether or not to co-author), quality (where to aim a product) and process (how to produce the text) (p. 5). Degn (2016) is also interested in how academics make sense of changing circumstances, especially during 'organizational turmoil and change' (p. 2). Drawn from organizational studies, her *sensemaking* framework considers that external pressures disrupt existing understandings and stimulate a process whereby organizational members must adapt to (make sense of) their circumstances, however ambiguous. Grant and Elizabeth (2015) interviewed women academics in New Zealand about the Performance-Based Research Fund, finding a range of responses (from pride and delight to anger and contempt) that did not fit into expected frameworks.

Taking these studies together, we surmise that academics will engage in processes of sensemaking in their efforts to interpret signals around requirements like research productivity; they will be making and re-making choices and decisions in relevant sites of negotiation around how aspects of their work contribute to desired outcomes, in a context where much is ambiguous and consequences unclear. Finally, even within a group that might be thought to have common interpretations, in new circumstances, there can still be an unexpected splintering of responses.

Canadian academe and the tensions of tenure

Canada has no national department of education. Instead, education, including higher education, is governed by the 10 provinces. The central government can, and does, influence the university sector indirectly, for example, through research council funding and grants for endowed university chairs. What the federal government cannot do is to proclaim a separation of research and teaching budgets or introduce a research assessment exercise. While, in theory, a province could do so, provincial efforts to influence university practices have usually remained at the level of influencing institutional policy and quality assurance mechanisms.

Despite some recent 'unbundling' (Macfarlane, 2011), for example, appointments to a 'teaching stream', and an increase in temporary positions without job security (Brownlee, 2015), the basic Canadian academic career structure consists of three ranks, assistant professor,[1] associate professor and full professor, all of whom do research, teaching and service. A recruit must first be hired into a *tenure-track position*, one that is expected to lead to permanence. If a review of their work is successful after a specified time, usually five or six years, the academic is awarded tenure, a permanent job that can be abrogated only under a few extreme conditions. At the same time or shortly after, s/he is usually promoted from assistant to associate professor and may stay at that rank until retirement or try for promotion to full professor at some future date. *It is important to note that an unsuccessful tenure review, if not reversed by appeal procedures, means the loss of one's job.*

Not only are the stakes high, but also the tenure review itself is extensive and labour-intensive, usually stretching over most of an academic year. The usual practice is for candidates to prepare a detailed dossier, including a CV, publications, course outlines and student course evaluations, narratives about their work, and any other relevant materials. The file is subject to peer review by internal and, in many cases, external assessors. The case may be adjudicated by several layers of committees and sometimes by senior management. Some (not all) institutions allow a second attempt and there are normally appeal procedures.

Along with other academics, ECAs will be evaluated in an annual performance review. Most also undergo a probationary or 'third-year' review, a kind of rehearsal for tenure. For all academics, the frequent reviews convey a message about rising standards and the need to move in directions that were not stressed in the past – obtaining external grants, accomplishing 'knowledge mobilization', accumulating high-prestige publications. For ECAs, the expectations may seem especially onerous, as they simultaneously need to hone their teaching skills and begin to be good institutional citizens.

There are differences between the American and Canadian versions of tenure. Canadian universities, while diverse, are nearly all public and not as varied or stratified as American ones. Administrators generally believe that the Canadian version is more transparent and fairer than the American one and the success rate appears to be higher, likely over 90%, even in the most research-oriented universities (Acker, Webber, & Smyth, 2012). Academic unions play a larger role in Canada (Dobbie & Robinson, 2008) and tenure review processes are spelled out in collective agreements or their equivalent and subject to bargaining. Tenure in Canada is not generally plagued by political interference as it has been in some American states (Flaherty, 2016).

What do we know about the Canadian tenure experience?

Apart from Horn's historical work (1999; 2015) on academic freedom and tenure, literature on tenure is almost entirely from the United States (see, for example, Chait, 2002; Lawrence, Celis, & Ott, 2014). American studies of ECAs generally find them grappling with a set of common conditions: managing conflicting time demands, preparing for class teaching, understanding tenure requirements, fitting in with colleagues and struggling to find work–life balance (e.g., Eddy & Gaston-Gayles, 2008; Murray, 2008). Other literature points to chronic disadvantages for women and minorities (e.g., Osei-Kofi, 2012; Tierney & Bensimon, 1996).

In Canada, Ornstein, Stewart, and Drakich (2007), using Statistics Canada data from the 1990s, concluded that time to tenure was similar for women and men, likely due to high success rates overall. Gravestock and Greenleaf (2008) have mapped tenure policies across Canadian institutions, and there are a few narratives of individual experiences as tenure candidates (Butterwick & Dawson, 2005; Kawalilak & Groen, 2010; Palulis, 2015) and as a faculty union grievance officer (de Montigny, 2011). As in the American literature, there are suggestions that individuals outside the mainstream have more problematic experiences with the process (Acker et al., 2012; de Montigny, 2011; Henry & Tator, 2012). The internationally comparative Changing Academic Profession (CAP) survey (Jones et al., 2012; Weinrib et al., 2013) did not ask direct questions about the tenure process, although noting that Canadian assistant professors are protected by strong unions, are well paid and show high levels of satisfaction similar to other faculty members. Qualitative studies include our own work (Acker et al., 2012; Acker & Webber, 2016a), which found pre-tenure academics struggling anxiously with the opaqueness of tenure guidelines, and a study in a newly designated university by Yeo, Bennett, Stoneman McNichol, and Merkely (2015), who argue that the character of the immediate surroundings is key to comprehending the ECA experience.

While some of this rather sparse and scattered Canadian literature on tenure alludes to corporatized and neo-liberal universities, it seems largely detached from the stream of critical commentary found internationally and in other Canadian writing (e.g., Bruneau & Savage, 2002; Chan & Fisher, 2008), which in turn makes few references to ECAs or tenure. We try to bridge this gap and add a Canadian perspective to the international literature, one that may suggest attending to local situations as much as global trends when considering 'the' measured university.

Our participants are engaged in sensemaking within multiple sites of negotiation. Tenure candidates have varied responses to the reward system and make decisions based on their personal circumstances and how they decode the messages of those who evaluate them. The sections that follow review the methods used and describe the participants, report findings under key themes and conclude with a discussion of how ECAs may be 'made to measure'.

Method

Between 2011 and 2014, the authors conducted semi-structured, qualitative, face-to-face interviews with 24 full-time tenured or tenure-track academics. Participants were drawn from ten universities in the province of Ontario across the spectrum of medical/doctoral, comprehensive and primarily undergraduate university types, and were equally divided among four subject fields, six each in education, geography, political science and sociology, and near-equally among career stages, seven assistant professors, eight associate professors and nine full professors. Interviews generally lasted about 90 minutes and were audiotaped and transcribed.

Our spotlight here is on the assistant professors, or ECAs, a group which contains five women (Ellie, Katie, Poppy, Tricia and Zoe) and two men (Kyle and Ryan) (names are pseudonyms). Five universities and all four subject fields are represented. One person is from an ethno-cultural minority group while the rest are White. Four hold doctorates from Canada, two from the United States and one from another country; all are Canadian. At the time of interview, two were in their thirties, four in early to mid-forties and one in early fifties, the age spread reflecting prior careers for some participants and the long time it may take to become established in academe. Five of the seven were married or partnered. Two had no children while the other five had either one or three children. Most appear to have solid middle-class backgrounds and two have a parent who is or was a university senior administrator.

The themes to be discussed below emerged from a process that began with the construction of the interview guide, itself resting on sensitization from literature reading and our previous research. As quality assurance offices were setting up in Ontario universities, and the province was prescribing that course outlines specify learning outcomes and programmes be reviewed on a rotating basis, we decided to ask academics how they understood and felt about accountability, performance, quality and equity and what was happening in their institutions. We added a number of other questions about academic background, the institutional context, academic freedom, whether circumstances were requiring adaptations of their work, satisfactions and dissatisfactions and demographic questions. Questions around 'performance' stimulated long exchanges, including thoughts on tenure and annual reviews. This article makes use of material mainly from those discussions, from an institutional context question about whether participants saw the universities being run like businesses (or not), and from the questions on satisfactions/dissatisfactions. Because the interviews were lengthy (usually about 30–40 typed single-spaced pages), we adapted a technique from McAlpine et al. (2013) of creating cameos that summarized the transcripts into 4–6 pages, looking back at the originals if necessary, but using the shorter versions to read and re-read and code selectively with this special issue in mind. What emerged from that exercise were five themes of measuring up, strategizing, romanticizing, criticizing and reconciling. Each of these themes included statements by the majority of the seven participants.

Findings

Measuring up

The 'measuring up' theme is the one closest to the special issue topic, including statements evoking evaluations, whether through a tenure, annual or probationary review or student evaluations of teaching. As has been suggested, the major challenge for assistant professors is achieving tenure and thus a permanent job that only extreme circumstances can dislodge. While Zoe, the youngest participant and in her first year in the Canadian position, indicated the least anxiety about tenure and evaluation more generally – 'I'm not that worked up about tenure, at least not yet' – others saw the upcoming tenure review as more central to their academic lives.

With less than a year remaining before submitting his dossier, Kyle talked about the criteria for tenure, which included 'teaching and research publications, output, how many publications do I have out'. Katie, at a similar stage, raised issues around the insecurity of being pre-tenure – 'rocking the boat as an assistant professor is truly not a good idea' – and the potentially serious consequences – 'my entire career is at stake right now, all of the years of post-graduate education are at stake right now'.

Annual reviews, which go by various names (performance review, activity reports and 'merit') were mentioned by five of the seven early career participants, as well as most others in the larger study. They require that details about all of the accomplishments of a given year be submitted for evaluation. The process varies by institution, usually involving a committee, the department chair and the dean. There might, or might not, be salary implications. Reported feedback varied from a one-page form letter (Katie) to sitting down with the dean talking about performance and goals for the future (Ryan).

Whether discussing tenure or annual reviews, assistant professors were usually critical of the process or the criteria. Regardless of university, it was generally understood that while teaching was important, research productivity was the key area of evaluation. Criteria might be too narrow: 'measured outputs' (Poppy); 'crude ranking of the journals' (Zoe). Documentation was a problem for Ellie: 'like with updating our resume, the CV, I don't have time to document every single thing that I do – it's too much but I know that this would be the way to go, right?' The use of external research grants as a performance indicator was clearly an issue for several in the group (Polster, 2007), especially given their inexperience in constructing applications and the low success rates anticipated. In Katie's university, 'there's a real focus on pulling in SSHRCs',[2] although, as Poppy pointed out, 'the teaching hasn't gone away'. These comments appear to go beyond those in the American literature about difficulties in time management and allude to changing and intensified requirements such as securing external competitive grant money early in one's career.

Participants disliked the use of student course evaluations for determining teaching competence, echoing literature that questions the validity and biases of these practices. Ellie noted that her 'accent' could be treated harshly in student responses. Zoe remarked that because the students are paying for tuition and other services, they begin to think that they are entitled to an 'A' grade in her class.

Kyle spoke thoughtfully about the difficulties of managing student complaints and knowing whether he has 'engaged the students… I'm never quite sure [laughs], I'm never quite sure'. While he prefers to think in terms of engagement rather than student course evaluations, the latter is a concern for tenure. Teaching a new course, 'I'm assuming I'm going to get a low teaching evaluation or lower compared to my other classes and I know I will have to account for that when I go up for tenure'.

Strategizing

In a previous study of academics close to the point of a tenure review, we found that some participants engaged in careful strategizing; many remarked upon the difficulty of knowing where they should put their energies when confronted with near-daily choices (Acker & Webber, 2016a; see also Nygaard, 2015). The theme of strategizing includes discussion of choices and balances that the participants identified (sites of negotiation) and ways they devised to adapt to real or imagined criteria by which they were to be judged.

Ryan wanted to know how many publications he would need: 'just give me a number'. Kyle had modified his research work, which in the past had been in an allied field with different norms, to match what he saw as a profile more suitable for his department. While repeatedly noting that no one had told him directly that such a change would be advisable, he had worked it out for himself after listening to colleagues' comments in other contexts: 'there is a normative assumption or expectation about what my scholarship is supposed to look like, and so I behaved accordingly'.

Katie's version of adaptation was to work herself into the ground: 'I work seven days a week. I'm exhausted and I'm still expected to perform'. She 'puts in anywhere from 50 to 80 hours a week, if not more'. Poignantly, she described her state of mind: 'I don't have a weekend off… I'm already burnt out… Do I work harder than my body will allow? Yes. Do I cry? Yes. Do I have anxiety? Yes'.

While not as obviously stressed as Katie, Ellie talked about being 'overwhelmed'. Time spent with her children competed with work time: 'Since [a leave] I have worked every day and every weekend and every night, give or take a few'. Close to a tenure review, Ellie worried that she should have been *more* strategic: 'I think I should have better planned writing more articles, looking at specific journals, been a bit more strategic in how I organized my time… there are many things to do all at once'.

Zoe, who was cross-appointed to two departments, was trying to decipher expectations of different subject fields. She explained: 'I'm looking for specific [mainstream] journals in [discipline] and I'm trying to fit my work into them, as opposed to allowing myself to do the work I want to do and finding the right home for it'. She hopes that if she could just publish in a journal specific to that discipline 'once or twice and prove to my [discipline] colleagues that I really am a [discipline person], I think that would be enough'.

Poppy spoke directly about strategy: 'very strategically how can I think about just expanding output in the next few years, pre-tenure, so that I will be counted in a way that shows performance' while regretting that she is unable to think about doing her 'best work'. Tricia, too, felt that the pressure to publish prolifically meant that some of her work was 'just okay' rather than 'great'.

Romanticizing and criticizing

Like respondents to the CAP survey (Weinrib et al., 2013), our participants at all career stages expressed largely positive sentiments about being an academic. However, in our study, the ECAs were the most effusive, frequently using the word 'love', and thus we labelled this theme as 'romanticizing'. Our qualitative approach showed that it was perfectly possible to 'love' one's work yet have significant criticisms of the workplace, and therefore we discuss 'romanticizing' and 'criticizing' together in this section.

Participants loved the research, the teaching and the flexibility of their work:

> I love teaching ... I have to enter into my little bubble but it gives me such a high ... I just love it. (Ellie)

> I love the research. I love the research. (Kyle)

> It's a great job, like in terms of life style, to have flexibility, to be able to, like, go on a class trip with my son, I feel so fortunate. (Tricia)

> It's great the flexibility that you have in your day to day life and your work schedule and being able to stay home in your jammies and write, and your ten-second commute from your bed to your desk by way of your coffee machine. (Zoe)

At the same time, and consistent with literature (Angervall, Beach, & Gustafsson, 2015), the women in the group spoke of how the job extended into every corner of their lives. Above, we quoted the comments of Katie and Ellie about being overworked. Zoe added: 'I feel like I'm always working and never working' (Zoe). Poppy echoed her point: 'When you go home, your work is still with you, either in your head or literally in that you are still doing it once you get home. So you can never sort of leave it', adding that 'overall I think the structure is not at all conducive to adapting to alternative life styles, work-life balance issues, all kinds of things ... Those pre-tenure years are crunched with reproductive years'.

Yet, they enjoyed the challenge. Katie was most explicit about the contradiction:

> You know work comes home with you all the time, grading comes home with you all the time, that's the downside of being an academic. It never leaves you ... I put in anywhere from 50 to 80 hours a week, if not more, sometimes 100 and you get paid the same, there's no overtime, and yet, some colleagues put in 20 or 30 ... *But that's the good part about academia, your ability to do it.* [our italics]. (Katie)

'Loving' the work did not mean that participants loved everything about the university and the academic world: in fact, they were surprisingly critical, a key point for our analysis. We have seen in previous sections that the criteria for assessing research output, the pressure to obtain external grants and the reliance on student course evaluations were points of disaffection.

In response to a question asking if they thought universities were operating like businesses (or not), a strong current of critique surfaced. Participants disliked: corporatization (Katie), 'branding and selling' (Zoe), merit schemes that institutionalized competition among colleagues (Ellie), the treatment of contingent staff (Zoe, Tricia), hiring more managers than faculty (Kyle), increasing class sizes to bring in money (Kyle, Tricia) and student consumerism (Zoe, Katie). Five of the seven (Katie, Kyle, Ryan, Tricia and Poppy) gave specific examples of programmes being under threat and/or needing to demonstrate their worth in narrow terms. For example, Ryan recounted meetings where the topic of discussion was 'we have a $165K shortfall, what are we going to do about it'. Tricia described pressures to 'develop more programmes that are practitioner-focused and that will make money'.

Reconciling

At first glance, there seems to be a contradiction between the extremely positive sentiments expressed by the ECAs about the satisfactions of academic life and the inclination to criticize their institutions and the ways in which they are being 'measured'. Untangling this conceptual knot is what we call 'reconciling'.

First, these assistant professors do not contest the right of the university to evaluate them. Generally, they accept the rhetoric of accountability for performance and say, despite reservations (often about the transparency of the process or the mode of feedback), that they appreciate the chance to reflect:

> It offers an opportunity for self-reflection, this opportunity to sit and think about what you've been doing, how you've been doing it. (Poppy)

> I believe that we do have to be accountable, we are paid with, largely, tuition money and public funding. (Katie)

> I like to be able to set goals and it gives me a framework to set goals. (Ryan)

Second, they are aware of how 'lucky' they are to have a tenure-track position.

> I did one year of sessional work and then a post came up in the department and that's when I applied. I was encouraged to apply and so it's really about being in the right place at the right time kind of thing and a whole lot of luck [laughs]. (Kyle)

> I can't believe this, like I can sit around, I get paid to sit around and think about stuff and write and I think it's a gift. (Tricia)

These academics are what Angervall et al. (2015) call 'the chosen, privileged and fortunate few' (p. 818). The 'being lucky' discourse comes into play when the participants see others much like themselves struggling, as Canadian universities have increasingly moved towards hiring cheaper, insecure, contingent faculty (also called adjuncts or sessionals) to fill teaching vacancies instead of investing in full-time tenure-track academics (Brownlee, 2015). Kyle commented: 'It's not lost on me the privileges that I have in this position. I see the part-timers, it's just brutal'. Zoe, too, criticized the way in which 'the business model' means 'hiring more and more adjuncts to come and teach the classes that our faculty don't want to teach ... adjuncts who faculty seem to think are completely interchangeable, completely disposable, and I think administrators are fine with that model'.

Third, to an extent, they have reconceptualized the tenure review as a *game*, one that the strategies described earlier will help them win. Their choices resemble those made by Nygaard's (2015) participants in the sites of negotiation she identifies. While there are other directions in which Tricia would like to go in her research, 'I don't have that kind of time, so I feel like it's a bit of a game. ... It's a bit of a game but if you don't play it, you're out, and I don't think that's in the long run what I want, I don't want to be out'. Kyle made a similar comment: 'these are the hoops that you have to manoeuvre through ... if I want to stay here, right, and I do want to stay here, right'.

Fourth, they believe that success in this 'game' will lead to a better future when the participants can enjoy the fruits of their labour, relax a bit and follow their own desires: 'life after tenure', perhaps another form of romanticizing. Tricia commented that after tenure, 'then I can sort of step back and do some real research or quality research'. Kyle had this vision: 'I know that once I have tenure, you know, fingers crossed, I won't be so rushed to get a publication out … right now I am rather preoccupied with quantity but that will stop after tenure'. He hopes to be able to achieve more depth in his work, 'engage with the debates'. Katie also anticipated a happier post-tenure world: 'My work–family and personal life balance is completely out of whack and I don't see any way to re-balance it until tenure occurs'.

Strategizing, game-playing and deferring gratification are typically individualistic ways of working through the difficult pre-tenure period. As ECAs will be called to account as individuals, this orientation makes sense. It is widespread in academe. At this stage, participants are not very involved in faculty association (union) activities or any protest movements. When asked about her university's faculty association, Zoe replied: 'Never heard of them'. They are immersed in their research and teaching, and it does not seem appropriate to 'resist' when the goal is so treasured.

Nevertheless, there are individual variations (Grant & Elizabeth, 2015). While Ryan is generally happy with his position and does not feel he is making compromises, he says at the end of his interview that he may not stay in academe. Ellie rejected parts of the dominant narrative. She described how young academics in a workshop on tenure showed concern about 'how to build their own portfolio, how to become successful. … how do I make sure that I publish enough', without questioning 'how to get through to students, how to teach, none of that'. Similarly, speakers at the workshop were saying 'don't get involved in administration, don't get into committees, don't volunteer your time, work on your publications, don't be too available to students'. She found it 'destabilizing because it didn't look at all like my reality'.

Conclusion

In comparing our results to the international literature, we see both similarities and differences. While for the Canadian academics continuous processes of evaluation create insecurity and uncertainty (an 'audit culture') and require continuous sensemaking in multiple sites of negotiation, externally imposed accountability mechanisms are not the main driver of these processes. It appears that traditional practices like tenure and annual reviews have joined forces with the intensification of work and expectations of performativity that are identified with the neo-liberal university. Insufficient resources and cutbacks also influence institutional, departmental and individual adaptations. What is also evident is that these junior academics manage to combine far-reaching concerns about university practices with a deep love for their work.

The title of this article is a pun. ECAs (indeed, all academics) could be seen to be 'made' (compelled) to measure, in this world of impact factors, citation indexes and other scores. While the tenure process in Canada has not been colonized by metrics, expectations that candidates will be producing publications in greater quantities and in better journals, gaining more grants, and scoring higher on student evaluations are very much in play. In another usage, in the world of tailoring, 'made-to-measure' is an adjective describing a customized product in between off-the-rack and bespoke. Off-the-rack would imply lesser quality and greater sameness, as in a chain store, while bespoke is the province of wealthy individuals who have each item created for them individually. A made-to-measure product is not originally designed for the customer but is tailored to their requirements.

So, too, we might consider our ECAs as resembling a made-to-measure product, as they strategize and alter their trajectories to craft a customized response to the generalized requirements of academic success in general and tenure survival in particular. On the whole, they create and deploy strategies to ensure that they meet ever-rising standards, because 'I don't want to be out' (Tricia). But this 'customization' means that even when they are all facing very similar challenges, they are not identical in their sensemaking, as Grant and Elizabeth's (2015) results would predict.

Both Ellie and to a lesser extent Ryan are mildly resistant to the dominant discourses. It may not be coincidental that Ellie and Ryan are the oldest in this group of assistant professors and have work experiences that go beyond the university. The others seem less able to imagine alternatives. Katie is working so hard that she experiences chronic anxiety and stress. Tricia, Kyle, Poppy and to an extent Zoe are reviewing their research and teaching with a strong intent to satisfy whatever is being asked of them, hoping that 'life after tenure' will give them greater freedom. Our interviews with newer associate professors do, indeed, suggest that they will feel freer post-tenure, although they face other evaluative procedures like annual reviews that continue to require conformity and strategizing, as well as increased administrative responsibilities (see Acker & Webber, 2016b, for cross-group comparisons). For ECAs, annual, probationary and tenure reviews were all part of the same apparatus and they did not make similar distinctions.

We believe it is important that all of the pre-tenure academics, however much they 'love' their jobs, have trenchant criticisms of the corporatized university and the ways in which evaluations proceed. In that sense, they do not appear to have become willing neo-liberal subjects (Archer, 2008). Is it a contradiction to criticize while conforming? Might this orientation among junior academics bode well for the future of the academy? Alternatively, will so many years of practising conformity create lifelong habits too difficult to dislodge? After all, 'playing the game' is not confined to novice academics (Lucas, 2006).

Current ECAs may not resemble their senior counterparts in years to come, as they operate from the start in a different, more neo-liberal environment replete with expectations for greater accountability, intensified workloads, demonstrable social impacts and chronic competition over scarce resources. There will be more annual reviews and future promotion prospects to consider as our ECAs move into middle and late career stages.

Notes

1. At times, North American terminology will appear in this article, that is, faculty for academic staff, professor for academic or lecturer and administration for management.
2. SSHRC (pronounced 'shirk') is an acronym for Social Sciences and Humanities Research Council, the granting body that provides most of the funding for research in the participants' subject fields.

Acknowledgements

We thank the Social Sciences and Humanities Research Council for support and Dr Victoria Kannen for research assistance.

Disclosure statement

No potential conflict of interest was reported by the authors.

Funding

This work was supported by Social Sciences and Humanities Research Council of Canada [grant number 410-2009-0581].

References

Acker, S., & Webber, M. (2016a). Discipline and publish: The tenure review process in Ontario universities. In L. Shultz & M. Viczko (Eds.), *Assembling and governing the higher education institution* (pp. 233–255). London: Palgrave Macmillan.

Acker, S., & Webber, M. (2016b). Uneasy academic subjectivities in the contemporary Ontario university. In J. Smith, J. Rattray, T. Peseta, & D. Loads (Eds.), *Identity work in the contemporary university* (pp. 61–75). Rotterdam: Sense.

Acker, S., Webber, M., & Smyth, E. (2012). Tenure troubles and equity matters in Canadian academe. *British Journal of Sociology of Education*, 33(5), 743–761.

Angervall, P., Beach, D., & Gustafsson, J. (2015). The unacknowledged value of female academic labour power for male research careers. *Higher Education Research & Development*, 34(5), 815–827.

Archer, L. (2008). The new neoliberal subjects? Young/er academics' constructions of professional identity. *Journal of Education Policy*, 23(3), 265–285.

Billot, J. (2010). The imagined and the real: Identifying the tensions for academic identity. *Higher Education Research & Development*, 29(6), 709–721.

Brownlee, J. (2015). Contract faculty in Canada: Using access to information requests to uncover hidden academics in Canadian universities. *Higher Education*, 70, 787–805.

Bruneau, W., & Savage, D. (2002). *Counting out the scholars: The case against performance indicators in higher education*. Toronto: Lorimer.

Burrows, R. (2012). Living with the h-index? Metric assemblages in the contemporary academy. *The Sociological Review*, 60(2), 355–372.

Butterwick, S., & Dawson, J. (2005). Undone business: Examining the production of academic labour. *Women's Studies International Forum*, 28, 51–65.

Chait, R. P. (Ed.). (2002). *The questions of tenure*. Cambridge, MA: Harvard University Press.

Chan, A., & Fisher, D. (Eds.). (2008). *The exchange university: Corporatization of academic culture*. Vancouver: University of British Columbia Press.

Clegg, S. (2008). Academic identities under threat? *British Educational Research Journal*, 34(3), 329–345.

Degn, L. (2016). Academic sensemaking and behavioural responses – exploring how academics perceive and respond to identity threats in times of turmoil. *Studies in Higher Education*. Advance online publication. doi:10.1080/03075079.2016.1168796

Dobbie, D., & Robinson, I. (2008). Reorganizing higher education in the United States and Canada: The erosion of tenure and the unionization of contingent faculty. *Labour Studies Journal*, 33(2), 117–140.

Eddy, P., & Gaston-Gayles, J. (2008). New faculty on the block: Issues of stress and support. *Journal of Human Behavior in the Social Environment*, 17(1/2), 89–106.

Enders, J., de Boer, H., & Leišytė, L. (2009). New public management and the academic profession: The rationalisation of academic work revisited. In J. Enders & E. de Weert (Eds.), *The changing face of academic life* (pp. 36–57). London: Palgrave Macmillan.

Flaherty, C. (2016, March 11). Fake tenure? *Inside Higher Education*. Retrieved from https://www.insidehighered.com/news/2016/03/11/u-wisconsin-board-regents-approves-new-tenure-policies-despite-faculty-concerns

Grant, B. M., & Elizabeth, V. (2015). Unpredictable feelings: Academic women under research audit. *British Educational Research Journal, 41*(2), 287–302.

Gravestock, P., & Greenleaf, E. (2008). *Overview of tenure and promotion policies across Canada*. Unpublished paper, University of Toronto. Retrieved from http://www.mtroyal.ca/cs/groups/public/documents/pdf/aptc_canada_tenurepolicies.pdf

Henkel, M. (2005). Academic identity and autonomy in a changing policy environment. *Higher Education, 49*, 155–176.

Henry, F., & Tator, C. (2012). Interviews with racialized faculty members in Canadian universities. *Canadian Ethnic Studies, 44*(2), 75–99.

Horn, M. (1999). Tenure and the Canadian professoriate. *Journal of Canadian Studies, 34*(3), 261–281.

Horn, M. (2015). Tenure and academic freedom in Canada. *Ethics in Science and Environmental Politics, 15*, 23–38. Retrieved from http://www.int-res.com/articles/esep2015/15/e015p023.pdf

Jones, G. A., Weinrib, J., Metcalfe, A. S., Fisher, D., Rubenson, K., & Snee, I. (2012). Academic work in Canada: The perceptions of early-career academics. *Higher Education Quarterly, 66*(2), 189–206.

Kawalilak, C., & Groen, J. (Eds.) (2010). Special issue: Perspectives – the road to tenure. *Journal of Educational Thought, 44*(1), 1–162.

Kreissl, K., Striedinger, A., Sauer, B., & Hofbauer, J. (2015). Will gender equality ever fit in? Contested discursive spaces of university reform. *Gender and Education, 27*(3), 221–238.

Lawrence, J., Celis, S., & Ott, M. (2014). Is the tenure process fair? What faculty think. *Journal of Higher Education, 85*(2), 155–192.

Leišytė, L., & Dee, J. R. (2012). Understanding academic work in a changing institutional environment. In J. C. Smart & M. Paulsen (Eds.), *Higher education: Handbook of theory and research* (pp. 123–206). Dordrecht: Springer.

Lorenz, C. (2012). If you're so smart, why are you under surveillance? Universities, neoliberalism, and new public management. *Critical Inquiry, 38*(3), 599–629.

Lucas, L. (2006). *The research game in academic life*. Maidenhead: Open University Press.

Macfarlane, B. (2011). The morphing of academic practice: Unbundling and the rise of the para-academic. *Higher Education Quarterly, 65*(1), 59–73.

McAlpine, L., Amundsen, C., & Turner, G. (2013). Constructing post-PhD careers: Negotiating opportunities and personal goals. *International Journal for Researcher Development, 4*(1), 39–54.

McAlpine, L., Amundsen, C., & Turner, G. (2014). Identity-trajectory: Reframing early career academic experience. *British Educational Research Journal, 40*(6), 952–969.

de Montigny, G. (2011). "Put on a happy face": Tenure, grievance, and governance. *Canadian Journal of Educational Administration and Policy, 125*. Retrieved from https://www.umanitoba.ca/publications/cjeap/pdf_files/de%20montigny.pdf

Murray, J. P. (2008). New faculty members' perceptions of the academic work life. *Journal of Human Behavior in the Social Environment, 17*(1/2), 107–128.

Nygaard, L. (2015). Publishing and perishing: An academic literacies framework for investigating research productivity. *Studies in Higher Education*. Advance online publication. doi:10.1080/03075079.2015.1058351

Olssen, M. (2016). Neoliberal competition in higher education today: Research, accountability and impact. *British Journal of Sociology of Education, 37*(1), 129–148.

Ornstein, M., Stewart, P., & Drakich, J. (2007). Promotion at Canadian universities: The intersection of gender, discipline, and institution. *Canadian Journal of Higher Education, 37*(3), 1–25.

Osei-Kofi, N. (2012). Junior faculty of color in the corporate university: Implications of neoliberalism and neoconservatism on research, teaching and service. *Critical Studies in Education, 53*(2), 229–244.

Palulis, P. (2015). Tenure (un)secure/d: As words go into labour. In E. Whittaker (Ed.), *Solitudes of the workplace* (pp. 80–99). Vancouver: University of British Columbia Press.

Polster, C. (2007). The nature and implications of the growing importance of research grants to Canadian universities and academics. *Higher Education, 53*, 599–622.

Shore, C., & Wright, S. (2000). Coercive accountability: The rise of audit culture in higher education. In M. Strathern (Ed.), *Audit cultures* (pp. 57–89). London: Routledge.

Tierney, W., & Bensimon, E. (1996). *Promotion and tenure: Community and socialization in academe*. Albany: State University of New York Press.

Uzuner-Smith, S., & Englander, K. (2014). Exposing ideology within university policies: A critical discourse analysis of faculty hiring, promotion and remuneration practices. *Journal of Education Policy, 30*(1), 62–85.

Vidovich, L., & Slee, R. (2001). Bringing universities to account? Exploring some global and local policy tensions. *Journal of Education Policy, 16*(5), 431–453.

Weinrib, J., Jones, G., Metcalfe, A. S., Fisher, D., Gingras, Y., Rubenson, K., & Snee, I. (2013). Canadian university faculty perceptions of job satisfaction. In P. Bentley, H. Coates, I. Dobson, L. Goedegebuure, & V. L. Meek (Eds.), *Job satisfaction around the academic world* (pp. 83–102). Dordrecht: Springer.

Wilson, M., & Holligan, C. (2014). Performativity, work-related emotions and collective research identities in UK university education departments: An exploratory study. *Cambridge Journal of Education, 43*(2), 223–241.

Yeo, M., Bennett, D., Stoneman McNichol, J., & Merkely, C. (2015). New faculty experience in times of institutional change. *Canadian Journal of Higher Education, 45*(4), 283–297.

Fear and loathing in the academy? The role of emotion in response to an impact agenda in the UK and Australia

Jennifer Chubb, Richard Watermeyer and Paul Wakeling

ABSTRACT
The research impact agenda is frequently portrayed through 'crisis' accounts whereby academic identity is at risk of a kind of existential unravelling. Amid reports of academics under siege in an environment in which self-sovereignty is traditionally preferred and regulation is resisted, heightened emotionalism, namely fear and dread, dominates the discourse. Such accounts belie the complexity of the varying moral dispositions, experiences and attitudes possessed by different individuals and groups in the academic research community. In this article, we attempt to examine the role of the affective in response to a particular research policy directive – the impact agenda. In doing so, we reveal the contributing factors affecting the community's reaction to impact. In cases where personal, moral and disciplinary identities align with the impact agenda, the emotional response is positive and productive. For many academics, however, misalignment gives rise to emotional dissonance. We argue that when harnessed, further acknowledgement of the role of emotion in the academy can produce a more socially and morally coherent response to an impact agenda. We review academic responses from the UK and Australia ($n = 51$) and observe a community heavily emotionally invested in what they do, such that threats to academic identity and research are consequently threats to the self.

Introduction

The emotional state of academic labour as it evolves in response to the challenges in higher education are frequently portrayed through 'crisis' accounts whereby academic identity is at risk of a kind of existential unravelling. Such diagnoses, however, belie the complexity of a rapidly changing organisational paradigm of higher education; the diversity of the academic research community; and the spectrum of cognate experiences, attitudes and moral dispositions. Amid such complexity and in the face of intensifying demands, the ability to distil a 'true' sense of academic identity is increasingly difficult – obscured by heightened emotionalism, particularly of fear and dread, which are yet to be fully explored.

Emotion, though prevalent in Western Philosophy through the discourse of Cartesian Dualism, remains 'rarely acknowledged and under or mis-theorised' in the context of higher education despite attempts to reconceptualise its relationship with rationality

(Beard, Clegg, & Smith, 2007, p. 236). Nevertheless, we find that emotion has a key influence in academic life particularly with respect to research. Much of the literature describes the tension between traditional notions of the academy as an 'emotion-free zone' to one where the role of the affective is acknowledged (Beard et al., 2007; Hey & Leathwood, 2009). Whilst the effects of emotion with respect to gender and teaching are well researched (Boler, 1999; Light & Cox, 2001), the role of emotion in response to recent higher education policy directives such as the impact agenda appears relatively under researched (Evans, 2004).

Reminiscent of what Beard et al. (2007, p. 237) refer to as the 'rational–emotional dilemma', we find academics struggling to reconcile their sense of identity and practice with profound change. The process of coping with change is emotionally laden and, therefore, inclined to produce partisan, embellished behaviours and hyperbolic testimony. Academics' identity politics are perhaps especially acute and exaggerated where in the academy, the status quo is traditionally preferred; where forms of regulation which might interfere with academics' right to self-sovereignty are fiercely resisted (Ahmed, 2003); and where organisational change of most kinds has until relatively recently been typified by a prevailing languor. Now, however, academics working in public universities increasingly find themselves subject to rapid rule-change through the reorganisation of higher education including globalisation, marketisation; metricisation; global recession (Marginson & Considine, 2000; Palfreyman & Tapper, 2014); and, in the UK especially, a politics of austerity in the distribution of public funds.

A slide towards a doomsday scenario for higher education (Bhattacharya, 2012) appears further hastened, if not normalised, where the everyday working conditions and ideological tenets of the academic profession are said to be in a state of continuous decline and erosion (cf. Giroux, 2014; Watermeyer & Olssen, 2016). Many commentators point to the detrimental impacts on the academic profession caused by neoliberalism, citing the precarity of the academic career; the fetishisation of competition (Naidoo, 2016); and the entrenchment of systems of control that are seen to erode academics' critical autonomy, freedom and agency.

Despite this, many academics persist, remaining dedicated to a role and field of inquiry they have heavily emotionally invested in. For every articulation of despair or despondency, a balance (of sorts) is recovered where a sense of commitment and/or love of what they do is asserted, despite the multiple, incongruous and seemingly grievous challenges they face. The emotional ties to academic labour are binding. They are exhibited in the kinds of vocationalism and hyper-professionality studied by Gornall, Cook, Daunton, Salisbury, and Thomas (2013) and the 'passionate attachments' explored by Hey and Leathwood (2009), marking academic life as all-encompassing and indivisible from other aspects of personhood. In some cases, the link between an academics' life and research is inextricable, as seen through the supposed phenomenon of 'mesearch' (Nguyen, 2015). Knowledge is, for personal and philosophical reasons, fiercely protected by its custodians: within this discourse, to be an academic is to *live* academia.

Of course, not all will be in a state of ideological conflict nor will they be necessarily ideologically bound. For some, existence in the neoliberal academy is less problematic and more easily negotiated. Smith (2012), for instance, refers to some academics exhibiting either conformist or flexible behaviours in response to the intensification of new managerialism in higher education. 'Flexians' are those perhaps most pragmatic and able to moderate their emotional investment in being an academic. Others might construe this as inauthenticity and a preference for playing the game; it might equally be a form of covert transgression. Either way, ideas of what it is to be an academic and how the academic role is configured and (self) presented are far more composite when understood in reference to underlying emotional frameworks.

Impact agendas in Australia and the UK

Both Australia and the UK have sought to introduce research policy which achieves economic and/or social impact. These policies envisage a potentially transformative role for knowledge produced through university research and are part of a broader trend to see universities as central to a knowledge economy (Etzkowitz & Leydesdorff, 2000; Gibbons et al., 1994). Such policies tend to eschew ideas of 'knowledge for its own sake', which might be conceived positively as an exhortation to avoid academic insularity; or alternatively more negatively as another instance of neoliberal performativity and a reduction of research to an investment intended to produce a (financial) return. Discussions of impact appeared first in Australia, before being taken up more forcefully in the UK, and finally returning to Australia. Whilst similar ideas have been raised in other countries such as Canada through knowledge mobilisation policies, Australia and the UK have been at the forefront of policies on research impact.

The focus of the accounts explored herein reflects the testimonies of academics responding primarily to an impact agenda in the context of research funding. The formal inclusion of 'pathways to impact' in grant applications for Research Council UK (RCUK) funding in the UK seeks to address how potential research will lead to economic and social impact. RCUK broadly defines impact as 'the demonstrable contribution that excellent research makes to society and the economy' (RCUK, 2011, p. 2). In the UK, assessment of impact accounts for a 20% measure of research quality in the 'Research Excellence Framework' (REF) – an exercise undertaken by funding agencies approximately every five years to determine the volume and quality of research undertaken in UK higher education institutions for the purpose of allocating mainstream quality-related research funding. Inevitably, the testimonies of UK academics provided herein may also reflect these changes. Here, REF impact is defined as 'an effect on, change or benefit to the economy, society, culture, public policy or services, health, the environment or quality of life, beyond academia' (REF, 2012). Within the context of the UK REF, impact was assessed through structured narrative case studies, where evidence was provided about how the underpinning research had caused change outside the academy. Impact case studies were assessed by expert panels who formed an overall view as to the reach and significance of the impact. Following a variety of concerns about impact as a component of the REF process and the value judgements made thereof (Martin, 2011; Samuel & Derrick, 2015), the recent Governmental Stern Review consultation in the UK (July 2016) announced a continued focus on impact in forthcoming assessments.[1]

Proposals to the Australian Research Council (ARC) similarly require a statement on impact. In 2016, the ARC consulted the sector with the Australian Academy of Technology and Engineering (ATSE) 'Research and Engagement'[2] consultation, in which views were sought on how to best implement a research impact agenda. This follows the ARC's shift towards an impact requirement in grant applications, the Excellence

Innovation Australia[3] (EIA) trial in 2012 and plans for impact to form part of Excellence in Research Australia 2017 (ERA).

Scholarly reactions to impact

Much has been written on the schism in higher education in which the traditional norms and ideals of sovereignty and a bounded territory of academe (Henkel, 2007) are seen to be threatened by 'new managerialism' arising from a neoliberal mandate (Deem, Hillyard, & Reed, 2007). The university, reported to be 'in crisis' (O'Shea, 2014) is seen to impair and inhibit the possibility of freedom and autonomy (Chubb & Watermeyer, 2016; Marginson & Considine, 2000). The inclusion of impact statements in both RCUK and ARC grant applications has prompted an emotional reaction from the scholarly community. Impact as a 'measure' of research quality has been deeply contested, seen as part of a growing 'audit-culture' (Cupples & Pawson, 2012; Lucas, 2006; Sparkes, 2007).

Characterised as a 'creeping assault' on freedom and agency (Hammersley, 2016; Holmwood, 2011), the impact agenda initially received a hostile reception by some members of the UK academic community (Braben et al., 2009; Collini, 2011; Watermeyer, 2012), and a similar 'chorus of dissatisfaction' was reported in Australia (Cuthill, O'Shea, Wilson, & Viljoen, 2014, p. 42; Donovan, 2008). Scholars describe how this has affected 'academic identities' (Delanty, 2008; Whitchurch, 2012; Winter, 2009) and, how this may have contributed to the erosion of academic virtues (Chubb & Watermeyer, 2016). By its critics, impact is deemed incongruent with traditional academic ideals (Harris, 2005; Lucas, 2006; Smith, 2012).

Much of the public debate concerning the reception of the impact agenda is characterised by academic *resistance*. In particular, voices which dominate the discourse are those whose research is less predisposed to impact (Braben et al., 2009; Gibbons et al., 1994). Here, such individuals and their 'tribes' (Becher, 1989; Biglan, 1973) have depicted a 'culture of fear' (Bhattacharya, 2012) and resistance in the academy, the result of which appears at first negative for the academy.

Notwithstanding disciplinary preferences and predispositions towards impact, support for the agenda (Becher, 1994; Leathwood & Read, 2012) comes from those who embrace and celebrate the non-academic influence of their work; those who pragmatically choose to adapt towards it (Smith, 2012), and those who recognise the opportunity and reward that may accompany it (Harris, 2005).

In this article, we explore the varying emotional responses of academics from the UK and Australia towards the research impact. Through the metaphor of a 'belt of resistance' which can be tightened or slackened, we attempt to elucidate the contributing factors to academics' reaction to an impact agenda. In so doing, we aim to use an emotional register as a way of further differentiating notions of academic personhood and the way with which it is conceived and exhibited in the milieu of the university's alleged existential crisis. In cases where personal, moral and disciplinary identities align with the impact agenda, the emotional response is positive and productive. For many, misalignment gives rise to emotional dissonance. Policy which pays no heed to the emotional register faces limited success. However, the difficulties arising from the impact agenda are not entirely externally imposed. The discourse which places academic identity at the centre of personhood – and whereby threats to academic identity are consequentially threats to the self – appears to be endogenous to academia.

Methods

Semi-structured interviews were conducted with 51 mid-senior career academics between 2011 and 2013 in the UK (30) and Australia (21) at two research-intensive universities. Interviewees were asked how they felt about the introduction of an impact agenda in terms of both funding and assessment in higher education research policy. Interviews were typically between 40 and 60 minutes in duration.

Interviewees represented a range of disciplines covering the arts and humanities (13), social sciences (12), engineering and the physical sciences (15), and life and natural sciences (11). Participants were selected based upon their grant-writing experience, specifically as principal or co-investigators on grant applications. Many also had experience as reviewers of applications and several had authored impact case studies for assessment purposes in their national context. Participants were recruited via research offices at both institutions. Whilst the aspiration was to achieve equal representation of men and women, this was not realised, principally due to an overrepresentation of men among grant award holders. There were 20 women and 31 men in the achieved sample.

The risk of harm to the participants was reduced by ensuring that they were making a voluntary informed decision to participate and anonymity was assured. Interviews were thematically analysed using qualitative analysis software NVivo 10 and a grounded theory approach was applied. Transcripts were coded according to the subjective, personal and emotional responses provided. Use of descriptive language – suggestive of positive, negative or neutral feelings towards the impact agenda – was also analysed. Themes were drawn inductively from the data. Informed consent to use the comments and testimonies of all participants was provided and where they are cited, their discipline and country are stated.

Findings

Academic testimonies were rarely dispassionate when responding to the emergence of an impact agenda. Instead, the majority of interviewees expressed an emotional attachment to their work and, as a consequence, the impact thereof.

Notwithstanding the potential for hyperbole or rhetoric, when asked to discuss impact, academics expressed emotions ranging from ambivalence and apathy – nervousness and vulnerability – to excitement, love, hate and distrust. For many of our interviewees, impact was seen as critical to their agency and identity; for others, it had the potential to threaten the very nature of what they do. Concurrent with an emotional commitment to or disassociation from impact, interviewees were nevertheless united in articulating the tensions related to having to account for the use of public funding and a sense of public responsibility.

Responsibility is not felt without complication and anxiety. For some, it carried a deep burden, tightening the belt of resistance towards an impact agenda, where self-justification was resisted and internalised. For others, it was an opportunity and resource, where emotion was harnessed in a positive and productive way. Impact is therefore either critical to academic agency – inherently related to motivation and responsibility; or is instead feared, where control and identity are lost through the experience of impact agenda.

Impact as critical to academic agency and personhood

Contrary to the 'siege-mentality' depicted by those critical of an impact agenda, several interviewees expressed a range of positive and affirming emotions when describing their feelings towards impact and in particular the *mechanisms* by which it can be achieved. Emotions such as passion, happiness, enjoyment, excitement and even love were expressed by academics whose agency and personhood appeared co-dependent upon 'making an impact'.

Importantly, those who expressed positive emotion did so with an accompanied sense of responsibility inherent to their perception of the academic role:

> It's sort of where my heart lies – quite deliberately and specifically working to apply the research that you are doing to real world political and social challenges across domains of theory and practice. (Politics, UK, Lecturer)

Here, impact was considered as inextricably linked, inseparable from the research itself: 'there's no point doing science unless you tell people' (Environment, UK, Professor). Understood as a core component of academic labour at least in certain disciplines, impact was therefore 'part and parcel' of the academic role. Notably, the most positive reactions towards impact came from those whose work was naturally predisposed to it and those who felt morally compelled to give back to society:

> Someone I know who got one of the largest grants ever said, 'I don't care if my research has impact – I'm doing this because I'm curious about this' and I just thought that was an appalling waste of tax payer's money to be able to get a lot of money to research something just because you're curious about it and not even see that down the road it might have impact. (Education, UK, Professor)

Often, moral compulsion was accompanied by a perceived sense of privilege. In this context, the existential purpose of academics was to contribute to society:

> We are paid from the public purse and we should be doing research-we are ridiculously privileged to work on whatever we like and it's wonderful, and to bend your mind a little bit to the fact that some of the stuff you do does have benefits outside the academy, and to put measures in place to make that happen, it's a minor tax. (Archaeology, UK, Professor)

> Well, what else are we here for? (Linguistics, Australia, Professor)

The tenor of interviewees' reactions often hinged principally upon the *type of research* they were conducting. Where research had obvious connections to real-world application, such as in the natural or social sciences, respondents were typically positively disposed to the impact agenda and did not exhibit great fear or anxiety. Here, impact was 'pretty much bread and butter stuff' and therefore 'not worth losing any sleep over': 'I don't think people should feel unduly stressed by it' (Physics, UK, Professor).

In addition, academics commonly expressed positive emotions for the mechanisms leading to impact. Depicted in several instances as fun, exciting, fulfilling, inspiring and engaging, several interviewees expressed their enjoyment and happiness at conducting public engagement and knowledge exchange activities. Many were enthusiastic and positive, indicating that to communicate research – and enjoying it – is not essentially at odds with academic personhood.

> It's an agenda I quite enjoy engaging with and I must say that going into the more practical, doing stuff that might actually change the way people manage things is probably much closer to what I set out to do as a scientist in the first place actually. (Biology, UK, Lecturer)

Rather, it was the bureaucratic burden seen to accompany impact which incited emotional distress and frustration, as well as a putative ongoing divorce of research and impact as distinct activities:

> Yeah I enjoy it, but I don't see that as being part of my research I see that as part of an education thing, as providing a service to the community–I see it as a service thing. (Finance, Australia, Professor)

Despite these accounts, impact is nevertheless predominantly seen to destabilise the traditional perception of academics whose role it is to purely teach and do research. It is here that control is lost and identity is seen to be at risk.

Loss of control and identity

Despite the presence of positive and enabling responses towards impact, the majority of interviewees described how the academic community was emotionally and morally conflicted through the experience of an impact agenda.

Accounting for much of the resistance was the perceived risk to freedom and autonomy, cited by a large proportion of participants. Over two-thirds repeatedly used words such as 'constrict', 'prescribe', 'limit', 'impair' and even 'stifle' or 'constrain' when describing how impact and other pressures arising from the managerialism in research affected their freedom and 'their ability to do things'. One interviewee optimistically exclaimed, however: 'you cannot stop me thinking about Keats in the morning!' (Literature, Australia, Professor). Notwithstanding the potential for emotional embellishment and sarcasm here, such comparisons imply that freedom is nevertheless potentially impaired.

Words such as; 'scary', 'threat', 'nervousness' and 'worry' littered the transcripts as many spoke of their 'frustrations', 'suspiciousness' and even 'resentment' of the impact agenda. Participants reported feeling 'sad', 'unhappy', 'jealous', 'anxious', 'demoralised', 'disillusioned' 'confused', 'hopeless', 'paranoid', 'vulnerable', 'scared', 'nervous' and 'depressed' about the impact agenda.

Despite an almost unanimous consensus that research paid for through public funds ought to be justified, for many interviewees, this was personally internalised, as though they themselves were being scrutinised and (de)valued. Here, we see responses in which the impact component is seen to 'threaten', 'destabilise' and 'demoralise' whole disciplines. This resulted in the expression of existential crises from individuals who felt that they had to 'justify their existence':

> I don't feel happy with it, and do I need to justify my job? How many levels do I have to justify it? (Music, Australia, Professor)

The effects of having to demonstrate research impact to the public received a hostile reception from some academics who felt personally attacked by the insinuation that academia was in some sense a discrete population of society, de-humanised in their ivory tower (Bok, 2003):

> Don't start me on the Ivory tower theory! No do start me! Yes, that is a word often used. The strange thing is that it's often used in a kind of out of context that implies that academics are not human. They're disembodied robots. Just because they work at a university they don't have lives, they don't have families, and they don't have to earn a living or pay their mortgages. Often it comes out as, 'oh what would you know about this, you're an academic'. It'll be about something like paying your mortgage, what do you think I know? I'm paying off my own, just like you. (History, Australia, Professor)

Academics expressed concerns not only for themselves but also for the ongoing stability of their discipline. Most notably, though not exclusively, participants who expressed fears relating to their discipline conducted less 'applied' types of research, such as those found in the theoretical humanities and physical sciences. Here, participants reported 'deep seated worry', 'frustration', 'struggle', 'fear', 'shock' 'hopelessness' and a range of other emotions: 'I sort of struggle' (Maths, Australia, Professor); 'I don't feel happy' (Music, Australia, Professor).

Feelings of dissatisfaction were accompanied in many cases by hopelessness and surrender:

> What we have now is a demoralizing, denigration of disciplines. (Philosophy, Australia, Professor)

> I get really sick because of the kind of research I do–I get pissed off at the idea that where you should put your funding is cancer research – that's the generic answer isn't it? (Music, Australia, Professor)

Humanities researchers in particular feared having to justify the *value* of their work and reconciling the work they do with the ability to prove or show (particularly) economic impact – they described their work as 'precious' and would happily 'scream and shout' about it (Music, Australia, Professor), in order to defend it:

> The agenda reinforces that the only valuable thing in life is money and that is deeply worrying. (Performance, UK, Professor)

In other theoretical disciplines, this position was mirrored. Academics predominantly from the physical sciences commented that impact was 'scary and really hard' because of the theoretical nature of the work they do (Maths, Australia, Professor); 'everyone is enormously worried' (Computer Science, UK, Professor). Many theoretically focused Australian academics also explained that an impact agenda would make many of them feel 'hopeless'. Here, worries related to a fear about government interference and instrumentalism in science:

> I tell you – it's serious, the scientific community is in shock ... It's a shattering blow to science – just this shaping of something, which is so precious, leave it damn well alone! (Chemistry, UK, Professor)

In addition, interviewees also described how some of these emotional reactions related to academic labour and job security. The pressures of new managerialism were reflected in many (perhaps hyperbolic) emotional responses from participants:

> You can easily lose your job, a previous dean was kicked out, you can lose your job if you question practices of a higher level, so everyone is vulnerable, and everybody is paranoid about losing their jobs. (Engineering Education, Australia, Professor)

Interviewees claimed that impact reduced the attractiveness of academic life to the extent that it influenced job decisions. Here, one participant explained how impact had affected their decision on whether to go for a promotion:

> Part of the reason I didn't put my hand up for [research leadership] role is, you know, this impact thing. (Literature, Australia, Professor)

Indeed, these pressures were felt by many on a very personal level, some participants claimed to be 'depressed' or 'sad'. These concerns were more readily expressed by women, but with some exceptions; 'I feel like crying about it sometimes' (Chemistry, UK, Professor). Australian participants were especially open about their emotions when describing the divergent pressures they faced:

> I got extremely depressed last year for the first time in my career and thought I can't do this anymore. (Education Engineering, Australia, Professor)

Another participant talked about how her life was a 'bloody nervous wreck' and that she did not feel happy because of the amount of stress she experienced in her career:

> You know, somebody would look at me from the outside and think ok, she's got over 100 publications, whatever – so she's got all these publications and she's had grants – she's doing this and she's going here, actually my life is a bloody nervous wreck. (Music, Australia, Professor)

The effects therefore are deep-seated and perhaps enduring, indicative of a broader set of concerns for academic labour.

A final justification for the tightening of a belt of resistance to an impact agenda is that many claimed that they did not feel that they were skilled enough to deliver it, which resulted in emotional distress and concern.

Regularly described as a 'mind-set barrier', impact was viewed by many academics as something which strayed from the normal occupations and skills traditionally associated with the academic role. Several participants welcomed this and described how the impact agenda was a good thing, as it challenged their abilities to 'think outside the box' but this was also seen as 'threatening' to academic identities many of whom confirmed that they naturally preferred to be left alone:

> I like what I do–but not on a stage. (Archaeology, UK, Professor)

There were fears that the impact requirement would result in a need to redefine the academic role. This was met with concern from over half of the participants who felt that this was at odds with their personalities: 'I think I'm one of those who aren't very out there and I'm actually fairly shy' (Health Sciences, Australia, Professor).

Personalities less inclined towards impact expressed how 'uncomfortable' or 'scary' it was to engage in knowledge exchange. A significant proportion of interviewees expressed a lack of confidence and fear when it came to their abilities to communicate their work to different audiences. Many put this down to a lack of training, their personality or their background, but, for many, it was also because they feared being the subject of mockery from their peers:

> I think a lot of academics are quite egotistic and you have to have a good ego to perform well in a film or on TV so they can walk around with puffed up breasts quite legitimately when you're on film whereas when you're on campus people think you're a jerk. (Archaeology, Australia, Professor)

> One is considered research output and the other is laughed at. The one that is laughed at reaches more people! (Music, UK, Professor)

Delivery of impact was regarded by many as a low-status activity; several claimed that it was not 'real research' and instead referred to it as 'pedestrian' or 'second-class', less 'highbrow' than pure research. Others claimed that such attitudes were borne out of 'professional jealousy' and snobbery (Music, Australia, Professor):

> Some of us might be perceived as unserious researchers if we engage with the public at a lower level where everyone can engage in debate. Frankly I think that type of academic snobbery is a bit archaic and outdated and I wouldn't want to bow to it. (Law, Australia, Professor)

Finally, the 'flexians' among our interviewees gave pragmatic responses to impact and called for 'balance' and 'proportionality'. As opposed to 'groaning about new policy' (Biology, UK, Lecturer), some academics advocated the need to simply 'get on with it' and to take control of the agenda:

> We can all sit back and whine about having to do it, but we could give our opinions and talk to people and have your input into what it looks like which might make it more helpful and more something that we can address – something we have all got a responsibility for. (Health Sciences, Australia, Professor)

The flexians held a minority view and nevertheless, it is clear that academics are highly invested in what they do. In particular, Australian participants on the whole were largely more emotional in their responses towards impact than those in the UK. This is perhaps indicative of the fact that an impact agenda was developed and in force in UK universities whilst only in its fledgling stages in Australia:

> The negative voices have fallen silent because they haven't got a choice. (Languages, UK, Lecturer)

A level of compassion towards those less able to conform to the requirement is perhaps therefore required from both the community that creates impact and that which requires it, in order to avoid a radical reconfiguration of the academic role altogether.

> John Paul Satre never taught at a university – I think you're going to have more of an intellectual life outside of the university. (Philosophy, Australia, Professor)

Discussion

Our initial intention to identify an emotional register that might show variance in the construction of academic personhood in the context of an impact agenda has, in these accounts, been largely upended by the domination of a sentiment of hopelessness and tales of lost or ceded power. Furthermore, a belt of resistance to an impact agenda has been shown to be ever tightening in parallel with the loosening of academics' sense of self-sovereignty.

Our interviews reveal a community with strong emotional reactions towards impact. For many of our interviewees, an impact agenda disrupted their sense of purpose as academic researchers – where panic was induced in terms of how they might maintain coherence with an adjusted version of their professional selves. However, this kind of panic appears at odds with another version of the implications of impact cited by a smaller subsection of our interview sample. This group perceived, within the impact agenda, a positive and logical drawing out or enhancing of the academic role through the figure of the public intellectual. For this cadre, impact provides an opportunity through which accountability and public disclosure confirm both their moral authority and the significance of their (public) role. An impact agenda was seen, therefore, to provide a platform from which academics can showcase not only to their public financiers but also to themselves (and each other) the efficacy of their research endeavours. For some, it appears to have provided a route to self-legitimisation and an affirmation of academic personhood and agency. However, as has been discussed, the majority of those who perceived the benefits of impact as a method of critical reflexivity and, therefore, self-justification, were also those whose research was oriented towards direct application or had a more proximate user-interface and whom we might also infer might more easily demonstrate causality between research outcome and user impact.

What some interviewees reported as the benefit of an impact agenda in instilling greater self-confidence in the presentation of their public personas, others claimed as a sense of alienation and fear, principally a fear of being ill-equipped or unsuited to tackle the associated risks of operating in the agora. The latter cited a sense of lost control and vulnerability in terms of the choreography of their public face; the risk perhaps of being fixed with a professional portraiture they might not recognise, like or agree with. This sense of vulnerability was further exacerbated where the risk of 'going public' might culminate in forms of professional penalisation such as lost esteem and status among academic peers.

A crucial aspect of interviewees' response is a concern with professional modesty and a perceived antagonism between their showing or 'selling' of their impact – in the pursuit of financial reward – and actually achieving scientific impact. For these academics, an impact agenda reinforces a market paradigm of research governance; the instrumentalisation and individualism of research cultures; and ostensibly, therefore, the predetermination and narrowing of their potential scientific, societal and economic contributions. In other words, these interviewees correlated an impact agenda with their professional enfeeblement, particularly in the terms of being self-directed and autonomous, and thereafter as detracting from the appeal of an academic career.

Ultimately, these accounts confirm an emotional register that is heavily weighted to a sense of fear and resistance to the perceived deleterious effects of an impact agenda on academic personhood or, more precisely, occupational welfare. We also identify an emotional split that separates from these a cohort for whom being impactful is less extrinsically motivated. These accounts also reflect not only academics' struggles with what are frequently invasive and professionally debilitative approaches to performance management, but the muddling of the notion of the public intellectual and a confusing of public accountability with performance-related auditability. No wonder then perhaps the symptomisation of professional distress takes centre stage in their reactions to an impact agenda.

And so, to conclude, these accounts indicate more of the kinds of vitriol and emotional turmoil that is seen to inform an increasingly homogenous characterisation of the university's existential crisis and unravelling of the academic profession. Yet, we also have here an emotional register, the needle for which gravitates towards fear, despondency and desperation but with the potential to oscillate towards a different underpinning value framework. That framework would see academic work as transcending and ultimately trumping the habitually stunted evaluative criteria applied in measuring what counts in higher education and which influences the contours of academic personhood. The challenge then for academics is almost one of escaping a belt of resistance towards an impact agenda and invoking a more 'authentic' sense of what academia is so that policy does not define but exemplifies the achievements of science. The need for recognition rather than dismissal of the role of emotion and affect appears therefore increasingly significant for an emotionally coherent academic community (Hey & Leathwood, 2009). Indeed, if the impact agenda is an emotional challenge for academics to go beyond, it signifies an opportunity for academic personhood to exceed the parameters of policy expectations.

Notes

1. UK Stern Review 2016. Retrieved from https://www.gov.uk/government/uploads/system/uploads/attachment_data/file/541338/ind-16-9-ref-stern-review.pdf
2. ATSE Research and Engagement Consultation 2016. Retrieved from https://www.atse.org.au/content/publications/reports/industry-innovation/research-engagement-for-australia.aspx
3. EIA Trial 2012. Retrieved from https://www.go8.edu.au/programs-and-fellowships/excellence-innovation-australia-eia-trial

Disclosure statement

No potential conflict of interest was reported by the authors.

ORCID

Jennifer Chubb http://orcid.org/0000-0002-9716-820X

References

Ahmed, S. (2003). The politics of fear in the making of worlds. *International Journal of Qualitative Studies in Education*, 16(3), 377–398.
Beard, C., Clegg, S., & Smith, K. (2007). Acknowledging the affective in higher education. *British Educational Research Journal*, 33(2), 235–252.
Becher, T. (1989). *Academic tribes and territories*. Buckingham: Open University Press/Society for Research into Higher Education.
Becher, T. (1994). The significance of disciplinary differences. *Studies in Higher Education*, 19(2), 151–161.
Bhattacharya, A. (2012). Science funding: Duel to the death. *Nature*, 488, 20–22.
Biglan, A. (1973). The characteristics of subject matter in academic areas. *Journal of Applied Psychology*, 57(3), 195–203.
Bok, D. (2003). *Universities in the marketplace: The commercialization of higher education*. Princeton, NJ: Princeton University Press.
Boler, M. (1999). *Feeling power: Emotions and education*. London: Routledge.
Braben, D., Allen, J. F., Amos, W., Ashburner, M., Ashmore, J., Birkhead, T., & Woodruff, P. (2009). Only scholarly freedom delivers real 'impact' 1: An open letter to Research Councils UK. *Times Higher Education*. Retrieved March 5, 2015, from http://www.timeshighereducation.co.uk/story.asp?storycode=408984

Chubb, J., & Watermeyer, R. (2016). Artifice or integrity in the marketization of research impact? Investigating the moral economy of (pathways to) impact statements within research funding proposals in the UK and Australia. *Studies in Higher Education*. doi:10.1080/03075079.2016.1144182

Collini, S. (2011). Research must not be tied to politics. *The Guardian*. Retrieved March 2, 2015, from http://www.theguardian.com/commentisfree/2011/apr/01/research-arts-and-humanities-research-council

Cupples, J., & Pawson, E. (2012). Giving an account of oneself: The PBRF and the neoliberal university. *New Zealand Geographer*, 68(1), 14–23.

Cuthill, M., O'Shea, E., Wilson, B., & Viljoen, P. (2014). Universities and the public good: A review of knowledge exchange policy and related university practice in Australia. *Australian Universities' Review*, 56(2), 36–46.

Deem, R., Hillyard, S., & Reed, M. (2007). *Knowledge, higher education, and the new managerialism: The changing management of UK universities*. Oxford: Oxford University Press.

Delanty, G. (2008). Academic identities and institutional change. In R. Barnett & R. di Napoli (Eds.), *Changing identities in higher education: Voicing perspectives* (pp. 124–133). Abingdon: Routledge.

Donovan, C. (2008). The Australian research quality framework: A live experiment in capturing the social, economic, environmental and cultural returns of publicly funded research. *New Directions for Evaluation*, 118, 47–60.

Etzkowitz, H., & Leydesdorff, L. (2000). The dynamics of innovation: From national systems and 'mode 2' to a triple helix of university–industry–government relations. *Research Policy*, 29(2), 109–123.

Evans, M. (2004). *Killing thinking: The death of the universities*. London: Continuum.

Gibbons, M., Limoges, C., Nowotny, H., Schwartzman, S., Scott, P., & Trow, M. (1994). *The new production of knowledge: The dynamics of science and research in contemporary societies*. London: Sage.

Giroux, H. (2014). *Neoliberalism's war on higher education*. Chicago, IL: Haymarket Books.

Gornall, J., Cook, C., Daunton, L., Salisbury, J., & Thomas, B. (Eds.). (2013). *Academic working lives: Experience, practice and change*. London: Bloomsbury.

Hammersley, M. (2016). Can academic freedom be justified? Reflections on the arguments of robert post and stanley fish. *Higher Education Quarterly*, 70(2), 108–126.

Harris, S. (2005). Rethinking academic identities in neo-liberal times. *Teaching in Higher Education*, 10(4), 421–433.

Henkel, M. (2007). Can academic autonomy survive in the knowledge society? A perspective from Britain. *Higher Education*, 26(1), 87–99.

Hey, V., & Leathwood, C. (2009). Passionate attachments: Higher education, policy, knowledge, emotion and social justice. *Higher Education Policy*, 22, 101–118. doi:10.1057/hep.2008.34

Holmwood, J. (2011). The idea of a public university. In J. Holmwood (Ed.), *A manifesto for the public university* (pp. 56–73). London: Bloomsbury.

Leathwood, C., & Read, B. (2012). *Final report: Assessing the impact of developments in research policy for research on higher education: An exploratory study*. Society for Research into Higher Education (SRHE). Retrieved March 3, 2015, from https://www.srhe.ac.uk/downloads/Leathwood_Read_Final_Report_16_July_2012.pdf

Light, G., & Cox, R. (2001). *Learning and teaching in higher education: The reflective professional*. London: Paul Chapman.

Lucas, L. (2006). *The research game in academic life*. Maidenhead: SRHE/Open University Press.

Marginson, S., & Considine, M. (2000). *The enterprise university: Power, governance and reinvention in Australia*. Cambridge: Cambridge University Press.

Martin, B. R. (2011). The research excellence framework and the 'impact agenda': Are we creating a Frankenstein monster? *Research Evaluation*, 20(3), 247–254.

Naidoo, R. (2016). *Higher Education Worldviews Competition Annual Lecture*. Retrieved August 6, 2016, from http://www.bath.ac.uk/management/news_events/news/2016/25-04-rajani-naidoo-higher-education-competition-worldviews-annual-lecture.html

Nguyen, V. (2015). Mẹ-search, hauntings, and critical distance. *Life Writing, 12*(4), 467–477.
O'Shea, É. (2014). Embedding knowledge exchange within Irish universities – International shifts towards a hybrid academic? *The All Ireland Journal of Teaching and Learning in Higher Education, 6*(1), 1391–1396.
Palfreyman, D., & Tapper, T. (2014). *Reshaping the university: The rise of the regulated market in higher education.* Oxford: Oxford University Press.
RCUK. (2011). *RCUK impact requirements*, p. 2. Retrieved March 6, 2015, from http://www.rcuk.ac.uk/RCUK prod/assets/documents/impacts/RCUKImpactFAQ.pdf
REF. (2012). *Assessment framework and guidance on submissions.* London: HEFCE (Updated).
Samuel, G., & Derrick, G. (2015). Societal impact evaluation: Exploring evaluator perceptions of the characterization of impact under the REF2014: Table 1. *Research Evaluation, 24,* 229–241.
Smith, K. (2012). Fools, facilitators and flexians: Academic identities in marketised environments. *Higher Education Quarterly, 66*(2), 155–173.
Sparkes, A. C. (2007). Embodiment, academics and the audit culture: A story seeking consideration. *Qualitative Research, 7*(4), 521–550.
Watermeyer, R. (2012). From engagement to impact? Articulating the public value of academic research. *Tertiary Education and Management, 18*(2), 115–130.
Watermeyer, R., & Olssen, M. (2016). 'Excellence' and exclusion: The individual costs of competitiveness. *Minerva, 54*(2), 201–218.
Whitchurch, C. (2012). Expanding the parameters of academia. *Higher Education, 64*(1), 99–117.
Winter, R. (2009). Academic manager or managed academic? Academic identity schisms in higher education. *Journal of Higher Education Policy and Management, 31*(2), 121–131.

Challenging a measured university from an indigenous perspective: placing 'manaaki' at the heart of our professional development programme

Nell Buissink, Piki Diamond, Julia Hallas, Jennie Swann and Acushla Dee Sciascia

ABSTRACT
Globally, universities show an outward strength partly built upon imported and exported commonalities that are measurable and therefore accountable, rankable and marketable. While there are advantages to this, it can create a barrier within each institution to acknowledging and valuing indigeneity, local flavour or special character. Such a barrier is present in Aotearoa, New Zealand, where it can be challenging to uphold obligations to the founding Treaty – Te Tiriti o Waitangi. This paper presents a case study that highlights our experience as academic developers in embedding a Māori value, manaaki, in the creation of a professional development programme and imported recognition scheme for university teachers. We were challenged to view the external visitors (the United Kingdom Professional Standards Framework (including the UKPSF)) as an opportunity for our land, to welcome them into our community using the protocols of the pōwhiri and to walk side by side with our colleagues, while aspiring to meet their needs. Embedding manaaki into a professional development programme has not been simply about being 'kind'. Manaaki is inseparable from a worldview that values and measures in a way that is fundamentally different to that of many modern European cultures. Within our University setting, manaaki as a measurement has sustained, nourished and uplifted both host (our team, our people, our University and our land) and visitor (the UKPSF and our participating colleagues) and it is continuing to challenge the existing view of measurement, cutting right through layers of institutional policy and practice. We are challenging the comfortable sameness, and the comfortably measurable sameness, in the global university. This case study aims to share the story behind the development of our programme, and will be of interest to those considering valuing indigeneity, local flavour or special character in a modern, measured university.

Introduction

Manaaki whenua, manaaki tangata, haere whakamua (Care for the land, care for people, go forward). (Māori proverb)

In an increasingly vanilla and globalised world, organisations such as universities tend to gravitate towards a comfortable and comfortably measurable sameness. Within this space it is not always easy to acknowledge or value indigeneity, local flavour or special character, yet for many peoples around the world to do so would be seen as a positive step. Further to this, in countries such as Aotearoa, New Zealand, there is also a legal duty through our founding Treaty – Te Tiriti o Waitangi – to ensure that our indigenous culture is fully integrated into all systems and organisations.

As a group of academic developers at a university in Aotearoa, it is important to us that we honour and embed the Treaty in all of our work. This paper shares how we strived to honour the Treaty in the importation of an external framework (Higher Education Academy United Kingdom Professional Standards Framework (HEA UKPSF)) and the creation of a professional development programme (Ako Aronui) to surround it. More specifically in this paper we share, as a case study, our focus on embedding an important Māori value, manaaki, through the development of a professional development programme for university staff that integrates traditional values, concepts, worldviews and philosophies.

While this case study is set in Aotearoa it is applicable globally to those involved in post-compulsory higher education who wish to embrace and sustain special character or local and indigenous knowledge whether that be a language, a way of life, a values system or an indigenous culture. This case will also have relevance to those interested in the burgeoning movement to bring affective values such as manaaki and kindness into the measured university.

The paper begins with a background to the Treaty, followed by a review of the literature related to the notions of manaaki and the measured university. Next the design of Ako Aronui is explained, the process and how what we did exemplified manaakitanga, the practising of manaaki. In order to fully convey the richness of the case study we have peppered the paper with quotes from one of our team, Piki Diamond. Piki is of Ngāpūhi and Ngāti Tūwharetoa iwi and has lineage to Britain and Ireland. Piki was not raised within either of her tribal regions; instead her whānau (family) were welcomed into the hearts of the iwi of Tauranga Moana, Ngai Te Rangi, Ngāti Ranginui and Ngāti Pūkenga. Piki explains:

> As Tauranga Moana opened their hearts my parents did the same, opening our heart, our home, welcoming whānau resettling to Tauranga Moana and children whose homes weren't so stable. I have realised I grew up in a privileged environment. Aroha (love) was abundant and expressed to us through actions of manaaki and tiakina (protection). Even angry words and tones of reprimand couched in actions of aroha, demonstrated that I had been spoken to because I was heading into an unsafe space. Actions spoke louder than the words and manaaki is the doorway to sanctuary.

Background to the case: Te Tiriti o Waitangi

Aotearoa, New Zealand, is an island nation situated in the South Pacific, where the indigenous Māori people signed an agreement with the British Crown in 1840 to ensure the retention of their lands, belief systems and language – however, this assurance has not been fully upheld, resulting in significant loss of language, culture and economic base (Smorti, Peters-Algie, & Rau, 2013). There is a lively history of establishing equity and cohesion between the two signatory parties, with Māori having a constant battle to uphold Te Tiriti o Waitangi. This conflict is seen and heard every day throughout the country, in every forum: education, industry, politics and the legal system (Borell, Gregory, McCreanor, Jensen, & Moewaka Barnes, 2009). Piki explains this struggle from her perspective.

> This battle is still alive and it will continue if we repeat past actions that have caused grievances. For me, it is not a fight against other races, though some do make it that. It is not about ego, nor is it political, in the Western sense that perceives progress and wellbeing as financial growth or the accumulation of possessions. This is tāngata mauri (collective consciousness, Māori ideals of politics). This is about life, this is about the land, this is about consciousness. Colonisation and industrial consciousness changed the face of our land. We call her Papatūānuku, Earth Mother. The new consciousness and its actions tipped her out of balance, spiralling her into devolution.

Through Piki's eyes, Māori have constantly struggled to be kaitiaki, custodians and carers of this land and this is done through values, language and protocols. Traditionally higher education institutions in Aotearoa have valued Eurocentric ways above indigenous knowledge and ways of being, because as a relatively young country, in terms of colonial settlement, our institutions of higher education have tended to look to 'international practice for its norms and values' (Prebble et al., 2004, p. 48). In order to successfully import a programme from Britain we had to change our mindset. As Piki explains,

> Our initial reaction to the idea of importing an accreditation scheme from Britain was, 'Great! Another form of colonisation'. But it was one we had to work with, and thankfully our whole team is sensitive to our country's history and know the wrongs that need to be righted. The drawing up of the Ako Aronui programme was not solely an intellectual pursuit. It was about restoring justice. It is about restoring balance.

Viewing the accreditation scheme through Piki's eyes required us to think about how such a balance may be achieved. We had to remember tikanga (protocol) and who both we and HEA are. We are tāngata whenua (people of the land, hosts) and they are manuhiri (visitors). Tikanga calls for us to manaaki, to follow protocol and care for the visitors. Through the welcoming ritual of pōwhiri, mutually beneficial relationships can be formed and in manaakitanga, manuhiri are welcomed to become whānau (family) with the tāngata whenua. Within the context of academic development, our team adopted the role of tangata whenua, set to manaaki our manuhiri – the HEA and eventually our participating colleagues.

Understanding manaaki

With its commonplace meaning, manaaki is hospitality, people caring for people and being kind (Moorfield, 2011). When manaaki is broken down into its compounds we can begin to see how manaaki also offers a measurement. The Qualifications Authority (New Zealand Qualifications Authority, 2013, p. 3) provide a number of ways of breaking down and explaining manaaki, and for this paper we draw on three of these:

(1) Manaaki – being careful with how we nurture and look after people and their mana.
(2) Mana-aki – taking care of and enhancing the mana of the people. This is what is measured.
(3) Mana-ā-kī – the power of the spoken word about the measurement. Mana-ā-kī reminds 'hosts to be expressive and fluent in welcoming visitors. It is also a reminder

to the tangata whenua (hosts) that the power of the word (or the words) of your manuhiri (guests) can sing your praises if your expression of manaakitanga is exemplary. But beware – it can also be detrimental, if manaakitanga is less than acceptable'. Mana-ā-kī reminds the tangata whenua that they need to be consistent and truthful in what they say, for actions will reveal any discrepancies and if what we say and/or do is not favoured by the manuhiri it can be detrimental to the tangata whenua and their project.

Mana is a concept that is integral to te ao Māori (the Māori worldview) and it attends to a person or people's prestige, influence and spiritual authority (Pere, 1997). Intrinsic to mana is humility and empowering others towards collective empowerment inclusive of oneself. The association of mana with manaaki is pivotal as it acknowledges that mana is being measured. Expressing manaakitanga is 'role modelling mana enhancing behaviour towards each other, taking care not to trample another's mana' (Williams & Broadley, 2012, 'Manaakitanga-Enhancement', para). Manaaki is demonstrated on a number of levels including one's relationship with the local environment as well as the dynamics of growing a healthy community (New Zealand Qualifications Authority, 2013). Piki explains further,

> When I say manaaki, I know what it looks like, feels like, sounds like. It is my lived experience, it's my ethical compass.

Here Piki has viewed manaaki as an ethical compass, one that guides decisions in her everyday life. Manaaki does this by providing a measure of things – affective values – which are so difficult to measure that they are often ignored (Buissink-Smith, Mann, & Shephard, 2011). This is possible because manaaki provides an alternative view of measurement based on an internal and external perception of how value has been demonstrated, rather than the western view of measurement which tends to be counted in terms of outputs. So, with manaaki there is measurement in that there is a judgement, evaluation or observation; however, the measurement relates specifically to the demonstration of an 'ethic of care' related to the well-being of yourself, others and the land (New Zealand Qualifications Authority, 2013). Specifically, the measurement relates to the uplifting (or not) of mana (prestige, authority, control, power, status, charisma, spiritual power or influence). A Māori proverb explains the measure by way of a cautionary reminder of the ramifications of not providing manaakitanga – 'Kai ana mai koe he atua; noho atu ana ahau he tangata' ('You are eating like a god; I am sitting here as a man') (Martin, 2008, p. 20). The measure inherent in this proverb can be applied to all types of relationships both between people and the environment, including the university. A university's teaching staff for example may feel like the University has everything (money, power, ranking, prestige, mana) while they do not feel their own mana is being enhanced as they are poorly welcomed, cared for or suitably resourced, and therefore, they may measure the University similarly.

The place of values such as manaaki in a measured university

We can see that when we look at a simple definition of manaaki it has a close relationship with values such as kindness, and kindness has been described as being 'out of place' in contemporary talk about higher education and higher education pedagogy (Clegg & Rowland, 2010, p. 722), in that it moves too far from the safety of a rationalist perspective and thinking behind the measured university – a university that has been described as a place where 'only the measurable matters' where, with entrepreneurialism at its heart, a particular 'careless' form of competitive individualism flourishes (Lynch, 2010, p. 55). Similarly, manaaki itself is a concept that is not often explicitly associated with mainstream post-compulsory higher education although it has been embraced in compulsory education. Manaaki is prominent in policy and practice in early childhood education as well as primary education in Aotearoa (New Zealand Qualification Authority, 2013). The national early childhood curriculum document, *Te Whāriki*, has been described as 'reflecting the partnership between Māori and The Crown inherent within Te Tiriti o Waitangi, New Zealand's founding document, and is an example of how traditional values, concepts, worldviews, and philosophies have been integrated into a modern, bicultural, educational document' (Rameka, 2011, p. 245). Furthermore, the concept of mana has been described as being 'central' to *Te Whariki* which states: 'Ko te whakatipu i te mana o te mokopuna te tino taumata hei whāinga ma tātou' ('Enhancing the power/status of the child is the highest objective for us all') (Rameka, 2011, p. 251). When manaakitanga is embedded in early childhood education it can be reflected in behaviours such as: 'showing respect and kindness to others, caring, sharing and being a friend', and it requires that learners 'develop empathy and connectedness with others, social and communal identities, and understanding of roles and responsibilities associated with those identities' (Rameka, 2011, p. 252). Manaaki clearly goes beyond simple kindness and is aligned throughout *Te Whāriki*, as a measurement and indeed as an assessment.

Manaaki is much less frequently mentioned in higher education literature or policy documentation, especially when we look outside of specific kaupapa Māori spaces such as Wānanga or Māori Departments. The limited existing literature in this area tends to not report on any actual application of manaaki in higher education, rather discussing the *potential* for the application of manaaki in higher education. Pio, Tipuna, Rasheed, and Parker (2014, p. 676), for example, recently raised the challenge of reimagining universities from an indigenous worldview with a 'foundation in Kaupapa Māori (the rights of Māori to be Māori), Manaaki (care/hospitality) and tino rangatiratanga (sovereignty)'.

It is clear that the emphasis and consciousness of honouring the Treaty through the delivering and enlivening of a bicultural curriculum has not become a norm in the university. There is no clear path to upholding Treaty obligations in Aotearoa; however, we are committed to fulfilling our educational obligations. This commitment can also be seen as part of a wider movement within measured universities internationally towards bringing back, remembering or reflecting on values. There are many examples in the literature that illustrate this shift towards values, and these stem from a variety of approaches and contexts (Burrows, 2012; Fortune, Ennals, Neilson, Bruce, & Bhopti, 2016; Samu, 2016). What these various authors describe or are advocating for is a return in higher education to basic human values and needs, highlighting the fact that many of our communities have become disconnected from the land and from each other. This aligns with the gaining of ascendancy in recent decades of indigenous worldview(s) in a world that is fragile, tired and unsustainable (Pio et al., 2014). In the process of flattening and globalisation, higher education institutions seem to have become koretake. In the Māori language the term koretake is used to mean useless, but a truer definition is rootless, without purpose and disconnected from origins. In many ways universities appear to have forgotten who they are and why they are here (Collini, 2012). This is why it is important to return to the basics, to go back to values, back to needs, to reconnect, to re-establish our roots and our purpose.

External measures and the HEA

The movement towards values described above is in part a reaction to an ongoing and powerful shift towards measurement in higher education, including an international trend to import external accreditation, recognition and measures into educational institutions (e.g., Harrison-Graves, 2016). Based on standardised notions of excellence, international and national measures have been widely employed across campuses including university-wide ranking of research performance, teaching quality and student experience (Hazelkorn, 2015). Specific to the professional recognition of teaching, many of the initiatives have been driven from outside the university by state and national bodies (Chalmers, 2011), and institutions in Australia, for example, have begun adopting the HEA's UKPSF (Beckmann, 2015) and the Australian University Teaching Criteria and Standards Framework (e.g., Chalmers et al., 2014).

The HEA framework has been offered in the UK since 2004 and has more recently been introduced into a small number of institutions in Australasia, led in part by the Australian National University (ANU). The HEA (2016) 'work(s) extensively in partnership with universities, bringing about change at institutional and departmental level to enhance the learning experience of students by improving the quality of teaching they receive'. The HEA enables participating or accredited institutions to frame their teaching professional development schemes within the UKPSF. Based on satisfactory evidence of professional practice, successful applicants are awarded one of four categories of Fellowship of the HEA (Beckmann, 2015). The recognition scheme is 'enacted in diverse ways by diverse institutions' (Beckmann, 2015), in that there is a focus through a framework of common standards but institutions are encouraged to develop and apply teaching development programmes fitted to the specific needs of their own staff (Parsons, Hill, Holland, & Willis, 2012). This advertised flexibility has encouraged variety in the courses put forward locally to support or surround the HEA framework. However, until 2015 no institution had also integrated the existing UKPSF with indigenous worldviews and values or special character.

The following section of the paper shares our case study; our journey of welcoming this 'visitor' – the UKPSF – to our University, a visitor that we saw as having the potential to provide a visible face for our drive towards creating a space and place for manaaki in our institution. In a context of international adoption of frameworks that are 'foreign', 'generic', 'flexible' or all of these things, we hope that this overview of our journey will provide inspiration or encouragement for others faced with a similar task (e.g., Chalmers et al., 2014).

The setting

This case study examines how manaaki was integrated into the Ako Aronui professional development programme at the Auckland University of Technology (AUT). It discusses how the programme was developed by a team of academic developers in the university's academic development unit, the Centre for Learning and Teaching (CFLAT). Two of the five academic developers who developed and implemented the Ako Aronui programme were Māori, and all five are the narrators and researchers behind this case study. This case study provides an understanding of their lived experiences. Not only do case studies focus on the perspectives of a group of people in order to 'understand their perceptions of events', but they also view the researcher as an integral part of the case (Cohen, Manion, & Morrison, 2011, p. 290), and as such 'may be linked to the personality of the researcher' (Verschuren, 2003, p. 133). Therefore one of the researchers, Piki, has been linked to this case by offering personal insights which are expressed throughout the article in the form of quotations.

The creation of Ako Aronui: AUT meets HEA

There is a dance that occurs when two entities meet with the intention of forming a union. This is a time of uncertainty, a time required to truly get to know each other. Māori formalise this dance, this initial encounter between tāngata whenua and manuhiri in pōwhiri. The authors, as the tāngata whenua, welcomed the manuhiri, the visiting HEA and the UKPSF. The CFLAT team working on this project held an ongoing concern around the question of how to meaningfully integrate the Treaty into our University's programmes. It was clear to all of us that contextualising the UKPSF to Aotearoa meant that it had to be connected or woven with te ao Māori. This convergence was not an instant or easy process, and it took time to understand how this could occur. Keeping our concerns in mind, the UKPSF was analysed and evaluated in relation to our contexts Aotearoa, te ao Māori, our University and individual philosophies.

As part of this analysis we wanted to ensure that any new teaching accreditation criteria could support existing policies and practices including the teaching excellence award criteria. In attending to the acknowledgement of Te Tiriti o Waitangi, the AUT Excellence in Teaching Awards and the Aotearoa National Tertiary Teaching Award criteria are provided in both English and Te Reo Māori. We wondered how the UKPSF would also translate and we questioned whether it could it be aligned within our current teaching award structures. It was of critical importance to us that the accreditation upheld the mana of the HEA whilst recognising and empowering our second group of visitors, in this instance the teaching academics in our University. We were informed by HEA that although the UKPSF could not be changed, it could be woven with kaupapa Māori, in order to recognise Māori knowledge and perspective. So began the development of the Ako Aronui programme.

The two Māori developers evaluated the dimensions and criteria of the UKPSF in relation to Māori concepts and overarching worldview. The team worked at creating a programme underpinned by the UKPSF that was a fusion of HEA, AUT and Māori, and together we developed the first version of the Ako Aronui programme. Below is an example of the Professional Values dimension of the UKPSF and its representation in Ako Aronui (Figure 1). The UKPSF is retained in the green text and then followed by the recontextualised statements.

The practice of these values encompass manaakitanga. For example, the original UKPSF Professional Value 2 states, 'Promote participation in higher education and

Figure 1. Contextualised Ako Aronui framework – Nga Uara: professional values.

equality of opportunity for learners', while the aligned value – Ako Aronui's Ngā Uara 2 – states 'Whakapiri, whakamana, whakamarama. Engage, empower and enlighten learners so that they can strive for tino rangatiratanga (self determination)'. In this instance, Ngā Uara 2 provides a pointer as to 'how' Value 2 can be achieved, and it re-positions the learner as the determiner and navigator of their learning. Underpinning concepts of engagement, empowerment, enlightenment and self-determination with manaakitanga recognises the role of the applicant throughout the new framework. To whakapiri (engage learners) the staff member (as a participant and applicant) should reflect practices of how they manaaki – welcome – their learners and create a safe space for learners to engage. Staff then needed to consider how they mana-aki the learners, that is to provide learning opportunities that draw on the learners' potential and acknowledge their achievements, thus helping them in experiencing a sense of whakamana (empowerment). Whakamārama are those moments when the learner is realising their potential, their tino rangatiratanga.

Embedding manaaki in Ako Aronui

> Kaua e takahia te mana o te tangata (Do not trample on the mana of the people). (Māori proverb)

Manaaki draws attention to the need to make meaningful connections, to care for people and to treat them with compassion. It brings an accountability that is based on the practice of values. Accordingly manaaki is measured by the practice of attending to the community and this involves remaining loyal to the community in which one serves. So it was vital that we practised and lived the values we had carefully weaved into the newly aligned framework. If we encouraged learner-loyalty or being learner-centred, for example, we had to ensure our own practice placed our loyalty with our academic and teaching staff. Our focus had to be on how the University and our team could support our academics, rather than asking how academics could support the University and its systems. The latter should be an incidental of the former. The mana of AUT should be raised as a result of our team encouraging and developing a culture focused on the well-being of people and underpinned by values. This relates to manaakitanga as an ethic of care which links directly to well-being (New Zealand Qualifications Authority, 2013). As such, the team set about ensuring that manaaki underpinned the Ako Aronui programme, in terms of our practice with staff. Being value-focused rather than content or system-focused we put people at the heart of the accreditation process. By focusing on manaaki first, we were reminded that we were walking alongside our colleagues, supporting them to tell and celebrate their teaching stories. Drawing on the explanations of manaaki given earlier as criteria for measuring manaaki, the following three sections provide examples of how we worked to embed the values of the Treaty through practising manaaki.

Manaaki – being careful with how we nurture and look after people

When we began the HEA accreditation journey, our team had no experience of the process, and only one other university in Aotearoa – Massey University – had engaged with them. In presenting the programme to our first group of staff we made this very clear, advising them that we were on the journey with them and would work towards providing them with knowledge and resources as they came to hand. We envisioned that the process would be collaborative, and in essence it was very much a 'let's give it a go' attitude. With this welcoming openness coupled with notions of ako (reciprocal learning) we took the opportunity to consult with the ANU. A contract with ANU enabled a cohort of 15 staff to obtain Fellowship under their accredited programme. This gave the group – including both the CFLAT team and other staff from across AUT – the opportunity to determine what was required for the written applications and how feedback could be provided. This support was invaluable for us as a team, and although the ANU accreditation staff did not explicitly approach their work from a viewpoint of manaaki, we learnt much from their 'down to earth' individualised approach to feedback. In our approach to welcoming our first group of applicants and in openly asking for help from ANU we aimed to be transparent and honest with our co-learners at AUT.

Drawing on the notion of manaaki, we organised events to develop a community of HEA applicants and to support staff to write their HEA submissions. These events were deliberately kept informal to encourage staff to feel comfortable sharing their stories with us and their peers. We did this by making time for hākarī – sharing kai (food) just to enjoy the company of the community. It was important that manaaki was practised in informal 'meet-ups' and workshops. This was done through balancing information-giving with social salutations, congratulations and invitations of sharing, the good and the ugly. Additionally, each teacher was matched with a mentor from the Ako Aronui team.

Mana-aki – taking care of and enhancing the mana of the people

We wanted to revive the celebration of good teaching to provide a space where staff could think about their academic practice and feel a member of a supportive learning and teaching community. We wanted staff to self-elect to participate, not to be told to do it. To empower applicants by letting them make decisions and to engage as they choose, we placed few restrictions on staff. While we had deadlines for submission we offered these as a guideline-only for the applicant, and clearly communicated that it was the applicant's responsibility to advance their application.

It was important that we took care of participating staff members by giving them the opportunity to reflect on themselves as a holistic 'person' with affective values in an institution of higher education. While mentoring applicants our team spent the time needed to get to know why staff were teaching, why they valued teaching and what their story was. We worked with applicants to ensure that their core values were woven throughout their application and that their passion for teaching shone. This has proven to be a strength of the programme and the team's ability to manaaki staff, guiding them through a reflexive process where staff are reminded of and celebrated for their passion for teaching. Accordingly upon 'graduation', the individual successes of staff were celebrated by their mentor, the team and the institution.

Mana-ā-kī – the power of the word

Mana-ā-kī refers to the power of the spoken word and it reminds the tangata whenua that they need to be consistent and truthful in what they say, for actions will reveal any discrepancies and if what we say and/or do is not favoured by the manuhiri it can be detrimental to the tangata whenua and their project (New Zealand Qualifications Authority, 2013). Our transparency and honesty aided in building trust with not only our applicants but also our wider community.

Mana-ā-kī has been invaluable to the ongoing recruitment and engagement of the Ako Aronui programme and the community. After an initial recruitment drive for the first phase of the programme – the development that has been discussed here – we have been able to rely on 'word of mouth' as our sole promotional channel. Positive recognition from the community gives mana to CFLAT. This demonstrated that our manaaki and service to our staff was appreciated and beneficial to the wider community. We are now into the second phase of the programme and while resource restrictions mean that we do not actively promote the programme, 'word of mouth' from our first cohort continues to spread and our Ako Aronui community is growing and staff remain eager to participate. Once staff have received recognition through HEA our team continues to enhance our relationship with them, and to date most 'graduates' look forward to becoming active participants in the community taking on ambassadorial, recruiting and mentoring roles – ensuring the scalability and sustainability of the programme – purely from their own enthusiasm and wanting. Their efforts and the efforts of our team help to ensure that the AUT's decision-makers see a culture that is becoming firmly established within the University where we value and recognise our people as people and not as commodities of production. Our growing community are 'waving the manaaki flag' at committee meetings, working parties, workshops, teaching spaces and in staff lunchrooms across our three AUT campuses. This is a beginning. AUT's values of aroha, tika and pono (integrity, respect and compassion) which tended to only appear in the policy documents are slowly being brought to life through the Ako Aronui programme and we have recently seen these values reflected in institutional job descriptions for example.

Through a similar 'word of mouth' process and mana-ā-kī, Ako Aronui has also gained national and international interest. Universities across Australasia and beyond have asked about the process and thinking behind embedding manaaki into the international accreditation process – in many cases with an interest in transferring our experience to recognising a special character or culture in their own institution.

Conclusion

This case study has illustrated our experience of acknowledging, valuing and sustaining indigeneity, local flavour or special character in a modern, measured university. Working collaboratively with an external model challenged us to view the external visitors as an opportunity for our land, to welcome them into our community using the protocols of the pōwhiri and to walk side-by-side with our colleagues, while aspiring to meet their needs and in turn those of the student community.

It has been a privilege to be able to embrace our indigenous culture and to contribute to the well-being of our nation. Manaaki as a measurement has uplifted both host and visitor, placing kindness, generosity and hospitality right at the centre of an institution where 'only the measurable matters'. For our team, as hosts, manaaki as a measurement brought an awareness to the team of our own actions, to ensure that what we espoused we practised. The result is an engagement from staff who appreciate the time and care that have been taken to bring a recognition programme to them and staff who continue to be active and supportive of our efforts.

Many universities that we have met with are watching our progress with particular interest – the most alluring aspect for external parties is the contextualisation of an imported framework to a local context. Ako Aronui is contributing to the development of our University's culture and community through its emphasis on acknowledging and celebrating the values of participants and the University – aroha, tika and pono (compassion, integrity and respect). Ako Aronui places manaaki at the heart of an ethical and good education, so that a member of the AUT academic community will be able to work in ways which are considered and self-determined. In their daily practice we have engaged our staff to: Manaaki – care for our learners and peers; whanaungatanga – build and maintain strong relationships; whakapiri – focus on the engagement and success of our learners; whakamarama – be enlightened and informed; auaha – be creative and innovative with their approaches to ako and whakamana – be empowered and confident in making decisions that support the well-being of the AUT community.

Embedding manaaki into a professional development programme has not been simply about being 'kind'. Manaaki is underpinned and inseparable from a worldview that values and measures in a way that is fundamentally different to that of many European-Industrialised cultures. Within our University setting, manaaki is continuing to challenge the existing view of measurement, cutting right through the many layers of institutional policy and practice. We are challenging the comfortable sameness and the comfortably measurable sameness in the global university. We know that making a change in a university, such as introducing a new graduate attribute, is best done with a fully integrated and embedded approach rather than as a token gesture or an 'add-on' (Spronken-Smith et al., 2016). Our key learning from this process has been that to truly integrate an indigenous value or viewpoint may involve an even bigger step – to challenge and question the very fabric of our measured institutions. What are we measuring? How are we measuring? What is the thinking behind the measuring? What and who are we valuing? Who are we rewarding? These questions all have follow-up questions, such as, who are we promoting? And, then further follow-on questions, such as, what sort of research output are we valuing? How does this translate to marketing, employability or university rankings? Being true to embedding manaaki is an ongoing process that is creating ripples across our institution that go well beyond a small group of academic developers simply being kind or welcoming in the delivery of their professional development programme.

This case study has focused on the development of the Ako Aronui programme and the creation of a space for considering manaaki as an alternative form of measurement, and what this might mean for the people and the land, as well as institutional policy and practice. We felt that the time was right for this development, this concerted move away from a measured vanilla sameness that was denying the rights of other opportunities to shine. As a team we encourage others to embrace and welcome international opportunities in a way that also lets their own special culture, flavour or character to have true voice and heart. Tīhei. Mauri ora! (Let there be life!).

Acknowledgements

We would like to acknowledge the first cohort of academics who with their willingness and enthusiasm continue to support, promote and participate in the development and practice of Ako Aronui. We would like to thank Emily Whitehead and Pam Wyse for always being there to help and enhance.

Disclosure statement

No potential conflict of interest was reported by the authors.

References

Beckmann, E. A. (2015, October). *Leadership through fellowship: Professional recognition as a pathway to improving scholarship of teaching and learning in Australian universities*. Presented at the International Society for the Scholarship of Teaching and Learning (ISSOTL), Melbourne.

Borell, B., Gregory, A., McCreanor, T., Jensen, V., & Moewaka Barnes, H. (2009). 'It's hard at the top but it's a whole lot easier than being at the bottom': The role of privilege in understanding disparities in Aotearoa/New Zealand. *Race/Ethnicity, 3*, 29–50.

Buissink-Smith, N., Mann, S., & Shephard, K. (2011). How do we measure affective learning in higher education? *Journal of Education for Sustainable Development, 5*(1), 101–114.

Burrows, R. (2012). Living with the h-index? Metric assemblages in the contemporary academy. *The Sociological Review, 60*(2), 355–372.

Chalmers, D. (2011). Progress and challenges to the recognition and reward of the scholarship of teaching in higher education. *Higher Education Research & Development, 30*(1), 25–38.

Chalmers, D., Cummings, R., Elliott, S., Stoney, S., Tucker, B., Wicking, R., & Jorre de St Jorre, T. (2014). *Australian university teaching criteria and standards project* (Final report no. SP12-2335). Department of Education, Australia. Retrieved from http://uniteachingcriteria.edu.au/wp-content/uploads/2013/11/Draft-SP12-2335-Project-Final-Report-21-July-2014.pdf

Clegg, S., & Rowland, S. (2010). Kindness in pedagogical practice and academic life. *British Journal of Sociology of Education, 31*(6), 719–735.

Cohen, L., Manion, L., & Morrison, K. (2011). *Research methods in education* (7th ed.). Oxon: Routledge.

Collini, S. (2012). *What are universities for?* London: Penguin.

Fortune, T., Ennals, P., Neilson, C., Bruce, C., & Bhopti, A. (2016). Collegiality, kindness and care in the measured university: Huh? In *Academic life in the measured university – pleasures, paradoxes and politics*. Retrieved from http://sydney.edu.au/education-portfolio/ei/cms/files/1A_Fortune.pdf

Harrison-Graves, K. (2016, April 22). *Universities in Australia and New Zealand are working with the higher education academy to reward and recognise great teaching*. Retrieved June 13, 2016, from https://www.heacademy.ac.uk/blog/universities-australia-and-new-zealand-are-working-higher-education-academy-reward-and-

Hazelkorn, E. (2015). *Rankings and the reshaping of higher education: The battle for world-class excellence* (2nd ed.). Basingstoke: Springer.

Higher Education Academy. (2016). Retrieved from https://www.heacademy.ac.uk/

Lynch, K. (2010). Carelessness: A hidden doxa of higher education. *Arts and Humanities in Higher Education, 9*(1), 54–67.

Martin, F. (2008). *Te Manaakitanga i roto i ngā ahumahi Tāpoi* [The interpretation of manaakitanga from a Māori tourism supplier perspective] (Unpublished master's thesis). Auckland University of Technology, Auckland, New Zealand.

Moorfield, J. C. (2011). *Te Aka: Māori-English, English-Māori*. Dictionary (3rd ed.). Auckland: Pearson.

New Zealand Qualification Authority. (2013, April). *Manaaki marae – Marae hospitality qualification review. Needs analysis*. Retrieved May 22, 2016, from http://www.nzqa.govt.nz/assets/qualifications-and-standards/qualifications/ManaakiMarae/May-2014-Prov-to-List/Manaaki-Marae-Needs-Analysis.pdf

Parsons, D., Hill, I., Holland, J., & Willis, D. (2012). *Impact of teaching development programmes in higher education*. Higher Education Academy. Retrieved from http://www.stlhe.ca/wp-content/uploads/2013/04/HEA_Impact_Teaching_Development_Prog.pdf

Pere, R. (1997). *Te Wheke: A celebration of infinite wisdom* (2nd ed.). Wairoa: Ao Ako Global Learning.

Pio, E., Tipuna, K., Rasheed, A., & Parker, L. (2014). Te Wero—the challenge: Reimagining universities from an indigenous world view. *Higher Education, 67*(5), 675–690.

Prebble, T., Hargraves, H., Leach, L., Naidoo, K., Suddaby, G., & Zepke, N. (2004). *Impact of student support services and academic development programmes on student outcomes in undergraduate tertiary study: A synthesis of the research*. Wellington: Ministry of Education. Retrieved March 28, 2016, from http://thehub.superu.govt.nz/sites/default/files/42269_ugradstudentoutcomes_0.pdf

Rameka, L. (2011). Being Māori: Culturally relevant assessment in early childhood education. *Early Years, 31*(3), 245–256.

Samu, T. (2016). Responding to the paradox of space, the politics of stewardship and the absence of pleasure: Pasifika teacher educators and the process of "becoming" academics in the Measured University. In *Academic life in the measured university – pleasures, paradoxes and politics*.

Sydney: University of New South Wales. Retrieved from http://sydney.edu.au/education-portfolio/ei/cms/files/1C_Samu.pdf

Smorti, S., Peters-Algie, M., & Rau, C. (2013). Engaging student teachers in sustainable praxis in Aotearoa/New Zealand. *Journal of Teacher Education for Sustainability, 15*(1), 5–14.

Spronken-Smith, R., McLean, A., Smith, N., Bond, C., Jenkins, M., Marshall, S., & Frielick, S. (2016). A toolkit to implement graduate attributes in geography curricula. *Journal of Geography in Higher Education, 40*(2), 254–266.

Verschuren, P. (2003). Case study as a research strategy: Some ambiguities and opportunities. *International Journal of Social Research Methodology, 6*(2), 121–139. doi:10.1080/13645570110106154

Williams, N., & Broadley, M. (2012). *Resource kit for student teachers.* Retrieved from https://akoaotearoa.ac.nz/download/ng/file/group-3993/resource-kit-for-student-teachers.pdf

Measuring the 'gift': epistemological and ontological differences between the academy and Indigenous Australia

Jonathan Bullen and Helen Flavell

ABSTRACT

This paper is drawn from our collective experience coordinating, and teaching in, a large common inter-professional unit on Indigenous cultures and health at an Australian university. Specifically, we use our lived experiences as Aboriginal and non-Aboriginal academics working interculturally to inform a theoretical discussion about how universities conceptualise 'quality' in learning and teaching for Indigenous studies and, more broadly, 'Indigenising the curriculum'. Drawing primarily on the work of Rauna Kuokkanen and the 'logic of the gift', we argue that the application of Western 'quality indicators' to learning and teaching for Indigenous content demonstrates an innate lack of institutional understanding of the complexities of teaching interculturally and the 'unlearning' which needs to occur for students to become critically self-reflexive and develop capacity for ontological pluralism (essential for graduate intercultural capability). According to Kuokkanen, for Indigenous people social order is maintained through giving and recognising the gifts of others, including the land; the logic of the gift, therefore, represents a radical critique of the entrepreneurial and measured university, which relies on one narrow idea of the world and human relationships. The transactional approach typically used to embed Indigenous knowledges into university courses thus illustrates the prevailing epistemic violence enacted on Aboriginal and Torres Strait Islander peoples. Importantly, in addition to Kuokkanen's work, we also apply Martin Nakata's notion of the 'cultural interface' to dissociate from essentialist notions of Indigeneity (and indeed the university) to imagine how Indigenous studies can open a dialogue about reciprocity, hospitality and the current limits of the academy's conceptualisation of 'quality'.

Introduction

We wish to acknowledge the *Nyungar Wadjuk* people as the traditional owners of the country on which this paper was conceived and written. We wish to acknowledge their continuing connection to land, sea and community and we pay our respects to them and their culture, and to Elders, past present and future.

This theoretical paper is based on our experiences as Aboriginal and non-Aboriginal academics coordinating, and teaching in, a large common inter-professional unit on Indigenous cultures and health in an Australian university (Kickett, Hoffman, & Flavell, 2014). In addition, we will draw on other experiences in formal academic roles aimed at increasing 'Indigenous[1] perspectives' to meet Key Performance Indicators (KPIs) aligned with Reconciliation Action Plans including delivering graduates with the intercultural capabilities – and will – to improve outcomes for Aboriginal and Torres Strait Islander peoples (Universities Australia, 2011). It is important to remember that current drives to include Indigenous Australian knowledge, history, and culture in higher education have been built on a long history of political activism by Aboriginal and Torres Strait Islander leaders working against colonising forces (Behrendt, 2013; Indigenous Higher Education Advisory Council, 2006).

Whilst our story takes place on *Nyungar Wadjuk boodja* (country) in Perth, Western Australia, it has relevance to any postcolonial context.[2] As suggested above, nothing we explore here either conceptually or theoretically is new; it is part of a colonial history spanning hundreds of years. The analysis undertaken through our experience mirrors relevant literature internationally (McLaughlin & Whatman, 2010). What our paper does, however, is apply theoretical debates about 'Indigenising the curriculum' to measures of 'quality' in learning and teaching. Not surprisingly, our experiences administering and teaching an 'Indigenous unit' illustrates the prevailing epistemic violence enacted on Indigenous peoples through enforcing a transactional approach to embedding 'relevant' content. Similarly, the application of Western 'quality indicators' to learning and teaching in Indigenous studies demonstrates an innate lack of institutional understanding of the complexities of teaching in this space and the 'unlearning' which needs to occur for students to become critically self-reflexive and develop the desired graduate cultural capabilities (Anning, 2010; Mackinlay & Barney, 2014; Mezirow, 1990). It is worth noting that 'cultural capability' or 'competence'[3] is highly contested with most non-Aboriginal academics having little or no understanding of the theoretical perspectives informing debates relating to these terms, nor the differences between cultural awareness, sensitivity, and safety (Bin-Sallik, 2003; McConnochie, Egege, & McDermmott, 2008; Taylor, Durey, Mullcock, Kickett, & Jones, 2014).

We have deliberately chosen to engage you as readers through subjectively embodying ourselves (Nakata, 2007a) in the text to argue that common sense assumptions and quality practices in higher education play a role in contributing to the disadvantage, suffering and, ultimately, premature deaths of Aboriginal and Torres Strait Islander peoples. For some of you that statement or positioning might mean you stop reading at this point, for others it may generate a liminal discomfort emanating from somewhere difficult to locate. Perhaps the discomfort manifests as a subdued optimism as the recognition that being challenged and made uncomfortable can be auspicious. Alternatively, perhaps, none of these scenarios resonate. Like the students who enter the unit explored here, your experiences, knowledge and identity will inform your expectations and reactions.

Our 'voice' for this paper is singular and multiple, moving in and out of our individual and collective selves in recognition of our plurality and that we – Aboriginal and non-Aboriginal people – must own the solution to how Aboriginal and Torres Strait Islander knowledge, history and culture might be 'embedded' in Australian higher education consistent with local cultural practices and the country we are a part of (Zubrzycki et al., 2014).

Who is speaking?

My name is Jonathan. I was born and raised in Western Australia. My mother is of *Bibbulman/Wadarndi* heritage on my grandfather's side and *Yamatji* from my Nan. My father is an English man born in Bristol. You might notice that like (or perhaps unlike) some Indigenous academics, I also acknowledge my non-Aboriginal heritage: it is a part of me. Formerly a co-coordinator of the unit, which is the focal point of this paper, I now work in an identified role embedding and integrating Indigenous perspectives into curricula across the university.

Briefly, as it is relevant to the paper's theme of 'measuring', I am mindful that not everyone will understand how nuanced the concept of identity can be in the Indigenous Australian tertiary space. Much of the challenge lies in people's external ascriptions, both black and white, of just who and what an Indigenous Australian is or can be. To some I am just Jon, an academic working in a challenging space within the tertiary setting; to others I am a representative of something that many academics just do not have the time for and/or interest in. And yet to others, I am an individual deemed to be somewhat fraudulent: an Aboriginal man in name only, a light skinned blackfella or an olive-skinned *wadjela* (European), someone who is representative of either the 'great white hope', or a continuing colonising force that sits under the umbrella of reconciliation. Hopefully the difficulty of positioning myself in terms of a guest (coloniser) or a host (Indigenous man) is made clear. The irony of my 'olive-skinned' aesthetic is that it in part opens the door personally and/or professionally through providing relative comfort for non-Aboriginal people who have engaged very little or not at all with Indigenous Australians. Whilst not without its utility, my ambiguous identity does indeed reflect the problematic nature of the intercultural space and the harsh terrain of epistemic ignorance this paper intends to seed.

My name is Helen, I'm *wadjela* or white person working and living on *Nyungar Wadjuk boodja* who has taught in the unit explored here. I find it difficult to situate myself as a *wadjela*. This is not because I am inherently uncomfortable with doing so, but rather because it is difficult not to sound tokenistic and superficial. What does it really mean to identify oneself as an uninvited guest in this country and what actions should accompany such a statement especially when you represent the privileged coloniser majority? Aboriginal cultural protocols are increasingly present in Australian higher education – welcomes and less formal acknowledgements of country – however, what does it mean and does it really signify a shift to 'Indigenise the academy'? The answer probably lies in my recent experience at the 2016 Office for Learning and Teaching Conference in Melbourne. There was a Welcome to Country by *Wurundjeri* Elder Mr Perry Wandin, but many in the audience, like a lot of students that academics complain about, were more engaged with their mobile devices. Similarly, the parallel session on Indigenous Education was attended by, maybe, 20 people, whilst the other sessions on assessment and employability were heavily subscribed. If the attendance at the Indigenous Education session is anything to go by, it appears that the majority of Conference attendees either felt Indigenous education was going well and did not need their attention, that it did not relate to their role as leaders in learning and teaching, or they had other priorities and/or felt they already knew enough. Following the formal Welcome to Country by Mr Wandin, what does this say about the capacity of non-Aboriginal academics to take the responsibilities of being a guest seriously or, indeed, to demonstrate hospitality to the 'other'? I would like to open a dialogue with you about how the academy could build on what is already happening and become both a better guest and host through a relationship built on an Indigenous notion of reciprocity.

Theoretical framework

We adopt the theoretical frameworks of two Indigenous academics to inform our discussion. Firstly, we explore Kuokkanen's (2007) theorisation of Indigenous epistemes as a gift to the academy to highlight the incommensurable alignment of capitalist axiology – typical of contemporary universities – with Indigenous Australian epistemology and ontology. According to Kuokkanen (2007), who is a Sami woman from Northern Europe, social order in Indigenous communities is maintained through giving and recognising the gifts of others including the land. Building on Derrida's work, she argues that 'The gift constitutes a specific logic that not only is different from that of the increasingly consumerist and careerist academy but also represents a radical critique of the logic of exchange' (Kuokkanen, 2007, p. 7). The application of quality metrics to 'Indigenising the curriculum' (e.g., numbers of courses with Indigenous content/non-Aboriginal student satisfaction with Indigenous units/students' achievement of cultural 'competency') not only illustrates the privileging of Western epistemology, ontology and axiology, but it also clearly highlights that 'Indigenous epistemes remain an impossible gift due to the prevailing epistemic ignorance in the academy' (Kuokkanen, 2007, p. 7). With the logic of the gift comes a form of generous hospitality that embraces the 'other' and recognises a multiplicity of reciprocal gift practices; in other words, it forms a framework for interaction which varies dependent on the local context, thereby challenging the logic of Western exchange (Kuokkanen, 2007). The theoretical framework for this dialogue is thus primarily informed by Kuokkanen's critique of the academy's sanctioned ignorance of Indigenous epistemes: 'How the academy is based fundamentally on a very narrow understanding of the world and human relationships' (Kuokkanen, 2007, p. 2).

The second theorist's work we adopt is that of Nakata (2007a), a Torres Strait Islander, and his conceptualisation of the 'cultural interface'; the complex and contested space which manifests at the juncture of different cosmological, epistemological and ontological positions. These differences, according to Nakata (2007a), must be recognised by anyone working in this space and that one cannot simply 'plonk' Indigenous content into the curriculum: 'Things aren't just black or white, and things cannot be fixed by simply adding in Indigenous components to the mix. This is a very complicated and contested space' (p. 8). As Nakata (2007a) argues, our collective understanding of Indigenous knowledge in postcolonial Australia – Indigenous and non-Indigenous – is mediated by Western discourses and intellectual traditions. Similarly, he warns against binary thinking, where Indigenous knowledges are unproblematically valorised in opposition to the overtly demonised Western other (Carey & Prince, 2015; Page, 2014). Nakata's work is widely recognised as a key theoretical approach to understanding what Indigenising curricula means in Australia, and has the potential to mean (Carey & Prince, 2015; Hook, 2013).

What we propose, therefore, is to recognise the impossibility of applying measures of quality to learning and teaching Indigenous Australian content. This is due to the contradictions inherent in continuing to unproblematically privilege Western capitalist knowledge systems (what is known, how it is known and by whom and how it is legitimised) to a way of being and knowing informed by the logic of the gift. Additionally, effective learning for Indigenous content – particularly when compulsory – is highly complex, contested and political (Leane, 2010; Page, 2014). As a consequence, and due to the academy's failure to be a reflexive host and tolerant of ontological pluralism (Gunstone, 2009; Hauser, Howlett, & Matthews, 2009), what often results is superficial learning (Page, 2014), overburdened staff (Page, 2008) and further disenfranchised Aboriginal communities (Miller, 2015). Through reflecting on our experience, we would like to contribute to the conversation begun by others (for example, the Australian Indigenous Studies Learning and Teaching Network, 2016; Fredricks, 2009; Hauser et al., 2009; McGloin, 2009; Moreton-Robinson, 2000; Nakata, 2007b; Nakata, Nakata, Keech, & Bolt, 2012; Page, 2014) to further the sector's understanding of 'Indigenising the curriculum', the learning and teaching context it requires, including the resources needed to support both students and staff at the 'cultural interface'.

Indigenous cultures and health

The unit which forms the basis for the dialogue undertaken here was a compulsory common inter-professional unit which has been taught to approximately 3300 students per annum from 19 to 27 health professions (from 2011 to mid-2016). A 12.5 (half credit) unit, it was introduced in 2011 as part of the common inter-professional first year at Curtin University's Faculty of Health Sciences.

Co-coordinated by Aboriginal and non-Aboriginal academics and taught by an intercultural team and jointly owned by the Faculty of Health Sciences and the Centre for Aboriginal Studies, it modelled effective intercultural partnerships (Kickett et al., 2014). Although the assessment tasks have been modified slightly since the unit's introduction in 2011, critical reflective writing focusing on the students' response to the content and their journey through the 12 two-hour weekly workshops remained constant (Mezirow, 1991). A deliberate approach to creating a safe environment for learning (Leane, 2010) was used to draw students into a conversation to reflect on and deepen their understanding of Indigenous Australia, white privilege, the impact of colonisation and past policies, intergenerational trauma and how this has shaped health behaviour and outcomes (Hendrick, Britton, Hoffman, & Kickett, 2014; Kickett et al., 2014). International students were engaged through a discussion on global Indigenous populations and/or ethnic minorities in their own countries (Kickett et al., 2014). In 2014, the team received a national teaching excellence award and, whilst the validity of such awards has been critically interrogated as measures of quality (see, for example, Probert, 2015), they are valued by universities as evidence of 'superior' student learning experiences. In this case, the national teaching excellence award epitomised the tensions at the cultural interface; a marketable moment for the University – in the same way the unit has been promoted during National Aboriginal and Islander Observance Day Committee Week – that obfuscates the site of struggle that the unit embodied.

Learning and teaching at the cultural interface

The student cohort

For those who work in this space, you have a sound understanding that teaching Aboriginal and Torres Strait content in a Australian contemporary university is highly complex (Page, 2014; Zubrzycki et al., 2014). This is, in part, because students are extremely diverse ethnically, culturally and racially and bring multiple experiences and perspectives to the classroom. The classroom can potentially include all of the following: white students (Australian and new migrants), students of colour (Australian and new migrants), International students, Indigenous Australian students (identifying and non-identifying), mature age students and refugees. All groups represent a range of socio-economic backgrounds (e.g., first in family to children of privileged professional parents and everything in between) and there is an increasing number of students with mental health issues (e.g., anxiety and depression) (Andrews & Wilding, 2004). Managing and unpacking 'culture' whilst maintaining a safe place for all to explore notions of 'Indigeneity' – including Aboriginal students – are, to say the least, challenging. The teaching was further complicated by the inter-professional, large first-year cohort.

Within such complex multicultural and disciplinary settings, what is desired is a transformational learning experience where students develop a critical and nuanced understanding of how their worldview (including their disciplinary/professional lens) can and does impede their capacity to be good hosts, tolerant of ontological pluralism. However, as has been observed by scholars in the field whilst transformation is desired, the 'unlearning' can fall short resulting in simplified binary thinking manifesting in 'primitivism/Indigenous vs modernity/non-Indigenous' (Nakata, 2012, cited by Page, 2014, p. 25). Significantly, such binaries are grounded in a Western model of exchange epitomised by the corporate university: there has been no transformation or decolonisation of knowledges, rather a simplistic exchange that cannot 'generate new knowledge to transform Indigenous social conditions' (Nakata et al., 2012, p. 121).

Much of the work done at the cultural interface would, ideally, have very little to do with the idea of 'transaction', that intrinsically inherent concept within the capitalist tertiary institution, but rather would focus almost entirely on a concept of transformation (Mackinlay & Barney, 2010); transformation built upon the foundation of reciprocity, relationships and recognition of the value of other ways of doing things and of shifting worldviews (Mezirow, 2000). It is at the juncture of transactional and transformational activity that all too often 'Indigenising the curriculum' falls short.

For example, students (who have come to be seen as, and consequently see themselves as, consumers) bring a transactional approach to their tertiary education experience. Students, who having experienced and adapted to a 'user pays' educational environment, apply this mentality to their learning often expecting a 'product' equivalent to their previous educational experiences. To illustrate the point, a student in her second teaching week of the unit emailed to say that the unit was taught incorrectly; that she would like to focus on more statistics, facts and figures, as opposed to an environment that encouraged and required students to critically reflect on, and engage with, the diversity of the classroom. The cultural interface needs to be unsettling if transformation is to be achieved; however, challenging students and engaging with concepts such as white privilege do not necessarily result in satisfied customers. Similarly, addressing deeply seated stereotypes and myths about Aboriginal people (e.g., 'they all have a problem with alcohol' and receive 'excessive government handouts') speaks deeply to national identity and the Australian egalitarian promise of a 'fair go for all' (see, for example, Henry & Tator, 1994). The identity issues raised often can, for some students, result in the need for support from the tutors and university counselling staff as well as time to resolve issues (not achievable within a 12-week teaching period). For some students, their own personal trauma can be drawn into the classroom, raising important questions around duty of care.

Opportunities for learning can be also lost in a teaching environment with large numbers of students (some of whom are learning in an online environment) where 'resisters' can become the focus (Page, 2016). In our efforts to deliver transformation for (virtually) all – as required by university measures of high student satisfaction, retention and achievement of learning outcomes – opportunities for not only learning but also building relationships with our students (essential to Indigenous pedagogies) are lost. What are the implications then for those teaching and administering units/courses at the cultural interface within an environment of massification and quality metrics?

Teaching staff

Teaching staff included Aboriginal, Torres Strait Islander and non-Indigenous people from a range of cultural and racial backgrounds. The emotional labour associated with teaching at the cultural interface for Aboriginal and Torres Strait Islander peoples has been documented (see, for example, Asmar & Page, 2009; Page, 2008). For Aboriginal and Torres Strait Islander peoples teaching this content is high stakes (outcomes directly impacting on family and community), requiring significant resilience and capacity to manage racism both overt (e.g., racist statements from students and colleagues) and covert (e.g., institutional racism). For most non-Aboriginal tutors, there is also some degree of emotional labour due to their investment in social justice and relationships with Indigenous Australians. It is important, however, to make clear that this emotional labour is not the same as it is not typically vested in familial and personal risk. Nor are non-Indigenous tutors required to repeatedly share traumatic and confronting stories from their past (including their family) to emotionally connect students with the lived reality of statistics. Ironically, whilst such units aim to develop graduates with the capacity to provide culturally safe health and social care services, Aboriginal and Torres Strait Islander academics are not afforded cultural safety within their own institutions (Bond, 2014). The emotional labour involved is commonly a dimension not even considered, let alone well understood, by those not engaged in this space. This includes those in senior decision-making roles – typically white and not provided with transformational learning opportunities – who formulate the policies, resourcing and quality measures that impact on the classroom, students and staff, and ultimately Aboriginal and Torres Strait Islander communities.

Therefore, effective learning and teaching in this complex space require a range of capabilities that are often unacknowledged and lack value in the academy. Some of the capabilities identified through community consultation as part of the Health Workforce Australia Aboriginal and Torres Strait Islander Curriculum Framework project (Department of Health, 2014) include the following:

1. Aboriginal and Torres Strait Islander content specific knowledge
2. Self-reflexivity – both in 'looking back' on one's life and in classroom practice
3. Highly developed facilitation skills – including the ability to facilitate courageous conversations [about race] (Singleton & Linton, 2006) and learning that inspires students to examine their beliefs in a safe learning environment
4. Robust skills in cross cultural facilitation and the capacity to develop challenging yet 'safe' teaching and learning spaces that do not resort to binary views but rather encourage students to explore multiple 'intercultural' perspectives in an open and transparent way
5. Deep understanding of the student learning journey specific to Aboriginal and Torres Strait Islander content
6. Ability to enact strategies of professional and personal self-care
7. Demonstrate intercultural partnerships, collaboration and engagement. (p. 19)

The failure to recognise and value these capabilities – as well as support staff to develop them – is based on a lack of understanding of the logic of the gift and an over-reliance on one knowledge tradition. In the rush to 'Indigenise the curriculum', there has been a tendency to assume that almost anyone can teach effectively in this space. This is a risky business which has the potential to reinforce racism, putting additional stress on other students and staff, particularly Aboriginal and Torres Strait Islanders. Put another way, those teaching must have undergone, sometimes to the point of crisis, the same transformational process of 'unlearning' which is being asked and expected of students.

Coordinating Indigenous studies units

As a coordinator of an Indigenous studies unit of this size, you need to not only be highly capable at managing and administering a large complex unit, but also serve simultaneously as a barrier and a bridge. This means you work to protect both staff teaching and student learning to ensure all have as safe a journey as possible. You must mediate the university's normative requirements around policy, practice and quality measures, whilst opening a space for Indigenous epistemology and ontology to exist in sufficient form to (hopefully) spark a transformational learning experience. This learning experience is not limited to enrolled students; it often means tutors (particularly those new to the cultural interface directed to service teach), colleagues and senior staff (including, potentially, your line manager). At the same time, you need to effectively build and strengthen relationships with community Elders to ensure the content and teaching are consistent with local cultural practices, and spend time supporting non-Indigenous staff and students whose journey of 'unlearning' has raised significant issues. More often than not, none of this relational and emotional labour is recognised in your workload. Nor is your capacity to undertake this work valued, including your cultural knowledge, resilience, collaborative facilitation skills and relationships. Of note, to be effective interculturally, you operate collectively – as much as possible within the context of your work environment – undermining capitalist notions of individualism and achievement. Questions raised about your qualifications and capabilities, as academic measures of capacity (where is your PhD?), override your cultural knowledge and intercultural skills (Behrendt, 1996).

At the cultural interface, the metrics used to measure effectiveness are misaligned – often violently – with the desired process of learning. This is most starkly illustrated through the use of anonymous student satisfaction surveys on learning and teaching to raise questions about quality and performance. As indicated earlier, transformational learning does not necessarily result in satisfied students; the cultural interface requires tolerance for ambiguity and feeling unsettled. Not every student has that capacity – and may hence be dissatisfied – and the constraints applied by university measures and economies of scale limit the learning that can occur. Time available for class discussion and effective facilitation of learning, for example, is an issue. A lack of knowledge by decision-makers thus results in under-resourcing; for example, rarely is there sufficient funding for ongoing, appropriate and relevant professional development for tutors and staff making decisions that impact on the unit. Additionally, the (often hidden) complexities (and workload) associated with managing a large Indigenous studies unit with an intercultural tutor team (often casual academics) increase the 'problem' of assuring the university's 'quality' measures. Workload is a sector-wide issue for academics (Bexley, James, & Arkoudis, 2011); however, one could argue that those involved in unit coordination in this space may be further overburdened. Deeply held personal commitments to change the status quo of Aboriginal and Torres Strait Islander peoples often result in extreme workloads of unacknowledged tasks limiting opportunities to progress higher degree research studies and careers, and impacting on personal relationships and health and well-being.

Implications for community

Whilst some would think it melodramatic to argue that transformational learning for students at the cultural interface is 'life and death', events emerging at the time we are writing this paper vehemently suggest otherwise. For Aboriginal and Torres Strait Islanders and engaged non-Indigenous people, the Four Corners' (Meldrum-Hanna, Fallon, & Worthington, 2016) report on the abuse and torture of youth in the Don Dale Northern Territory juvenile detention centre was unsurprising. Mainstream Australia was reportedly shocked. However, as Shaylene Solomon, a former child youth worker in Queensland attests, this sort of abuse is rife nationally and has been ongoing for centuries (Anderson & Ferguson, 2016). The criminal justice system is, of course, only one government-run institution that perpetuates racism, resulting in appalling outcomes for Aboriginal and Torres Strait Islanders: reduced life expectancy, high rates of children being removed and suicide, over-representation in detention, poor health and education and low rates of home ownership and employment (Eckermann et al., 2010; Turale & Miller, 2006). The events viscerally portrayed in the Four Corners' programme in July 2016 illustrate that colonial violence is not an historical artefact, but the lived experience of contemporary Aboriginal and Torres Strait Islanders.

Inappropriate attempts to, as Nakata has described, 'plonk' Indigenous content into the curriculum will not achieve the fundamental systemic transformation of graduates and institutions so desperately needed. As we finalise writing this paper, there is criticism from Aboriginal leaders about the constitution of the planned Royal Commission into the treatment of youth in the Northern Territory detention centres. Unsurprisingly, and yet again, the initial response from the government was to appoint a non-Aboriginal commissioner to lead another enquiry to investigate 'Indigenous issues'. This transactional, 'measured' approach to dealing with the 'Indigenous problem' fails to consider alternative, collaborative, creative and forward-focused solutions informed by other ways of knowing and being in the world. What is evident in the federal government's response is a lack of capacity to understand the limits of Western knowledge systems or a disposition to engage 'in open, exploratory, and creative inquiry into these difficult intersections, whilst building language and tools for describing and analysing what they engage with' (Nakata et al., 2012, p. 121). The failure of universities to be comfortable with ontological pluralism will result in graduates who are ill equipped to change the institutions they work in and imagine new languages to address the social inequities facing Aboriginal and Torres Strait Islanders. Ideally, the learning achieved in Indigenous studies would follow the process described above by Nakata. However, whilst some progress has been made, learning is constrained through the academy's impatience with, and inattention to, the 'other'. In the words of Kuokkanen (2007), without accepting our responsibilities to the 'other', different ontological understandings are not possible; what is required is 'a different temporality, one that challenges today's dominant preference for quick fixes and for cost-effectively mass producing graduates within pre-determined time frames' (pp. 11–12).

Discussion

If the purpose of transformative Indigenous educational experiences is to shake up, to place the student and educators in positions of discomfort and at times crisis – epistemologically and ontologically – then new measures of learning and teaching 'quality' must be imagined. Ironically, baseline measures of student dissatisfaction, if reliably captured, might tell a story in terms of how well Indigenous studies units are fulfilling their intended purpose. Current quantitative measures that fail to capture the impact of the unit described here are self-perpetuating as they misrepresent what is happening at the cultural interface. Instead, measures that could determine students' progress with possible key threshold concepts (e.g., their level of comfort with the discomfort associated with ontological pluralism) would be more appropriate and could enable adaptive, scaffolded learning experiences. As Page (2014) attests, however, more research is required to understand how students learn Aboriginal and Torres Strait Islander content. This research might help make clear what indicators could predict the likelihood of transformation. Questions arise, of course, about the willingness of universities to consider different conceptualisations of 'quality' and their associated time frames.

For example, whilst students often fail to understand Indigenous notions of reciprocity and hospitality, so do many of the academics who have 'Indigenous' KPIs. It is important to keep in mind that relationships between Indigenous and non-Indigenous Australians have always been articulated in terms of property relations (Nicholl, 2004). Highly transactional approaches to being inclusive of Indigenous content, within the always 'overcrowded' curriculum (Nakata, Nakata, & Chin, 2008), clearly illustrate a lack of understanding of the gift. 'I'll do something for you, if you do something for me', is a common experience for Aboriginal academics charged with embedding Indigenous content. There is a personal toll when faced with this mantra of capitalist exchange (particularly against the backdrop of land theft and dispossession), although often a superficial understanding of reciprocity and hospitality emerges for the non-Aboriginal academic through the process.

Given the contested space, limited resources and small (but growing) numbers of Aboriginal and Torres Strait Islander academics, there is ongoing potential for practices to lapse back to familiar Western 'ways of doing and knowing'. This work to 'Indigenise curriculum' and transform students' worldview is, therefore, always at risk of being undone. This is particularly so when individual champions in senior roles move on (Department of Health, 2014).

The lack of understanding of the gift results in a worsening of outcomes for Aboriginal and Torres Strait Islanders. 'Tick the box' approaches to KPIs embedded in strategic plans can function to let non-Indigenous people not only achieve what they need to advance their careers, but also allow them to feel better without any transformation: of both themselves and students. It is the how – how Indigenous content is included and taught – which is a more meaningful 'measure' as it indicates the level of intercultural understanding in the university (Biermann & Townsend-Cross, 2008).

More culturally appropriate approaches, for example, that incorporate Indigenous Australian epistemes could be considered as the mechanism to identify and measure 'quality'. Wright's framework (Wright, O'Connell, Jones, Walley, & Roarty, 2015) for building mental health agencies' capacity to improve service delivery through ongoing, sustained relationships with local Elders is one possible way forward. Through building reciprocal relationships with Elders that respect local protocols and build trust, universities could develop their capacity for creating new languages to express and explore 'quality' at the cultural interface. In a university with meaningful cultural capability, local Elders would determine whether graduates are practice-ready to work with community.

Our paper has been critical of the epistemic violence inherent in the attempt to quantify learning in Indigenous studies, as well as an ignorance of the complexities of effective learning at the cultural interface. This work is not the sole responsibility of Aboriginal and Torres Strait Islander academics – to include and teach Indigenous studies – it must be a shared responsibility built on reciprocity, respect and hospitality. Non-Indigenous academics must become active allies with a willingness to be vulnerable and open to the 'other'.

Notes

1. In respect of the diversity of Indigenous Australians, 'Aboriginal and Torres Strait Islander' has been used in this paper to refer to the original custodians and guardians of the land which makes up what is now known as Australia. However, at times, 'Indigenous' and 'Indigenous Australians' are also used as these are terms often found in the literature exploring Aboriginal and Torres Strait Islander content and perspectives in higher education. We acknowledge that many of these terms are contentious and problematic and that Aboriginal people prefer to be identified by their language group. We respectfully apologise for any offence that may be caused.
2. We are not suggesting to collapse the diversity of Aboriginal and Torres Strait Islanders, but rather make reference to the many shared experiences of colonised Indigenous peoples.
3. It is generally accepted that 'competency' is inappropriate as it implies an end point, rather than the life-long process involved in becoming effective interculturally. Additionally, Aboriginal and Torres Strait Islanders are, very reasonably, resistant to notions that anyone outside their communities can be culturally competent in their culture (MacMillan, 2013; Taylor et al., 2014).

Acknowledgements

We would like to acknowledge all the people involved in conceiving, designing, teaching and supporting the unit explored here over the years it has been taught. The unit was made possible by many people including community members who generously shared their stories, which featured in the Vodcasts. A special and heartfelt thanks also goes to Louise Austen for her comments on, and suggestions for, this paper.

Disclosure statement

No potential conflict of interest was reported by the authors.

References

Anderson, B., & Ferguson, Z. (2016, July 30). Former worker claims abuse was rife at Cleveland youth detention centre in Queensland. *ABC Online*. Retrieved from http://www.abc.net.au/news/2016-07-30/new-claims-of-abuse-at-cleveland-youth-detention-centre/7674896

Andrews, B., & Wilding, J. M. (2004). The relation of depression and anxiety to life-stress and achievement in students. *The British Psychological Society, 95*, 509–521.

Anning, B. (2010). Embedding an Indigenous graduate attribute into University of Western Sydney's courses. *The Australian Journal of Indigenous Education, 39*(S), 40–52.

Asmar, C., & Page, S. (2009). Sources of satisfaction and stress among Indigenous academic teachers: Findings from a national Australian study. *Asia Pacific Journal of Education, 29*(3), 387–401. doi:10.1080/02188790903097505

Australian Indigenous Studies Learning and Teaching Network. (2016). *Australian Indigenous studies learning and teaching network*. Retrieved from http://www.atsis.uq.edu.au/?page=199124

Behrendt, L. (1996). At the back of the class. At the front of the class: Experiences as Aboriginal student and Aboriginal teacher. *Feminist Review, 52*, 7–35.

Behrendt, L. (2013). Foreword. In G. Foley, A. Schapp, & E. Howell (Eds.), *The Aboriginal tent embassy: Soverignty, black power, land rights and the state* (pp. xxiii–xxiv). Hoboken: Taylor and Francis.

Bexley, E., James, R., & Arkoudis, S. (2011). *The Australian academic profession in transition: Addressing the challenge of reconceptualising academic work*. Melbourne University. Retrieved from http://www.cshe.unimelb.edu.au/people/bexley_docs/The_Academic_Profession_in_Transition_Sept2011.pdf

Biermann, S., & Townsend-Cross, M. (2008). Indigenous pedagogy as a force for change. *The Australian Journal of Indigenous Education, 37*(Suppl.), 146–154.

Bin-Sallik, M. (2003). Cultural. Safety: Let's name it! *The Australian Journal of Indigenous Education, 32*, 21–28.

Bond, C. (2014). When the object teaches: Indigenous academics in Australian universities. *Right Now – Human Rights in Australia*. Retrieved from http://rightnow.org.au/opinion-3/when-the-object-teaches-indigenous-academics-in-australian-universities/

Carey, M., & Prince, M. (2015). Designing an Australian Indigenous studies curriculum for the twenty-first century: Nakata's 'cultural interface', standpoints and working beyond binaries. *Higher Education Research & Development, 34*(2), 270–283.

Department of Health. (2014). *Aboriginal and Torres Strait Islander health curriculum framework*. Canberra: Australian Government. Retrieved from http://www.health.gov.au/internet/main/publishing.nsf/Content/aboriginal-torres-strait-islander-health-curriculum-framework

Eckermann, A.-K., Down, T., Chong, E., Nixon, L., Fray, R., & Johnson, S. (2010). *Binan Goonj: Bridging cultures in Aboriginal health* (3rd ed.). Chatswood: Elsevier.

Fredricks, B. (2009). Look before you leap: The epistemic violence that sometimes hides behind the word 'inclusion'. *The Australian Journal of Indigenous Education, 38*, 10–16.

Gunstone, A. (2009). Whiteness, Indigenous peoples and Australian universities. *Australian Critical Race and Whiteness Studies Association e-Journal*. Retrieved from http://www.acrawsa.org.au/files/ejournalfiles/44acrawsa517.pdf

Hauser, V., Howlett, C., & Matthews, C. (2009). The place of Indigenous knowledge in tertiary science education: A case study of Canadian practices in Indigenising curriculum. *The Australian Journal of Indigenous Education, 38*, 46–57.

Hendrick, A., Britton, K. F., Hoffman, J., & Kickett, M. (2014). Developing future health professionals' capacities for working with Aboriginal and Torres Strait Islander peoples. *The Australian Journal of Indigenous Education, 43*(2), 154–164.

Henry, F., & Tator, C. (1994). The ideology of racism: Democratic racism. *Canadian Ethnic Studies, 26*(2), 1–14.

Hook, G. (2013). Towards a decolonising pedagogy: Understanding Australian Indigenous studies through critical whiteness theory and film pedagogy. *The Australian Journal of Indigenous Education, 41*(2), 110–119.

Indigenous Higher Education Advisory Council. (2006). *Improving Indigenous outcomes and enhancing Indigenous culture and knowledge in Australian higher education, including the IAHEC conference report 2005 and the IHEAC strategic plan 2006–2008*. Retrieved from http://foi.deewr.gov.au/documents/improving-indigenous-outcomes-and-enhancing-indigenous-culture-and-knowledge-australian

Kickett, M., Hoffman, J., & Flavell, H. (2014). A model for large scale, interprofessional, compulsory cross-cultural education with an Indigenous focus. *Journal of Allied Health, 43*(1), 38–44.

Kuokkanen, R. (2007). *Reshaping the university: Responsibility, Indigenous epistemes, and the logic of the gift*. Vancouver: UBC Press.

Leane, J. (2010). Aboriginal representation: Conflict or dialogue in the academy. *The Australian Journal of Indigenous Education, 39*(S), 32–39.

Mackinlay, E., & Barney, K. (2010). Transformative learning in first year Indigenous Australian studies: Posing problems, asking questions and achieving change. *The International Journal of the First Year in Higher Education, 1*(1), 91–99.

Mackinlay, E., & Barney, K. (2014). PEARLs, problems and politics: Exploring findings from two teaching and learning projects in Indigenous Australian studies at the University of Queensland. *The Australian Journal of Indigenous Education, 43*(1), 31–41.

MacMillan, F. (2013). *Position paper – Culturally responsive health care*. Retrieved from http://iaha.com.au/wp-content/uploads/2013/09/Position_Paper_Culturally_Responsive_Health_Care.pdf

McConnochie, K., Egege, D., & McDermmott, D. (2008). Issues in cultural competence. In R. Ranzijn, K. McConnochie, & W. Nolan (Eds.), *Psychology and Indigenous Australians: Effective teaching and practice* (pp. 191–206). Newcastle Upon Tyne: Cambridge Scholars.

McGloin, C. (2009). Considering the work of Martin Nakata's 'cultural interface': A reflection on theory and practice by a non-Indigenous academic. *The Australian Journal of Indigenous Education, 38*(1), 36–41.

McLaughlin, J., & Whatman, S. L. (2010). *Decolonising curricula in an Australian university: Re-imagining curriculum through critical race theory*. Paper presented at the World Congress in Comparative Education Conference, Istanbul, Turkey. Retrieved from http://eprints.qut.edu.au/42551/

Meldrum-Hanna, C., Fallon, M., & Worthington, E. (Producers). (2016). Australia's shame. *ABC four corners*. Sydney: Australian Broadcasting Corporation.

Mezirow, J. (1990). How critical reflection triggers transformative learning. In J. A. Mezirow (Ed.), *Fostering critical reflection in adulthood: A guide to transformative and emancipatory learning* (pp. 1–20). San Francisco: Jossey-Bass.

Mezirow, J. (1991). *Transformative dimensions of adult learning*. San Francisco, CA: Jossey-Bass.

Mezirow, J. (2000). *Learning as transformation: Critical perspectives on a theory in progress*. San Fransico, CA: Jossey-Bass.

Miller, M. G. (2015). Consultation with Aboriginal and Torres Strait Islander people in early childhood education: The impact of colonial discourses. *Adult Education Research, 42*, 549–565.

Moreton-Robinson, A. (2000). *Talkin' up the white woman: Indigenous women and white feminism.* St Lucia: Queensland University Press.

Nakata, M. (2007a). The cultural interface. *The Australian Journal of Indigenous Education, 36*(S), 7–14.

Nakata, M. (2007b). *Disciplining the savages: Savaging the disciplines.* Canberra: Aboriginal Studies Press.

Nakata, M., Nakata, K., & Chin, M. (2008). Approaches to the academic preparation and support of Australian Indigenous students for tertiary studies. *The Australian Journal of Indigenous Education, 37*(Suppl.), 137–145.

Nakata, M., Nakata, V., Keech, S., & Bolt, R. (2012). Decolonial goals and pedagogies for Indigenous studies. *Decolonization: Indigeneity, Education & Society, 1*(1), 120–140.

Nicholl, F. (2004). 'Are you calling me a racist?' Teaching critical whiteness theory in Indigenous sovereignty. *Borderlands Ejournal, 3*(2). Retrieved from http://www.borderlands.net.au/vol3no2_2004/nicoll_teaching.htm

Page, S. (2008). Beneath the teaching iceberg: Exposing the hidden support dimensions of Indigenous academic work. *The Australian Journal of Indigenous Education, 37*(Suppl.), 109–117.

Page, S. (2014). Exploring new conceptualisations of old problems: Researching and reorienting teaching in Indigenous studies to transform student learning. *The Australian Journal of Indigenous Education, 43*(1), 21–30.

Page, S. (2016). *Using the threshold concepts framework to explore student learning in Indigenous studies.* Paper presented at the HERDSA Conference 2016: The shape of higher education, Fremantle, Western Australia.

Probert, B. (2015). *The quality of Australia's higher education system: How it might be defined, improved and assured.* Sydney: Office for Learning and Teaching.

Singleton, G., & Linton, C. (2006). *Courageous conversations about race.* Thousand Oaks, CA: Corwin Press.

Taylor, K., Durey, A., Mullcock, J., Kickett, M., & Jones, S. (2014). *Developing Aboriginal and Torres Strait Islander cultural capabilities in health graduates: A review of the literature.* Adelaide: Health Workforce Australia.

Turale, S., & Miller, M. (2006). Improving the health of Indigenous Australians: Reforms in nursing education. An opinion piece of international interest. *International Nursing Review, 53*(3), 171–177.

Universities Australia. (2011). *Guiding principles for developing Indigenous competency in Australian universities.* Canberra. Retrieved from https://www.universitiesaustralia.edu.au/uni-participation-quality/Indigenous-Higher-Education/Indigenous-Cultural-Compet#.Vs0wMPl97IU

Wright, M., O'Connell, M., Jones, T., Walley, R., & Roarty, L. (2015). *Looking forward project: Final report.* Subiaco, Western Australia. Retrieved from http://aboriginal.telethonkids.org.au/media/2030482/LFP-final-research-report-2015-ecopy.pdf

Zubrzycki, J., Green, S., Jones, V., Stratton, K., Young, S., & Bessarab, D. (2014). *Getting it right: Creating partnerships for change. Integrating Aboriginal and Torres Strait Islander knowledges in Australian social work education and practice.* Sydney: Australian Government. Retrieved from file:///C:/Users/227369D/Downloads/ID11_2003_Zubrzycki_Report_2014%20(1).pdf

Target-setting, early-career academic identities and the measurement culture of UK higher education

Jan Smith

ABSTRACT
Early-career academics are subject to a barrage of formal measurements when they secure a first academic post in a UK university. To support this process, guidance is provided by universities on what is measured, though this can lack disciplinary nuance. This article analyses the perceptions of a sample of social scientists of the process of target-setting during their academic probationary periods, showing that the perceived surveillance regime legitimates particular academic identities. I show how, for those who took part in this study, the currently instantiated competitive UK measurement culture can produce conformative subjects who frustrate institutional rhetoric.

I don't think it's too much measurement, but it's bad measurement, it's a shame.

Early-career academics (ECAs) are subject to a barrage of measurements when they secure a first academic post in a UK university in response to the surveillance regimes that now form part of the corporatised university environment globally (Lynch, 2010). Targets are set and monitored regularly[1] as new academics strive to establish independent academic identities. What constitute desirable targets for institutional satisfaction remain opaque to individuals, who turn to generic advice provided by Human Resources Departments that lack disciplinary nuance (Becher & Trowler, 2001). Consideration of the affective dimensions (Clegg, 2008) of a permanent measurement culture (Davies & Petersen, 2005) is now foregrounded in literature on academic identities where care and collegiality (Lynch, 2010) are being superseded by individuation (Macfarlane, 2007) and competitiveness. As Ball (2003, p. 216) argues, this requires people to perform in material and symbolic ways in response to systems of control and surveillance rooted not in academics' desires but 'institutional self-interest' (Ball, 2003, p. 218) as corporatised managerialist imperatives overtake virtuous conceptions (Macfarlane, 2007) of academic service.

Affect is an important dimension of research on contemporary conditions of academic work environments as marketisation privileges a target-setting culture. Shin and Jung (2014) use regression analysis on a large international data set to categorise national HE systems into high/low job satisfaction and high-/low-job stress working environments, in which the UK scores poorly. Stensaker (2015) theorises organisational identity as a device to explore university working environments, where brand and marketing focus change at an institutional level. Any university, however, is reliant on the work of its individual academics, and an exploration of how ECAs recognise and acclimatise to managerialist demands (Sutherland, 2015) is timely, given the impact of market-orientated policy drivers (McGettigan, 2013; Shin & Jung, 2014). The aim in this article is to relate the idea of 'identity-trajectory' (McAlpine, Amundsen, & Jazvac-Martek, 2010, p. 129) to the lived experience of beginning work in a national but highly stratified HE system exhibiting high stress and low satisfaction (Shin & Jung, 2014). The opacity of the UK's academic probation system can indicate a mismatch between Sutherland's (2015) conceptions of objective and subjective career success and induce individual behaviours that support what Ball (2003, p. 236) calls 'cynical compliance'.

The measurement culture in UK universities

Much measurement in universities is subsequently used in league tables (Times Higher Education, 2016) that reflect perceptions of increasing surveillance experienced by academics (Davies & Petersen, 2005, in an Australian context; Gill, 2009, in the UK; Grant & Elizabeth, 2015, in New Zealand). These measurements frequently focus on research – outputs, grant capture – and evolve over time. The UK was an early advocate of a 'Research Assessment Exercise' (now the Research Excellence Framework [REF]) in the 1980s, since adopted by Australia in the form of the ERA (Australian Research Council, 2015) and New Zealand's PBRF (Grant & Elizabeth, 2015). In addition to the REF, underpinning this study is a raft of other measurement technologies that vary in relation to both national HE systems and the positioning of institutions within the national hierarchy. In the UK, the Russell Group of 24 research-intensive institutions (of which the research site is one) tend to follow the processes in Table 1, but variations exist in the sector for universities which align more closely with different mission statements. For illustrative purposes, Table 1 summarises some things measured in UK HE that impact directly on ECAs in relation to teaching and research roles; management and governance data requirements are not included, as these demands commonly fall to those with different responsibilities.

Universities now compete globally in recruitment terms, driven by what McGettigan (2013) calls the 'Great University Gamble': a free-market ideology that seeks to prioritise the private good (and minimise public funding) of universities. One outcome of this process is a need to measure – inputs, outputs, processes, quality – and the list is additive: in the UK, research impact, for instance, is a recent practice instantiated for the REF in 2014 and the newest demand is the Teaching Excellence Framework (TEF), introduced from 2016 (Business Innovation & Skills [BIS], 2016). The extent of surveillance (Davies & Petersen, 2005) poses challenges to all, but particularly ECAs as they establish their independent academic identities. As Shin and Jung (2014) note, implementing reforms associated with 'New Public Management' are clear indicators of high stress for those working in UK HE, and this manifests itself from the beginning of the academic probation period (APP). The propensity for measurement in UK HE may be a distinct barrier for new international colleagues: the proportion of non-UK staff recruited to UK universities currently stands at 29% (Higher Education Statistics Agency, 2016). The importance ECAs attach to both objective and subjective measures of career success (Sutherland, 2015) suggests that the globalisation of the search for academic talent may expose new academics

Table 1. An outline of possible teaching and research-related required reporting mechanisms for academics.

Measurement tool	Description of purpose	Level of granularity
Transparent Approach to Costing (TRAC)[a]	Feeds into funding formula with different activities costed at different rates; forms the basis for a university's financial allocation	Individuals account for how they spend their time in a given period (may include weekends). Universities return aggregate data to funding agency to account for proportion of funds spent on each activity. Annual activity for all academic staff
Research Excellence Framework (REF)[a]	To distribute research funding via competitive national formula	Individuals make claims about research output and significance; departments develop submissions; institutions strategise according to current parameters. REF is every 5–7 years, but data collection a permanent feature for all academic staff (every accepted publication needs to be deposited, be peer-reviewed, journal impact factor, rating for REF categories). Published
National Student Survey (NSS)[a]	To measure student satisfaction annually via unified national tool to publish league tables of performance	Final-year undergraduates provide data. Department-level and institution-level data are used internally to guide developments/policies and externally for league table claims. Related to MEQ (below). Annual activity that Academic staff must promote. Published
Module Evaluation Questionnaires (MEQ)[a]	To measure student satisfaction at modular (course) level, usually via standard institutional instrument	Academic staff administer for each module taught. In some institutions, academics responsible for analysing responses and creating action plans. Data collection/analysis potentially several times a year, feeds into institutional reporting mechanisms annually. Often published internally
Programme Reports[b]	To assure quality, internally	Annual report analysing admissions and performance data (includes MEQ – above, and possibly NSS data). Individuals feed to programme leader level, to faculty level
External Examiner Reports[b]	To assure quality, internally/externally	Annual report analysing processes and performance. Scrutiny at individual module (course) level, feeds forward to department/faculty. Published
Quality Assurance Agency (QAA) Review[b]	To assure quality, nationally	Institutions inspected. Draws on NSS, MEQ, Programme Reports, External Examiner Reports. Every five years. Published
Appraisal[a]	To monitor staff performance	Individuals make claims about responsibilities/levels of performance. Departments manage roles/responsibilities, institutions use to guide strategic developments. Annual activity for all staff
Probation – initial[c,d]	To set probationary targets	New academics set performance goals for six-, 18-month and three-year intervals. Department and Faculty scrutinise. One-off activity for individuals
Probation – mid-term[c,d]	To review/revise performance targets	New academics review performance at six and 18 months, may revise goals. Department and Faculty scrutinise. One-off activity for individuals
Probation – final review[c,d]	To monitor performance	New academics provide evidence of meeting targets. Department and Faculty scrutinise. Continued employment confirmed or terminated, or probation extended. One-off activity for individuals
Teaching Excellence Framework (TEF)[e]	To promote high-quality teaching	New process for measuring the quality of teaching using existing metrics. Potentially three-yearly exercise using institutional-level data with the intention of department-level scrutiny in future. Full details currently being established

[a]All academic staff will include ECAs.
[b]May include ECAs.
[c]Exclusively for ECAs.
[d]All institutions implement academic probation and target-setting, but the focus varies according to mission statements. Research-intensive HEIs privilege publication/grant capture targets.
[e]New requirement impacts on all staff with teaching duties.

to 'normative prescriptions' (Stensaker, 2015, p. 105) of their career trajectories that are important for policy and practice development. It is also instructive to reflect on the many measurements in higher education that originate in the UK that are subsequently exported to other geographies.

Many of the mechanisms presented in Table 1 use numerical data to form judgements, although reports, reviews and appraisals can draw on more narrative data from senior staff. For ECAs in many research-intensive institutions, however, probationary paperwork requires individuals to set out the number and quality of papers published (measured by REF rating and/or journal impact factor) and institutional policy is likely to exist on a minimum Module Evaluation Questionnaire (MEQ) scores. These performance indicators form part of Strathern's (2000) 'audit culture', are monitored across institutions for all academics but play an especially important role in determining appropriate performance levels (Davies & Petersen, 2005) for ECAs. **Required** reporting targets are outlined in Table 1, but there are also expectations regarding service, knowledge-exchange, outreach and impact that remain implicit.

Current conditions of academic work dictate competing priorities, as Sutherland (2015) points out, privileging compliance with managerialist demands. ECAs must, within four months of taking up post in the study university, complete a binding probationary agreement, a high-stakes process embedded within complex institutional and external policy drivers. As Shin and Jung (2014) report, measurement associated with managerial reforms are a source of stress, amplified by the probationary target-setting process. In the UK, ECAs are conscious **not** of rewards for particular behaviours (Davies & Petersen, 2005), but instead of the punitive conditions attached to not meeting targets set as part of the APP, an oppositional stance to the neoliberalised institutional culture. To explore lived experiences of ECAs subject to this complex target-setting culture, I draw on two key frameworks for the utility of their sensitising concepts (Blumer, 1954), before analysing how this process feels in the UK's ever-shifting measurement culture.

Identity-trajectory

The longitudinal work undertaken by McAlpine et al. (2010) reports the generative concept of 'identity-trajectory' connecting the biographical baggage that ECAs bring with them to the perceived demands of their current contexts. This often includes significant geographical relocation (McAlpine, 2012). Given the temporal scope of probation in the UK context, and the proportion of international staff beginning their careers here, considering the impact of both institutional and individual factors in academic identity development is important. The APP works as an early conditioning mechanism, positioning those subjected to it in relation to Strathern's (2000) audit culture. The process requires all ECAs to submit themselves to very specific targets that embrace the intellectual, the institutional and the networking strands that McAlpine et al. (2010) elaborate.

Intellectually, McAlpine et al. (2010) foreground contribution demonstrated by artefacts, whilst Clegg (2008) and Skelton (2012) also note that biographies and values play key roles. As noted in Table 1, identities are initially required to be performed on paper in the probationary process. Individuals' experiences of novel structuring demands are related to their goal of 'intentional navigation in the complexity of the academic world' (McAlpine et al., 2010, p. 137) but 'affirmation' may reside some distance from everyday lived reality and therefore not come from a professionally significant other. Agency, in the sense of exercising control over one's direction in academic life is both 'real and imagined' (Billot, 2010, p. 709) in relation to perceptions of either the immediate or the more diffuse employing context. Self-surveillance[2] coexists with satisfying the 'greedy institution['s]' (Wright et al., 2004, p. 144) desire for a wider gaze in complex ways where interactions are not well understood. Intention, which in the McAlpine et al. (2010) model supports the past–present–future trajectory of academic identities can thus give rise to disruptions where the measurement culture does not align with what Archer (2000, p. 77) calls the 'continuous sense of self'.

The institutional emphasis is critical: as Stensaker (2015) points out, external pressures are exerted on institutional dynamics to address systemic reforms. Within this complex setting, ECAs need to interpret the demands of their new context in short order for the APP, with a more or less well-developed sense of it (Trowler & Cooper, 2002; Trowler & Knight, 1999). Resources provided at the institutional level (McAlpine et al., 2010) may favour particular activities (Skelton, 2012) or ways of being (Clegg, 2008; Davies & Petersen, 2005). For ECAs, any conflict between personal agendas and institutional priorities (Sutherland, 2015) has the potential to disempower: with limited experience and faced with an opaque process, framing appropriate ambitions can have a destabilising effect on probationers' academic identities.

Trowler and Knight (1999) emphasise the importance of the local in inducting ECAs to their new work contexts and this notion of networking is taken up by McAlpine et al. (2010) and extended to include the inter/national, an important point given how many academic staff are globally mobile. For probationers, particularly those immediately post-PhD, these networks will include previous supervisors – with whom they now need to compete for funding – mentors, and other recent doctoral graduates who face similar challenges but in differing contexts. The variability of academic practices within an institution (Smith, 2010) can render any advice from outside sources commonly available to ECAs, however well-meaning, problematic.

Teaching and learning regimes

ECAs, as Trowler and Knight (1999, p. 178) suggest, join a specific 'cultural configuration' of academic practices, shaped by local discourses, some of which may appear alien or troublesome (Perkins, 2008) but are vitally important to the probationer wanting to 'fit in' to their new department. The immediate network for ECAs is, then, what Trowler and Cooper (2002, p. 221) characterise as a 'Teaching and Learning Regime' with its 'constellation of rules, assumptions, practices and relationships' to be acquired and demonstrated to the satisfaction of an as yet not necessarily well-understood 'other' who controls the probationary process. TLRs (Trowler & Cooper, 2002) feature eight 'components' concerned with highly situated academic practices: identities in interaction; power relations; codes of signification; tacit assumptions; rules of appropriateness; recurrent practices; discursive repertoires; and implicit theories of learning and teaching. As Trowler and Cooper (2002) caution, these components form a dynamic whole and disaggregating them is wise only for analytic purposes. For this reason, only three of these 'moments' (Trowler, 2008, p. 51) are of most interest in this article – power relations, discursive repertoires and codes of signification – as they are particularly illuminative in understanding the process of probationary target-setting for ECAs but the evidence presented below can also be read against other 'moments' with ease.

Power relations exist in every educational setting but, in UK universities, are communicated to ECAs in at least two potentially conflicting ways: the discursive repertoires and recurrent practices within an academic department (Trowler & Cooper, 2002), and through the institutional structures imposed by the probationary process (Smith, 2010). The first channel of communication is subject to perceptions of local power hierarchies, whilst the second is represented by the measurement imperatives outlined in Table 1, which also form a basis for the discursive repertoires available to ECAs. Overt surveillance (Davies & Petersen, 2005) makes clear what is valued and how it needs to be represented. The measurement regime induces a particular form of performativity (Ball, 2003) for individuals, departments and institutions, not necessarily well aligned as Billot (2010) suggests. Complex forms of identities and practices can be seen to be reducible to crude measurements that can be interpreted in various ways. The language implicit in measurement tools can thus challenge discursive repertoires employed at multiple levels (Trowler & Cooper, 2002), including the values base (Skelton, 2012) that individuals bring to academic work.

Taking the ideas of power, language, practices and relationships further, Trowler and Cooper (2002, p. 228) posit 'codes of signification' as a constellation of factors influencing 'dispositions in the attribution of meaning and emotion'. For ECAs establishing independent academic identities, codes of signification manifest themselves in the probationary agreement. Measurable targets must be specified in paperwork common to every department or faculty, unrelated to disciplinary and other local nuances (Becher & Trowler, 2001; Trowler & Cooper, 2002; Trowler & Knight, 1999). The goal-setting objective of probation thus becomes divorced from local academic practices: there is a minor focus on citizenship (Macfarlane, 2007), emphasis on more easily countable research outputs (Wilsdon, 2015), and a standard form of teaching evaluation via the MEQ (see Table 1). From the earliest days of an academic career, indulging in quantifying the self is an institutional requirement and a process that does not engage with affective dimensions of academic work (Clegg, 2008) or take account of an ethos of care (Lynch, 2010). Measurement in academic life in the form of probationary target-setting for ECAs thus legitimises particular behaviours that connect to Shin and Jung's (2014) categorisation of UK HE as a high-stress environment.

Exploring ECAs' experiences

Volunteers for this study were sought from an ECA population with recent experience of the target-setting process in a research-intensive university. Six social scientists (from a population representing many disciplines) came forward. Narrative-style interviews (Riessman, 2008) were undertaken with the gender-balanced sample. The fine-grained and contextually sensitive nature of the data gathered gives rise to serious ethical considerations: individuals' experiences are unique, but institutions indulge in practices that may easily identify them. For this reason, echoing Hemer (2014), I used an inductive approach to thematising interview responses, and present only limited direct quotation below. Extensive extracts risk identification, not only of participants, but non-participant others implicated in probationers' narratives (Mattingly, in Riessman, 2008), though this may lead to a charge of over-interpretation. Analysis sought evidence of the existence of power relations, discursive repertoires (Trowler & Cooper, 2002) and the concomitant affective dimensions (Clegg, 2008) of academic identity-trajectory (McAlpine et al., 2010) drawn from literature work. Beginning academics bring with them biographies and sets of practices learnt elsewhere, and must fit these to their new cultural configurations (Trowler & Knight, 1999) as best they can.

The uniqueness of individual accounts cautions us against extrapolating 'truths' from such accounts, but Polkinghorne (1995, pp. 12–15) makes an important distinction between 'narrative analysis' where stories are the outcome of research, and 'analysis of narratives', where common themes may be discerned. Following the latter approach, data are presented here from an analysis of a small number of richly detailed accounts gathered from an 'experience-centred narrative' (Squire, 2008, p. 41) perspective. The process of target-setting was the focus of interview encounters with individuals with very recent experience of satisfying the APP regime. This approach does not dwell on concrete events, but seeks instead to explore how ECAs are 'imbricated in narrative' (Squire, 2008, p. 43) as they seek to develop their academic identity-trajectories (McAlpine et al., 2010) within unfamiliar TLRs (Trowler & Cooper, 2002), bringing diverse biographies and experiential learning moments to bear on a rigid institutional structure.

The unit of analysis is the co-constructed narrative (Riessman, 2008) as ECAs interact with the interviewer. The focus here is on key messages, the 'what' of probationary experience that the narrator wished to communicate (Riessman, 2008) whose import is marked in particular emphases in interview encounters. What is foregrounded is influenced by pre-existing theoretical constructs available to participants and interviewer in relation to purpose. Though promising to take an hour of their time, most interviews lasted longer than this, as participants were keen to situate their experiences in ways that 'traverse temporal and geographical space' (Riessman, 2008, p. 23): they recognise their contributions as in part stemming from their backgrounds, but also located firmly in the cycle of preparing and having approved their probationary paperwork. The 'badge' of 'approval' came to be significant in the analysis, though I am mindful that the audience for a narrative (Riessman, 2008; Squire, 2008) influences its production. The aim here is to represent, rather than generalise, and in the analysis, I try to reflect this by giving voice to ECAs' experiences, though the interpretations are mine alone.

The sensitising concepts (Blumer, 1954) present in the literature review for this article were not the starting point for analysis but, in interrogating interview data, it became clear that TLRs (Trowler & Cooper, 2002), identity-trajectory (McAlpine et al., 2010) and the very specific measurement culture (Shin & Jung, 2014) engendered by the probationary regime were keenly felt. As can be seen by the quote that opens this article, the idea of measurement as it currently operates does not sit well: 'bad measurement' or dissonance (Smith, 2010) permeates interview talk that is ill at ease, as Macfarlane (2007) suggests, with any notion of contemporary collegiate academic identities. Within and across interview readings, the powerful technologies of TLRs and measurement emerged and this shapes the analysis that follows.

Small, institutionally based samples need to be humble in their claims, although this does not make them untrustworthy. As we try to get at what matters in the probationary experience, what 'counts' came to dominate interview encounters. I hope what follows does not 'essentialise' or 'other' (Cousin, 2006) ECAs as particular performative subjects (Ball, 2003) and instead serves to liberate rather than domesticate which Land (2004, pp. 177–179) expresses as the desire to either critique or comply with a dominant culture that – when applied to ECAs – what matters is to design intellectually productive and achievable individual aspirations. To this end, the next section draws from participants' testimony on the three sensitising elements of Trowler and Cooper's (2002) TLRs elaborated earlier and subsequently McAlpine et al.'s (2010) notion of identity-trajectory, before closing comments on how academic identities are coming to be shaped by the practices of the measured university.

Power relations: policy and the personal

The structure provided by an institution's probationary policy works mostly, in effect, as a stricture in its archaic sense of 'binding tightly'. Trowler and Knight (1999) argue strongly against technical–rationalist models of induction but the distance between formal, collective probationary requirements and the notion of belonging in academic life remains. The narratives explored in this section vivify, with two exceptions, the gap between institutional beliefs in the process of socialisation and the lived experiences of those subjected to it. The local locus of control and informality that Trowler and Knight (1999) advocate is yet to be realised:

> As a PhD student I never had the feeling of making the wrong choices but here I have that daily. If I spend time doing this, am I doing the right thing? Do 'they' – I don't formulate 'they' as a person – think I should be doing something else? (F)

The surveillance technology of the probationary process is disembodied and in some ways dehumanised:

> … you have this rigmarole of ticking boxes which means setting unambitious targets, it's not very inspiring but you don't want to be a 'hostage to fortune', I was warned off of that. (F)

'They' – representing a research-intensive institution with global aspirations – assert that they want ambitious targets in the three traditional areas of academic practice outlined in the probationary paperwork (research, education and citizenship), but the probationary process appears to operate in a climate of fear and uncertainty influenced by a highly individualised (Macfarlane, 2007) and non-caring culture (Lynch, 2010) that may be interpreted in gendered ways:

> It all becomes an exercise in following a performative script … (M)

These contrasting positions illustrate the power of the probationary target-setting process either as antithetical to both intellectual and institutional agendas, or as simply a game to be played. There appears to be no concrete reconciliation between organisational rhetoric (Stensaker, 2015) shaped by the measurement culture of external policy drivers and individuals' personal aspirations suggested by Billot (2010) as a way forward in an increasingly commodified higher education environment (McGettigan, 2013). The implications of this dichotomy are explored further below. Closing the gap between institutional and individual goals (Billot, 2010) is the work of examining the immediate work environment that ECAs join, most often characterised by departments or schools; vision and leadership at this level inculcate particular cultures and practices that use existing expertise productively or otherwise (Macfarlane, 2007).

Discursive repertoires: the language of fitting in

Everyone has been so nice. (F)

The probationary procedure communicates institutional wishes and desires but local practices influence socialisation processes in particular ways (Trowler & Cooper, 2002), some of which align more positively than others. I argue that probationary academics join highly situated TLRs (Trowler & Cooper, 2002) rather than distant and perceived bureaucratic institutions: departmental discourses and interactions are important in shaping individuals' practices and aspirations. Any distance between 'espoused theories' and 'theories in use' (Schon, 1984) has the potential to induce anxieties in the probationary process. How 'nice' colleagues are (locally) and the need to fit in with their practices do not translate easily to the perception of sterile institutional requirements:

> The 3 years is difficult because it's not in your control, no-one can tell you what you're going to be doing, how many students, what courses, admin roles. You have to **trust** people what they tell you and I struggled with that. (F, my emphasis)

> It [the probationary paperwork] got rejected because I didn't set an MEQ [module evaluation questionnaire] target because it's team-taught but I got explicitly asked to include that and that really annoyed me because I don't want to be appraised on a measure that doesn't appraise **my** work, it's annoying and I felt, I did not need this shit ... (M, my emphasis)

The locus of control in these quotes is firmly rooted in individuals' perceptions of their own practice: they want to 'own' the means of judgement, but it is striking how strongly this emphasis on individuation misaligns with current practices. 'Trusting' others, and recognising contributions – 'there is now some differentiation in the questions to separate out the teaching strands ... ' (M) – present clear challenges to the formation of academic identities for ECAs located in departments that espouse their institution's focus on quantifying selves (Davies & Petersen, 2005). Conflicting messages are prevalent in the processes of academic probation that give rise to difficulties for ECAs. Trowler and Cooper (2002) summarise neatly a long-standing preoccupation with the psychologised individual as the unit for analysis in professional development programmes common in the UK which contradicts what they recognise as far more socially situated and relational work contexts (see also Sutherland, 2015). This is a paradox that plays itself out in the academic probationary period and is recognised, if not actually resolved, by the discursive repertoires that ECAs join.

Clegg's (2008, p. 343) notion of 'principled, personal autonomy' is absent from these accounts in exchange for compliance with institutionally decreed alternative visions of the 'teacher's soul' (Ball, 2003). Billot's (2010) argument for a closer alignment of institutional and individual goals is available to only two participants in this study, both male, who appear to have access to powerful resources:

> Oh that [probationary target setting] was very straightforward because I've got a very experienced mentor who knows what's required. (M)

> I was told to scratch the first year because it'll run away with you, you spend it getting to know how things work ... (M)

Mentors, for these male academics, include professors in their respective departments and the power of local discourses is acknowledged. In contrast, the female academic whose quote opens this section has been appointed two female mentors, one of whom has only recently been promoted to Senior Lecturer level. The male academic who contests his department's practices about team-taught judgements refers openly to having a recently promoted female professor as his mentor. This is not to suggest that particular mentors take their roles any less seriously than others, but does perhaps trouble the notion that equitable access to resources (material and discursive) may proceed along gendered lines. Lynch (2010) argues that caring responsibilities are influential, and here whether these manifest through personal circumstances or by institutional stereotype can be traced through the language in use in these responses: either trust in others, or a bridling at co-ownership in relation to target-setting.

Codes of signification: challenges to identity-development

> Well, it's scholarly schizophrenia isn't it? (M)

This comment was not meant to offend: it simply illustrates an increasingly commonplace experience of academic life where probationary lecturers find themselves positioned by an institutional discourse that they are well placed to critique, but find far harder to escape:

> Everyone knows it's a management technology but then they tell you, be careful what you promise because it's a legal relationship and how you say things and it makes you less ambitious, I think. (F)

The target-setting nature of the APP can be disempowering, an example of what Morrish (2015) portrays as 'anticipatory audits' and 'demands for post-hoc justification'. The link to an audit culture (Strathern, 2000) is clear. A constant focus on the required reporting mechanisms sketched in Table 1 as examples of institutional accountability legitimises a particular form of academic identity:

> I got asked whether my form could be used as an example by the Head of Department. This is my first proper job so I don't know what's important but it shouldn't be targets, it should be ambitions … The notion of tying me down to things I need to show in three years' time is obnoxious to me because it precludes other opportunities. (M)

A culture of conformity is now being produced in UK universities that supports Billot's (2010) challenge of more closely aligning individual and institutional objectives. Rather than furthering a notion of 'working in concert' (Billot, 2010, p. 720), however, the experiences from most participants in this study suggest instead that this process of alignment disempowers and constrains ECAs. Whilst academic probation is a long-standing process in UK universities, it is not a static instrument. There is evidence of a creeping incrementalism:

> I submitted 3 weeks ago and got revisions from the HoD as the new guidelines came out so I needed to change my paperwork and re-submit. (F)

The 'code of signification' (Trowler & Cooper, 2002) is clearly interpreted here – by both Head of Department and probationer – as a domesticating agenda (Land, 2004) or a 'management technology' in the participant's words. The historical tripartite academic role that Macfarlane (2007) argued was being eroded is now fragmented (Macfarlane, 2016) under the weight of target-setting. Skelton (2012) uses this notion of fragmentation to illustrate how a changing values base can alienate some academics, whilst McGettigan (2013) and Stensaker (2015) show how institutional identities become more pressing in a competitive market. Reconciling the institutional–individual as Billot (2010) recommends becomes harder with every additional demand placed on academics, and ideas of measuring, monitoring and care raise pressing questions for ECAs explored in the following section.

Identity-trajectory

The autonomy of probationary academics is recognised in their pursuit of goal-setting behaviours provided that these are congruent with the wider surveillance economy (Davies & Petersen, 2005). An accommodative local ethos may be superseded by bureaucratic superstructures which can undermine the three elements of identity-trajectory development: intellectual; institutional and networking posited by McAlpine et al. (2010). Personal aspirations – and the intention to do meaningful work – were strongly expressed by participants in this study. Similar to their Canadian counterparts reported in McAlpine et al. (2010), the interdependence of their personal research agendas, networks and new institutional homes was recognised, and the potential to build on previous relationships was noted. However, the overt target-setting culture militates against exploring what should be a productive temporal dimension of academic identity formation:

> It makes you very individualistic ... I didn't put in any joint publications [as targets] with previous colleagues because that doesn't depend on me. (F)

> I'm incredulous that someone would expect me to set targets that far in advance without being able to interact with them ... I'm not sure whether it's a system of surveillance or a system for career development, that's not entirely clear. (M)

> I know I need to develop my networks, but how do you do that? (F)

These are painful narratives. The strictures of probationary target-setting required by institutions constrain the ambitions of the ECAs they purport to support. The local, as argued for by Trowler and Knight (1999), is usurped by a perceived wider gaze: 'I assume, metaphorically, that it's the DVC [Deputy Vice-Chancellor] but there's someone behind that ... ' said one female respondent, assigning power some distance from the 'cultural configuration' (Trowler & Knight, 1999) of the department. All but one of the participants were within months of gaining their doctorates, often seen as a time of significant intellectual growth, independence and contribution, but perceptions of satisfying the measurement culture embedded in the probationary agenda negated such explorations.

Personal responsibility does not appear to be a problem – participants commonly voiced an aspiration to 'be the best I can' – but ambition and risk, touchstones of significant research, are rejected in favour of the 'unambitious' (F) and the safe: 'if you've got something in the bag, put it in ... ' (M). Inducing defensive responses or game-playing strategies are presumably not the intention behind institutional policies, though this appears to be the effect on some ECAs. The nature of the probationary target-setting process emphasises individuation (Macfarlane, 2007) and induces a reluctance to develop new networks or further enhance existing ones as probationary targets. The self-censorship of relationship-building of the intellectual kind appears to preclude serendipitous opportunities in deference to required managerialist box-ticking, potentially constraining fulfilment in identity-trajectory (McAlpine et al., 2010) work.

Probationary tensions: domestication or liberation?

The academic probationary process serves many purposes in the measurement culture of UK universities: in the study site, the APP privileges research (outputs and income) but also functions to regulate teaching performance through MEQ scores and mandating professional development (Trowler & Cooper, 2002). Targets are also required in relation to citizenship (Macfarlane, 2007), but the university-wide surveillance instrument is silent on issues of care (Lynch, 2010), networking (McAlpine et al., 2010) and personal investment (Clegg, 2008). More personally focused intellectual and networking strands of McAlpine et al.'s (2010) model are subsumed by the institutional mores highlighted by Shin and Jung's (2014) assertion of the high-stress UK HE environment, or Sutherland's (2015) concern with the tension between objective and subjective measures of career success. Agentic energy is devoted to avoiding failure in meeting 'unambitious' APP targets.

Rather than a tool of liberation, where ambitions can be expressed, the probationary process operates as a compliance-inducing domesticating technology (Land, 2004). ECAs censor themselves in relation to targets, not wishing to be judged against goals outside their personal control, giving rise to the paradox of a measurement culture that begets not itself, but its antithesis. For many respondents, ambition – emancipatory critique in Land's (2004, p. 179) conceptualisation – is curtailed and a domestication that 'emphasizes adherence to expressed policy' (Land, 2004, p. 179) – or in this case, very specific targets – prevails. ECAs submit to a 'normative ... naturalizing and legitimizing' (Land, 2004, p. 189) effect. Each iteration of the institution's probationary guidelines predictably calls for ever-greater measures of performance: higher MEQ scores, larger grants, the promise of increased research productivity. Under such circumstances, academic identity-trajectories prove problematic as intellectual, individual and networking aspirations (McAlpine et al., 2010) are subordinated to meeting performative demands. The punitive framing of performance management (Shin & Jung, 2014) sends messages about the value of particular activities (Hemer, 2014) for ECAs seeking to understand new work environments.

A very real sense of visibility and monitoring is palpable and positions ECAs in ever-more intricate webs of performativity. Simultaneously, in this sample, ECAs express their concerns over limiting their horizons but not their ultimate ambitions, in pursuit of compliance with the domesticating regime of the APP. It is hard to see how the current framework for measurement in UK universities supports ECAs in their goals if they fear the domesticating repercussions that result from not satisfying a distant – and disembodied – 'other'. Ball's (2003, p. 236) 'cynical compliance' comes to the fore in the testimony here: as institutions privilege an increasingly narrow sense of target-setting, they undermine their own marketisation ambitions.

The performative culture acknowledged by many authors is writ large in the determination to maximise league table visibility by universities. In practice, however, the 'conformative subject' emerges who frustrates institutional ambition by privileging agentic desires, illustrating the limitations of particular forms of measurement. 'Bad measurement

... ' cannot induce behaviours valued by corporatised universities in response to the continuing sense of economic imperative (BIS, 2016) rewarded by successive neoliberal government agendas. Re-introducing an element of trust in the work contract between universities and their academics has the potential to reinvigorate motivation towards a productive identity-trajectory for ECAs. Further domestication through widely applied targets has the potential, it appears, to satisfy a measurement culture at the expense of a much-needed growth one.

Notes

1. In the UK, this process is known as academic probation and typically lasts from one to three years. It differs from the US sense of probation that applies to students who are underperforming.
2. I am grateful to a (deliberately unnamed) participant for seeing this in an earlier discussion of the findings long before I did.

Disclosure statement

No potential conflict of interest was reported by the author.

References

Archer, M. (2000). *Being human: The problem of agency*. Cambridge: Cambridge University Press.
Australian Research Council. (2015). *Excellence in research for Australia*. Retrieved July 29, 2016, from http://www.arc.gov.au/era-2015
Ball, S. (2003). The teacher's soul and the terrors of performativity. *Journal of Educational Policy*, 18(2), 215–228.
Becher, T., & Trowler, P. (2001). *Academic tribes and territories: Intellectual enquiry and the culture of disciplines*. Milton Keynes: SRHE/Open University Press.
Billot, J. (2010). The imagined and the real: Identifying the tensions for academic identity. *Higher Education Research & Development*, 29(6), 709–721.
Blumer, H. (1954). What is wrong with social theory? *American Sociological Review*, 19, 3–10.
Business Innovation & Skills. (2016, May). *Success as a knowledge economy: Teaching excellence, social mobility and student choice*. Retrieved July 29, 2016, from https://www.gov.uk/government/uploads/system/uploads/attachment_data/file/523546/bis-16-265-success-as-a-knowledge-economy-web.pdf
Clegg, S. (2008). Academic identities under threat? *British Educational Research Journal*, 34(3), 329–345.
Cousin, G. (2006). Threshold concepts, troublesome knowledge and emotional capital: An exploration into learning about others. In J. H. F. Meyer & R. Land (Eds.), *Overcoming barriers to student understanding: Threshold concepts and troublesome knowledge* (pp. 134–147). London: RoutledgeFalmer.
Davies, B., & Petersen, E. B. (2005). Neo-liberal discourse in the academy: The forestalling of (collective) resistance. *LATISS: Learning and Teaching in the Social Sciences*, 2(2), 77–98.
Gill, R. (2009). Breaking the silence: The hidden injuries of neo-liberal academia. In R. Flood & R. Gill (Eds.), *Secrecy and silence in the research process: Feminist reflections* (pp. 228–244). London: Routledge.
Grant, B., & Elizabeth, V. (2015). Unpredictable feelings: Academic women under research audit. *British Educational Research Journal*, 41(2), 287–302.
Hemer, S. (2014). Finding time for quality teaching: An ethnographic study of academic workloads in the social sciences and their impact on teaching practices. *Higher Education Research & Development*, 33(3), 483–495.

Higher Education Statistics Agency. (2016). *HESA staff record 2014/15*. Retrieved March 15, 2016, from https://www.hesa.ac.uk/pr/3843-press-release-228

Land, R. (2004). *Educational development: Discourse, identity and practice*. Buckingham: SRHE/Open University Press.

Lynch, K. (2010). Carelessness: A hidden doxa of higher education. *Arts and Humanities in Higher Education*, 9(1), 54–67.

Macfarlane, B. (2007). *The academic citizen: The virtue of service in university life*. Abingdon: Routledge.

Macfarlane, B. (2016). From identity to identities: A story of fragmentation. *Higher Education Research & Development Virtual Special Issue*. Retrieved July 29, 2016, from http://explore.tandfonline.com/content/ed/academic-identities-vsi

McAlpine, L. (2012). Academic work and careers: Relocation, relocation, relocation. *Higher Education Quarterly*, 66(2), 174–188.

McAlpine, L., Amundsen, C., & Jazvac-Martek, M. (2010). Living and imagining academic identities. In L. McAlpine & G. Akerlind (Eds.), *Becoming an academic* (pp. 125–154). Basingstoke: Palgrave Macmillan.

McGettigan, A. (2013). *The great university gamble: Money, markets and the future of higher education*. London: Pluto Books.

Morrish, L. (2015). *Raising the bar: The metric tide that sinks all boats*. Retrieved March 15, 2016, from https://academicirregularities.wordpress.com/2015/11/26/raising-the-bar-the-metric-tide-that-sinks-all-boats/

Perkins, D. (2008). Beyond understanding. In J. H. F. Meyer, R. Land, & J. Smith (Eds.), *Threshold concepts within the disciplines* (pp. 3–19). Rotterdam: Sense.

Polkinghorne, D. E. (1995). Narrative configuration in qualitative analysis. *International Journal of Qualitative Studies in Education*, 8(1), 5–23.

Riessman, C. K. (2008). *Narrative methods for the human sciences*. Thousand Oaks, CA: Sage.

Schon, D. (1984). *The reflective practitioner: How professionals think in action*. Basic Books.

Shin, J. C., & Jung, J. (2014). Academics' job satisfaction and job stress across countries in the changing academic environments. *Higher Education*, 67, 603–620.

Skelton, A. (2012). Value conflicts in higher education teaching. *Teaching in Higher Education*, 17(3), 257–268.

Smith, J. (2010). Forging identities: The experiences of probationary academics in the UK. *Studies in Higher Education*, 35(5), 577–591.

Squire, C. (2008). Experience-centred and culturally-oriented approaches to narrative. In M. Andrews, C. Squire, & M. Tamboukou (Eds.), *Doing narrative research* (pp. 41–63). London: Sage.

Stensaker, B. (2015). Organizational identity as a concept for understanding university dynamics. *Higher Education*, 69, 103–115.

Strathern, M. (2000). *Audit cultures: Anthropological studies in accountability, ethics and the academy*. Abingdon: Routledge.

Sutherland, K. (2015). Constructions of success in academia: An early career perspective. *Studies in Higher Education*. doi:10.1080/03075079.2015.1072150

Times Higher Education. (2016). *World university rankings 2015–16*. Retrieved July 29, 2016, from https://www.timeshighereducation.com/world-university-rankings/2016/world-ranking#!/page/0/length/25/sort_by/rank_label/sort_order/asc/cols/rank_only

Trowler, P. (2008). *Cultures and change in higher education*. Basingstoke: Palgrave Macmillan.

Trowler, P., & Cooper, A. (2002). Teaching and learning regimes: Implicit theories and recurrent practices in the enhancement of teaching and learning through educational development programmes. *Higher Education Research & Development*, 21(3), 221–240.

Trowler, P., & Knight, P. (1999). Organizational socialization and induction in universities: Reconceptualizing theory and practice. *Higher Education*, 37, 177–195.

Wilsdon, J. (2015). *The metric tide: Report of the independent review of the role of metrics in research assessment and management*. Retrieved July 29, 2016, from http://www.hefce.ac.uk/pubs/rereports/Year/2015/metrictide/Title,104463,en.html

Wright, M. C., Assar, N., Kain, E. L., Kramer, L., Howery, C. B., McKinney, K., ... Atkinson, M. (2004). Greedy institutions: The importance of institutional context for teaching in higher education. *Teaching Sociology, 32*(2), 144–159.

The missing measure? Academic identity and the induction process

Jennie Billot and Virginia King

ABSTRACT
The effectiveness of academic induction is under-monitored by higher education institutions (HEIs) despite growing evidence that some academics, facing increased expectations and rising accountability within higher education (HE), perceive a lack of support from their institution. In this paper, we argue that HEIs should follow the example of other sectors to promote socialisation through adequate and supportive scaffolding of the multiple responsibilities that new academics are required to take on. We offer a dual lens into the induction of early career academics in the contemporary university. Using corpus analysis techniques, we survey recent research into induction from the fields of HE studies and of human resources (HR). The HR literature displays a greater emphasis on organisational socialisation but also on performance measures. Secondly, drawing on an empirical study of researcher experiences within a measured and funding-directed environment, we surface the challenges faced by new academics and the tensions of juggling multiple roles and identities. We find that induction programmes that encourage and educate individuals to take responsibility for their socialisation can enhance positive outcomes. Paradoxically, traditional, one-size-fits-all, induction that focuses on the 'doing' of academic practice leaves individuals unequally prepared for academic life. The empirical study findings echo claims in the literature that communities of practice can act to positively support newer academics. The induction challenge then is to provide personalised, professional scaffolding for scholarly development and to monitor its effectiveness, while seeking opportunities to build a more supportive academic culture.

Introduction

The induction process for new academic staff aims to ensure a smooth transition into the specific context and requirements of an institution and takes different forms. It could be a requirement to attend a brief orientation session on joining a higher education institution (HEI), attendance at a series of self-selected workshops, completion of mandatory online tutorials or a pedagogical training programme, or combinations of these. Additionally, it may include 'buddying', mentorship, office-sharing, team-teaching or research collaborations. Essentially, induction comprises 'professional practices designed to facilitate the entry of new recruits to an organisation and to equip them to operate effectively within it' (Trowler & Knight, 1999, p. 178). While it is known that, for some staff, the HEI induction process can prove ineffective (Mathieson, 2011; Nadolny & Ryan, 2015; Smith, 2010; Walker, 2015), the success of academic induction is under-researched and under-monitored by HEIs. This situation is ironic given the levels of measurement currently existing within HEIs and has implications for staff engagement and development.

How do academics experience induction? In their study of health practitioners, Ennals, Fortune, Williams, and D'Cruz (2015) identified that induction frequently focuses on the 'doing' of academic work, rather than the 'being, becoming and belonging' (p. 5). Induction that focuses on the doing of academic work, particularly within the limits, measures and required productivity by which an academic is currently defined (Billot, 2011), misses the integral nature of identity formation (becoming). Negotiating this academic terrain involves more than simply understanding roles and responsibilities (Fortune et al., 2016) for it is where a professional identity is forged.

Fitzmaurice (2013) and Sheridan (2013), amongst others, identify academic identity as ongoing construction, deconstruction and reconstruction of personal and professional identities. Furthermore, academic identity, while fluid and multifaceted, draws on both disciplinary affiliation and the institutional context (Smith & Rattray, 2016). To become effective practising academics (Browning, Thompson, & Dawson, 2014), there needs to be strong alignment between an institution's drive for their academic staff to be productive in the current competitive marketplace and the support given to new staff, as they transition (Billot, 2011). Internationally, global rankings influence staff recruitment policies (e.g., by targeting early career academics from highly ranked institutions) and staff progression (e.g., using bibliometrics to rank staff research effectiveness) (Hazelkorn, 2015), but rankings only indirectly affect factors that are not measured, such as day-to-day support for academic staff. Significantly, a growing body of research into academic staff turnover highlights a perceived lack of support from the institution as a reason for leaving it (Gourlay, 2011; O'Meara, Lounder, & Campbell, 2014; Smith, 2010; Watanabe & Falci, 2016).

In this paper, we offer a dual lens into the induction of early career academics in the contemporary university. Using corpus analysis techniques, we survey recent research into induction, comparing that of higher education (HE) and human resources (HR) to expose their different emphases. Secondly, drawing on an empirical study of researcher experiences within a measured and funding-directed environment, we surface the challenges faced by new academics and the tensions of juggling multiple roles and identities. By providing both the corpus analysis and findings from the empirical study, we offer a way to view their alignment, identifying potentially different ways in which new academics can experience academic induction which help to explain why academics may find their induction unsatisfying or unsupportive.

Contextualising the corpus approach

A review of the themes within recent research into academic induction was undertaken to help locate our small-scale case study within the measured university landscape. Drawing on previous studies (Clouder & King, 2015; King, 2013), this review of the literature employed 'corpus analysis' techniques. Corpus analysis uses computing power to examine a body of words, combining quantitative techniques (such as comparing word frequency) and qualitative techniques (such as word-usage contexts) (McEnery & Hardie, 2012). As a research approach, corpus analysis is beginning to gain ground amongst educational researchers: recent examples in *Higher Education Research & Development* include two which compare and contrast university strategic usage (Efe & Ozer, 2015; Mampaey, Huisman, & Seeber, 2015), Pilcher and Richards (2016) which looks at lecturers' language and Hanna (2016) which explores student writings.

The corpus approach is thought to provide an impartial means of analysing large volumes of text because it uses software to locate frequent patterns of word usage (Kennedy, 1998).[1] However, there is a danger that 'a [single] corpus approach may yield numerous "so what" findings, where the frequency patterns simply confirm the expectations of people who are reasonably au fait with the society that the texts come from' (Baker & Levon, 2015, pp. 231–232). One way of overcoming this problem is to compare one corpus with another since this permits similarities, differences and unique characteristics to be revealed (Kilgarriff, 2001).[2] Additionally, a concordance tool can be used to examine the usage contexts of a particular word and of words which often occur close together, but not necessarily side-by-side (Kennedy, 1998). By using a variety of corpus techniques to increase the accuracy of findings,[3] corpus analysis results can complement, or enhance, the findings of purely qualitative research (Baker & Levon, 2015). However, success relies on the initial capture of an appropriate body of text which will act as the corpus (Baker & Levon, 2015; McEnery & Hardie, 2012).

Literature review using corpus analysis

Creating the induction research corpora

For this research, a corpus was created from data held in the Scopus™ database (www.scopus.com) of academic publications.[4] A Scopus search was devised which selected abstracts of documents published since 2011 in the broad field of HE, allowing for alternative names for induction (e.g., orientation, transition) and synonyms for early career academics (e.g., new faculty, teacher-educator), and which largely excluded irrelevant documents.[5] A comparison corpus was created using a similar Scopus search to extract abstracts concerning induction in the HR research field.[6] Neither the HE nor the HR corpus was a perfect or complete representation of induction research; rather, each provided an easily captured and useful snapshot of current research in their field, and hence were comparable. Up to this point, any valid literature search approach would have been equally effective in providing a body of data for further analysis.

Analysing the corpora

The extracted abstracts, together with their titles, authors and keywords, were loaded into the Voyant Tools™ corpus analysis environment (www.voyant-tools.org)[7] so that the themes underpinning each corpus could be revealed using Voyant's keyword-listing tool. Individually, these lists of unusually frequent vocabulary may be unsurprising, but comparatively, they are significant since they highlight the different foci of the two sets of research into induction. The HE corpus included the keywords 'development', 'learning' and 'training' which were neither part of the original search terms nor functional terms within the article abstracts which made up the corpus. By contrast, the HR corpus themes were signalled by the keywords 'performance', 'measurement' and 'relationship'.

The frequency and close occurrence of the terms 'development', 'learning', 'training' and 'program' in the HE corpus suggested that 'doing' activities represented an important theme in the underlying HE induction literature: this was confirmed by detailed examination through the concordance. As shown in Figure 1, these words all occurred less frequently in the HR corpus despite its greater size and smaller vocabulary. In particular, 'training' was used less than half as often as in the HE corpus. Neither corpus appeared to emphasise the 'being' aspect of employment since the term 'identity/identities' appeared equally infrequently in both. Although support for 'becoming' and 'belonging' through reference to 'community/ies' was found twice as often in the HE corpus as in the HR corpus, the HE concordance revealed that these tended to represent individual or pilot initiatives, or their recommendation by theorists in response to an identified need. Furthermore, the HE corpus evidenced a desire by those undergoing academic induction for supportive communities of practice or learning which was not mirrored in the HR corpus.

The major themes of relationships and of performance in the HR induction data were relevant but little evidenced in the HE data. The frequency of the word 'performance' was due, in part, to a concern in HR research with measuring individual and corporate activity in the light of particular variables. The term 'measure/s/ment' occurred six times as often as in the HE corpus. Although 'relationship' occurred in the HR corpus as a functional term within article abstracts (e.g., the relationship between stages in a project), it more often signalled a *social* perspective in the underlying research which reported relationships between employees, managers or customers; and between people and departments or organisations. Of particular note was the term 'organisational socialisation' and the

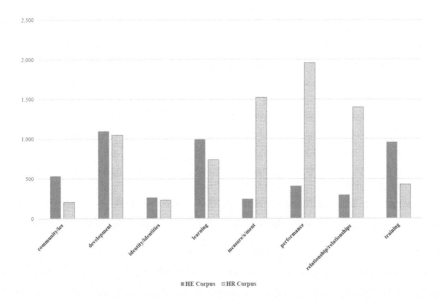

Figure 1. A comparison of usage frequency of significant words in the HE and HR corpora.

newer 'onboarding' which were used in the HR corpus to describe the way new recruits are integrated. Concordance entries confirmed an organisation-level concern with new employee socialisation in the HR corpus which could not be found in the HE corpus, and which may account for the lack of demand for support communities in the HR corpus.

Reference to the use of mentors; mutual support and practice, research, learning and teaching in relation to academic identity were all at low levels of frequency in the HE corpus. One interpretation of this shortage of clear induction themes would be that education research presents a patchy use of a disparate set of induction activities across a variety of HE contexts. Another interpretation could be that, other than training courses and, occasionally, mentoring, effective induction practice initiated by institutions for academic staff did not make a significant showing in the literature we examined.

Our intention in taking this corpus analysis approach was to examine relevant induction literature from a global and impartial perspective. The analysis contributes some new insights on the process of induction in HE compared to other sectors. In order to explore how academics actually experience their early introduction to, and employment in, the academy, we now refer to a research study positioned in a New Zealand university.

Case study and findings

A recently completed empirical study (Billot, Pacheco, & Codling, 2016) examined the experience of researchers in relation to their research activity and the support provided by their university. The study was undertaken in a teaching and research university in the North Island of New Zealand and aimed to access the voices of academics who research within a measured and funding-directed environment. Data collected from conversations with new and emerging academic researchers are relevant here in terms of how well-aligned induction is structured for these particular academic needs. The research employed a case study integrated approach (McAlpine & Norton, 2006) that acknowledges the relevance of context, with collection of both qualitative and quantitative data. The analysis took into account the academic's assessment of their own needs, as well as the conditions and interactions that support those needs. An electronic survey and focus group discussions comprised the data collection methods. An initial call went out for survey participants, followed by a second one for the focus groups.

The online survey contained closed and open-ended questions, with most questions referring to the time spent on research; expectations for research productivity; perspectives on the research support infrastructure and support from managers and recommendations for increased support for research. Survey respondents comprised 178 researchers from a total population of 981 permanent academic staff, 652 of which were research-active and eligible to participate. While the study invited all researching academics to participate, new and emerging researchers were self-identified in the study as a particular cohort during their participation in focus group discussions. Their perspectives provide pertinent input to this paper. These focus group participants each held a role that comprised teaching, research and service responsibilities (which could include institutional committee membership or contributions to professional leadership or peer-mentoring initiatives). In alignment with Mathieson (2011), whose empirical study findings emphasised the importance of academic voice, the discussions encouraged the participants to consider their socially situated positioning and participation in professional practices.

Findings from the survey phase inform the broader context. Survey questions focused on participant demographic information to ascertain faculty location, degree of experience and qualification across the sample. Nearly 60% held a doctorate; 55% had been at the university for more than five years; 21% were in the professoriate, 57% were lecturers or senior lecturers and the rest were researchers holding other managerial or academic positions. For the respondents, on average, 35% of the average weekly academic workload is spent on research, with 33% of researchers identifying that they experienced unclear research expectations. Lack of time was identified as the most significant challenge, with 11% meeting research expectations by using their personal time. While almost half of the respondents experienced adequate support for their research activity, the remainder felt that research support was insufficient or less than adequate. Constructive suggestions were made in terms of how additional support mechanisms and strategies could be implemented. Overall, these survey findings help to sketch a picture of the research environment that new and emerging researchers will enter. Induction then becomes a crucial introduction for newer academics, particularly for meeting the research expectations within their academic role.

The focus group participants of newer academics/emerging researchers demonstrated a strong capacity to reflect on their current circumstances within the study discussions. While many of the challenges were shared with more experienced researchers, such as experiencing pressure to undertake several roles in a time-pressured environment as well as manage large workloads, several were clearly linked to being a newer academic. The participants identified three distinct areas that influence their ability to progress as newer researchers, which could be initially addressed through a comprehensive induction programme. A sense of isolation, lack of confidence and need for support that specifically targets their needs were identified as crucial for assisting newer academics. While viewing themselves as competent researchers, they claimed that they were 'new and emerging', indicating less certainty on how to progress to become experts in their area. They identified confidence in their capabilities on entering the institution and learning to be productive researchers, but a sense of being overwhelmed clouded a clear forward direction. Feeling isolated was common amongst the participants, with a typical reticence to ask more experienced academics for assistance. At the same time there was concern that senior researchers were too busy to support their less-experienced colleagues and did not proactively involve the latter in their research activities. One member put this quite forcefully:

> It's the blind leading the blind in a lot of cases and it's not that we don't have phenomenal people, but most of the people who are really research-active, really important people, are far above and far too busy doing their research, to actually work with the people at the bottom ... (A)

These newer academics struggled with multiple responsibilities citing insufficient time to manage both teaching and research expectations. They recommended scheduled non-teaching time that would allow for research conversations and collaborations. Strong support for networks and research communities (real and virtual) was called for, although there was a sense that these were not easy to find. One focus group member said that:

> It's a bit like researching in a vacuum, and so you would expect ... that there's a whole university that's trying to develop research and growth in research and the skills, that there

would be communities that you could join to develop your skills, no matter where you were in the process, but I don't find that. (J)

As emerging researchers, the participants experienced differential support within the university. In some cases, support was easily accessible while in other schools it was harder to find. Further, as reflected in Wilson's (2012) work there are often differentials in information sharing which can inhibit the enhancements of a research community. According to one participant:

> The tension of course is that whilst you've got all these different cultures if you like, research cultures, for want of a better term, whilst that's really good for those schools that do something, there are some schools that don't. So what you have then is inequity across the university and that's why sometimes you look at the whole. There can be differences within that whole as long as there is a total environment where everybody gets support. In this university there's a lot of fragmentation about the support levels. I think … there are some that don't [get support], and that is the problem. (Y)

There were suggestions of how to address such frustrations and concerns, including support and mentoring from more experienced colleagues who could share their expertise and skills. Such positive relationships would not only enhance the University's research culture but also increase the sense of a collective research community. One potential way in which this process could be supported is through adept middle managers/leaders who could provide a positive link between the University's strategic direction for research and a broader, more responsive approach to researchers' challenges and needs. Such a move involves a cultural shift whereby the needs of emerging researchers become prioritised to ensure a sustainable researcher community.

These academic perspectives, focused on being a newer researcher, confirm the currency of earlier studies' findings regarding poor academic induction support, including Mathieson (2011), Smith (2010) and Trowler and Knight (1999). Locke, Whitchurch, Smith, and Mazenod (2016) recently identified that newer academics are faced with multiple dilemmas on how to consolidate their position; the participants in this study voiced this concern as one of their primary challenges. They were apprehensive about the lower flexibility of some career paths which could affect longevity of career development and stability. New academics may encounter constraints in employment pathways, reducing surety of employment. The study participants noted the increase in fixed term and casual contracts which inevitably affect engagement in meeting the challenges of the academic domain (Wilson, 2012).

The issues raised by the participants have an impact on the development of an academic and professional identity. Much time is spent on the 'doing' rather than the 'being' or self-representation (Trede, Macklin, & Bridges, 2012). Jawitz (2009) contends that professional identity development is consistently connected to daily practice and values that inform ways of being, so being and doing need to be a personally coherent synthesis of practitioner, researcher and teacher. If we accept Jawitz's premise, then addressing the uncertainty and ambiguity for newer academics (teachers and researchers, or a combined role) is crucial yet an ongoing challenge. As academics, the participants were not entrants to the university but new and emerging researchers. In some ways it might be considered that they had already moved through the very early stage of becoming accustomed to the academic workplace. In fact what was interpreted from the participants' discussion was that, although more familiar with the university environment and systems, they still felt a sense of isolation and a need for support.

In this paper, we focus on early induction as, ideally, a supportive experience. The findings of this empirical study identify that becoming confident as an academic is an ongoing process and induction into all aspects of being an academic is just the first step.

Discussion

The findings of this empirical study add depth to our corpus analysis which identified that educational research places less emphasis than does HR research on relational and community developments, when providing induction for new staff. Furthermore, our corpus analysis suggests that the shortcomings of academic induction internationally make our case study participants' experiences not uncommon. In HE, greater stress is given to role expectations during induction processes rather than scaffolding for an individual's academic and career socialisation. We claim that when induction incorporates supportive and collegial networks which are aligned with mechanisms for individual proactivity, this can have continuing positive outcomes for both the individual and the institution. Further, it becomes apparent that managers of new staff comprise a crucial element for supporting development in this phase of employment. However, to date, induction programmes have been based on the transmission of information around practices with less evaluation undertaken on the effectiveness of this approach (Trowler & Knight, 1999). In this scenario, the 'recruit learns to fit in or be an outsider' (p. 180) and the overt is given priority over the tacit, 'the corporate over the local, the formal over the naturally occurring, structure over action' (p. 191). Trowler and Knight call for induction and socialisation to work together and their implementation to be in the hands of local leaders. This appears to be the dominant approach reported in the HR literature we surveyed through corpus analysis. The HE corpus indicated that academic induction has yet to progress from training to 'organisational socialisation', and the case study illustrated the effects on individuals who experience induction as inadequate in terms of support. The sense of isolation, lack of confidence and unsatisfied training needs reported by participants signal an ineffective induction process which is undermining their academic identity.

Wenger (1998) believed that identity, as a concept, acts as a pivot between the individual and their social context. Thus a good starting point for developing a sense of belonging and acceptance within a university is through the interactions and relationships with people in the workplace (Remmik, Karm, Haamer, & Lepp, 2011), as suggested by the HR corpus. Remmik et al. (2011) claim that these more informal relationships can help newer academics learn and adjust quickly and can introduce new knowledge into the institutional community. Further, Hemmings (2012) emphasises how 'confidence begets confidence' (p. 182) especially for early career researchers, and that mentoring, networking with colleagues and personal skill development (such as time management and career planning) have significant parts to play. These approaches are common outside the HE sector (Korte, Brunhaver, & Sheppard, 2015).

Since novice academics are unsure of their place in the organisation, Remmik et al. (2011) claim that 'discovering what it means to be an academic, and what the culture of their particular unit is, and how to relate to it, [were] the key issues affecting their professional identity development' (p. 195). We would argue that this is an aspect of academic induction that could be more actively supported by HEIs.

In their extensive study of early career academics in New Zealand universities, Sutherland, Wilson, and Williams (2013) identified that new academics were more satisfied when they had some control over their working conditions. As we also claim, Sutherland et al. recommend proactivity for new academics, encouraging them to plan and seek support for their own professional development, agency that helps to build confidence in teaching and research. This approach is complemented by their academic leaders identifying their particular needs and where support is most appropriately accessed. Such support could contribute to the academic staff retention strategies that Hazelkorn (2015) notes are beginning to be adopted to improve institutions' positions in ranking tables. This would suggest that a whole-organisation approach to measuring the success of induction is desirable, mirroring the induction practices in other sectors which the HR corpus revealed. Hence, linking induction to retention could underpin institutional strategies to 'measure the right things' (Altbach, 2006, p. 3).

While the HR corpus emphasised performance measurement, this was not strongly evidenced in the HE corpus, suggesting that performativity is not associated with HE induction literature. However, our case study findings resonate with the academic realities identified for those in teaching and learning by Locke et al. (2016), who report that in HE in the UK, measures for greater accountability and demands for improved efficiency have become 'even more acute' (p. 4). While these pressures impact directly on current academic staff, there is a wider implication for institutional sustainability, namely the need to attract, prepare and support newer academics with clear career pathways. Currently there is a concern that after gaining one's first academic position, emerging academics are faced with multiple dilemmas on how to consolidate their position. The challenge of managing a complex academic role has been noted within the Vitae Researcher Development Framework in which a teaching lens has been incorporated (Vitae, 2016). While the framework acknowledges that qualified academic staff need to engage in continuing professional development to support teaching and researching practice, there is an underlying acceptance that learning and becoming a scholar is an ongoing journey which begins as a new academic.

Mathieson (2011) queries the focus on a centralised induction process and recommends that academics need to examine their particularised working context and develop their own agentic pathway through becoming an academic. This would mean a rethink on how induction is structured and implemented, and should involve the socialisation process that is so closely linked to individual practice. Grappling with the challenges of managing these responsibilities is a unique experience, so that through a greater understanding of the nuances of these challenges, induction programmes can be tailored appropriately. While Trowler and Knight (1999) undertook their study in 1997–1998, their findings provide insights since the context for HE was undergoing change during their research. Despite 15 years having passed, their recommendations find resonance today with claims that developing one's professional identity is connected to daily practice and values that inform ways of being (Gale, 2011; Jawitz, 2009; Trede et al., 2012). Further, as Bolden, Gosling, and O'Brien (2014) in their study of academic responses to leadership in HE noted, academics need 'a sense of shared identity and belonging to an identified community' (p. 764).

Our corpus analysis revealed an academic induction process focused on training rather than socialisation, and our case study echoed this. While we support a centrally provided induction programme which can ensure a consistent approach to institutional practices, we also champion individuals taking responsibility for their own development within an organisation that promotes socialisation. Our research into the development of an identity within the academy suggests that academics need to work both individually and collectively to enhance their position in the academic community (Billot & King, 2015). The participants in the empirical study voiced a need for increased academic support from their own institutional community and this resonated with similar findings within the HE literature. Thus, while individual agency is an essential component of being a newer academic, there can be great benefit in belonging to, and participating in, healthy communities of practice that support and scaffold academic development. Yet there is a tension here, for individuality can potentially collide with broader community objectives. The participants in the New Zealand study pointed to a need to enhance an institutional research culture which supports collaborative engagement. These elements all have implications for how new academics find their academic place. Further research is needed into how HE institutions can foster a cohesive culture while also supporting academic individuality, and could perhaps identify directions for leaders of future strategic change.

Conclusion

In the contemporary HE sector, the increasing level of managerialism has impacted upon academic practices and academic identity formation (Smith & Rattray, 2016). As external reforms drive institutions to respond by increasing levels of accountability and economic efficiency throughout the workforce, so academics experience prescription in their academic lives (Huang, Pang, & Yu, 2016) particularly within their academic practices. We argue that a well-designed induction can provide the transformative vehicle for developing as a newer academic. Without such introductory support, there is the risk that new academics become overly challenged to find their place in the academic community, impacting on identity formation and potential disengagement.

Our case study suggests that, through harnessing their individual agency, new academics can develop necessary skills for negotiating this complex academic terrain. Being proactive is one potential way of managing the system and forging a preferred identity, or one that aligns with the environment with which they identify. When adequately informed and prepared, academics have the ability to 'negotiate their values, locations and roles through the process of prioritising' (Huang et al., 2016).

Entering the complex academic landscape has been described as a journey of surviving and thriving as an academic (Mathieson, 2011), often with teaching, research and service comprising an academic's responsibilities (Walker, 2015). Compliance to newer institutional norms requires a full understanding of expectations so induction has an important place in employment initiation. However, the induction design needs to be carefully crafted to encourage and educate individuals to take responsibility for their socialisation while integrating support structures that include networking and peer-mentoring to enhance positive outcomes. These contribute to confidence-building which Hemmings (2012) believes is the cornerstone of effective career scaffolding. Paradoxically, traditional, one-size-fits-all, 'doing'-focused induction leaves individuals unequally prepared for academic life. Such measures have implications for support by perceptive managers and leaders. Billot and King (2015) claim that academics need a clearer understanding of the 'rules of the game' which are often not easy to identify. Through understanding the academic domain, leaders can facilitate a collegial pathway for community engagement and an increased 'sense of citizenship' (Bolden et al., 2014, p. 765).

Fortune et al. (2016) claim that one needs to perceive that one belongs before one can develop an identity. This calls for 'a space that supports identity shift and scholarly growth [that] must be attentive to being and belonging, not just doing' (p. 11). However, our analysis of HE studies literature and recent case study suggest that academic induction may not provide the supportive socialisation that is seen in other sectors. The induction challenge then is to provide personalised, professional scaffolding and scholarly development. Perhaps measuring the effectiveness of existing academic induction is the only way to achieve this?

Notes

1. Corpus analysis often begins by identifying 'key words' (vocabulary that is unusually frequent compared to standard usage) and 'collocates' (words which occur unusually frequently together). Combining key words with their collocates provides insight into the dominant themes in a corpus (Baker & Levon, 2015).
2. The comparison corpus could be one of the widely available reference corpora (Kennedy, 1998), or a specifically created corpus (Kilgarriff, 2001).
3. The concordance tool can provide text extracts which exemplify a key theme (see, for example, Hanna, 2016). Corpus analysis software may also provide visualisation tools which help to reveal the underlying structures and idiosyncrasies of a text (see, for example, Pilcher & Richards, 2016). Although it is currently unusual for educational researchers to employ specialist corpus analysis software, useful results can still be obtained with smaller data sets by using spreadsheet or 'manual' text analysis, as Efe and Ozer (2015) and Mampaey et al. (2015) demonstrate.
4. An initial search of Scopus selected over 700,000 documents covering various different kinds of 'induction', yet many relevant to the induction of academic staff were not found by the search because they did not specifically use the word 'induction'.
5. The final HE studies corpus held 1535 abstracts.
6. The HR corpus held 1189 abstracts.
7. Voyant reported that the HE corpus comprised 343,921 words and 21,675 unique word forms. The HR corpus comprised 448,125 words and 21,355 unique word forms, making it about a third larger than the HE corpus, but with a slightly smaller vocabulary.

Disclosure statement

No potential conflict of interest was reported by the authors.

References

Altbach, P. (2006). The dilemmas of ranking. *International Higher Education, 42*(1–3). Retrieved from http://ejournals.bc.edu/ojs/index.php/ihe/article/view/7878/7029
Baker, P., & Levon, E. (2015). Picking the right cherries? A comparison of corpus-based and qualitative analyses of news articles about masculinity. *Discourse & Communication, 9*(2), 221–236. doi:10.1177/1750481314568542
Billot, J. (2011). The changing research context: Implications for leadership. *Journal of Higher Education Policy & Management, 33*(1), 37–46. doi:10.1080/1360080X.2011.537010
Billot, J., & King, V. (2015). Understanding academic identity through metaphor. *Teaching in Higher Education, 20*(8), 833–844. doi:10.1080/13562517.2015.1087999

Billot, J., Pacheco, G., & Codling, A. (2016). *The reality of being a researcher in a New Zealand university*. Higher Education Research and Development Society of Australasia Conference: *The Shape of Higher Education*. Perth. Retrieved from http://herdsa2016.org/

Bolden, R., Gosling, J., & O'Brien, A. (2014). Citizens of the academic community? A societal perspective on leadership in UK higher education. *Studies in Higher Education*, 39(5), 754–770. doi:10.1080/03075079.2012.754855

Browning, L., Thompson, K., & Dawson, D. (2014). Developing future research leaders: Designing early career researcher programmes to enhance track record. In T. Bromley (Ed.), *Vitae occasional papers: Volume 1. The impact of researcher development* (pp. 15–18). Cambridge, UK: Careers Research and Advisory Centre (CRAC).

Clouder, L., & King, V. (2015). What works? A critique of appreciative inquiry as a research method/ology. In J. Huisman & M. Tight (Eds.), *Theory and method in higher education research* (pp. 169–190). Bingley: Emerald Group. doi:10.1108/S2056-375220150000001008

Efe, I., & Ozer, O. (2015). A corpus-based discourse analysis of the vision and mission statements of universities in Turkey. *Higher Education Research & Development*, 34(6), 1110–1122. doi:10.1080/07294360.2015.1070127

Ennals, P., Fortune, T., Williams, A., & D'Cruz, K. (2015). Shifting occupational identity: Doing, being, becoming and belonging in the academy. *Higher Education Research & Development*. doi:10.1080/07294360.2015.1107884

Fitzmaurice, M. (2013). Constructing professional identity as a new academic: A moral endeavour. *Studies in Higher Education*, 38, 613–622. doi:10.1080/03075079.2011.594501

Fortune, T., Ennals, P., Bhopti, A., Neilson, C., Darzins, S., & Bruce, C. (2016). Bridging identity 'chasms': Occupational therapy academics' reflections on the journey towards scholarship. *Teaching in Higher Education*. doi:10.1080/13562517.2016.1141289

Gale, H. (2011). The reluctant academic: Early career academics in a teaching-oriented university. *International Journal for Academic Development*, 16(3), 215–227. doi:10.1080/1360144X.2011.596705

Gourlay, L. (2011). 'I'd landed on the moon': A new lecturer leaves the academy. *Teaching in Higher Education*, 16(5), 591–601. doi:10.1080/13562517.2011.605548

Hanna, B. E. (2016). Eating a home: Food, imaginary selves and Study Abroad testimonials. *Higher Education Research & Development*, 35(6), 1196–1209. doi:10.1080/07294360.2016.1160876

Hazelkorn, E. (2015). *Rankings and the reshaping of higher education: The battle for world-class excellence* (2nd ed.). Basingstoke: Palgrave Macmillan.

Hemmings, B. (2012). Sources of research confidence for early career academics: A qualitative study. *Higher Education Research & Development*, 31(2), 171–184. doi:10.1080/07294360.2011.559198

Huang, Y., Pang, S.-K., & Yu, S. (2016). Academic identities and university faculty responses to new managerialist reforms: Experiences from China. *Studies in Higher Education*. doi:10.1080/03075079.2016.1157860

Jawitz, J. (2009). Academic identities and communities of practice in a professional discipline. *Teaching in Higher Education*, 14(3), 241–251. doi:10.1080/13562510902898817

Kennedy, G. (1998). *An introduction to corpus linguistics*. Abingdon: Routledge.

Kilgarriff, A. (2001). Comparing corpora. *International Journal of Corpus Linguistics*, 6(1), 97–133. doi:10.1075/ijcl.6.1.05kil

King, V. (2013). Self-portrait with mortar board: A study of academic identity using the map, the novel and the grid. *Higher Education Research & Development*, 32(1), 96–108. doi:10.1080/07294360.2012.751525

Korte, R., Brunhaver, S., & Sheppard, S. (2015). (Mis)Interpretations of organizational socialization: The expectations and experiences of newcomers and managers. *Human Resource Development Quarterly*, 26(2), 185–208. doi:10.1002/hrdq.21206

Locke, W., Whitchurch, C., Smith, H., & Mazenod, A. (2016). *Shifting landscapes: Meeting the staff development needs of the changing academic workforce*. York: Higher Education Academy.

Mampaey, J., Huisman, J., & Seeber, M. (2015). Branding of Flemish higher education institutions: A strategic balance perspective. *Higher Education Research & Development*, 34(6), 1178–1191. doi:10.1080/07294360.2015.1024634

Mathieson, S. (2011). Developing academic agency through critical reflection: A sociocultural approach to academic induction programmes. *International Journal for Academic Development*, 16(3), 243–256. doi:10.1080/1360144X.2011.596730

McAlpine, L., & Norton, J. (2006). Reframing our approach to doctoral programs: An integrative framework for action and research. *Higher Education Research & Development*, 25(1), 3–17. doi:10.1080/07294360500453012

McEnery, T., & Hardie, A. (2012). *Corpus linguistics: Method, theory and practice*. Cambridge, UK: Cambridge University Press.

Nadolny, A., & Ryan, S. (2015). McUniversities revisited: A comparison of university and McDonald's casual employee experiences in Australia. *Studies in Higher Education*, 40(1), 142–157. doi:10.1080/03075079.2013.818642

O'Meara, K. A., Lounder, A., & Campbell, C. M. (2014). To heaven or hell: Sensemaking about why faculty leave. *Journal of Higher Education*, 85(5), 603–632. doi:10.1353/jhe.2014.0027

Pilcher, N., & Richards, K. (2016). The paradigmatic hearts of subjects which their 'English' flows through. *Higher Education Research & Development*, 35(5), 997–1010. doi:10.1080/07294360.2016.1138455

Remmik, M., Karm, M., Haamer, A., & Lepp, L. (2011). Early-career academics' learning in academic communities. *International Journal for Academic Development*, 16(3), 187–199. doi:10.1080/1360144X.2011.596702

Sheridan, V. (2013). A risky mingling: Academic identity in relation to stories of the personal and professional self. *Reflective Practice: International and Multidisciplinary Perspectives*, 14, 568–579. doi:10.1080/14623943.2013.810617

Smith, J. (2010). Forging identities: The experiences of probationary lecturers in the UK. *Studies in Higher Education*, 35(5), 577–591. doi:10.1080/03075070903216650

Smith, J., & Rattray, J. (2016). Preface: Mapping the terrain of identity-work research. In J. Smith, J. Rattray, T. Peseta, & D. Loads (Eds.), *Identity work in the contemporary university* (pp. vii–xiii). Rotterdam: Sense.

Sutherland, K., Wilson, M., & Williams, P. (2013). *Success in academia? The experiences of early career academics in New Zealand universities*. Wellington: Ako Aoteoroa National Centre for Tertiary Teaching Excellence.

Trede, F., Macklin, R., & Bridges, D. (2012). Professional identity development: A review of higher education literature. *Studies in Higher Education*, 37, 365–384. doi:10.1080/03075079.2010.521237

Trowler, P., & Knight, P. (1999). Organisational socialisation and induction in universities: Reconceptualising theory and practice. *Higher Education*, 37, 177–195. doi:10.1023/A:1003594512521

Vitae Careers Research and Advisory Centre. (2016). *Teaching lens on the Vitae Researcher Development Framework and the UK Professional Standards Framework*. Retrieved from https://www.vitae.ac.uk/vitae-publications/rdf-related/teaching-lens-on-the-vitae-researcher-development-framework-rdf-apr-2013.pdf

Walker, P. (2015). The globalisation of higher education and the sojourner academic: Insights into challenges experienced by newly appointed international academic staff in a UK university. *Journal of Research in International Education*, 14(1), 61–74. doi:10.1177/1475240915571032

Watanabe, M., & Falci, C. D. (2016) A demands and resources approach to understanding faculty turnover intentions due to work–family balance. *Journal of Family Issues*, 37(3), 393–415. doi:10.1177/0192513X14530972

Wenger, E. (1998). *Communities of practice. Learning, meaning and identity*. New York, NY: Cambridge University Press.

Wilson, L. (2012). Welcome on board: Designing support interventions to meet the needs of new part-time lecturers. In F. Beaton & A. Gilbert (Eds.), *Developing effective part-time teachers in higher education: New approaches to professional development* (pp. 117–133). Abingdon: Routledge.

Lost souls? The demoralization of academic labour in the measured university

Paul Sutton

ABSTRACT
In this conceptual paper, I contend that the soul of academic labour is becoming lost in performativity. Performativity, I explain, is a form of regulation and control that deploys technical rationality and judgements to incentivize and punish academics. Indeed, performativity is central to the culture of measurement within contemporary universities. This, I contend, is demoralizing academic labour as performativity only measures and values those dimensions of academic labour that can be captured by quantitative performance indicators. To critique this process, I firstly locate performativity within a moral economy perspective. I argue that the university economy is no longer structured by the moral norm of education as a public good. It has been restructured, commodified and marketized by neo-liberal capitalism. Secondly, I explore how the reorganization of institutional practices and academic identity within the university by performativity wreaks terror in the academic's soul. Thirdly, I critique the unsatisfying post-structural reduction of the soul to a synonym for subjectivity and offer a sociological conception of the soul as the spiritual dimension of academic labour emerging from deep, rich social relations of production. My conjecture is that the soul is the moral energy and purpose central to species-being: the peculiarly human ability to transform the socio-human world for the good of all. Finally, I suggest that within the soulless technical measure of academic labour that now dominates the university lies the possibility for developing a more soulful normative measure. My aim then is to articulate a dialectical humanist conception of the soul of academic labour in order to critique the reductive positivism of the measured university.

Introduction: the de-moralized economy of the measured university

> Moral economy studies the moral norms and sentiments that structure and influence economic practices, both formal and informal, and the way in which these are reinforced, shaped, compromised or overridden by economic pressures. (Sayer, 2007 p. 262)

In their discussion piece, *Against academic identity*, Neary and Winn (2016) argue that interest in academic identity is a reflection of a wider concern with the nature of academic labour. They declare that the concept 'fails to deal with real nature of work in capitalist society' (Neary & Winn, 2016, p. 409). In addition, they argue that dominance of post-structural conceptions of identity that celebrate difference – gender, ethnic, sexual, etc. – has led to an accommodation with, rather than the overthrow of capitalism, the real cause of the subordination of labour. Hence, the concept of academic identity should be 'abolished'. I share Neary and Winn's position on the subordination of academic labour by capitalism and the deleterious effects of post-structuralist conceptions of identity. However, rather than seeking to abolish the concept of identity, I want to work 'in-against and beyond' it (Holloway, 2010).

To achieve this end, I conceptualize academic labour as an expression of what Marx (1997) called 'species-being': the peculiarly human ability to transform both the socio-human world and ourselves for the good of all. Furthermore, I speculate that species-being has a moral dimension: it is an expression of the human soul. In addition, I conceptualize the soul as the 'moral energy' that gives purpose and value to social labour (Marx, 1997, p. 81). Thus, unlike Neary and Winn's political economy, I seek to explore an aspect of the moral economy of academic labour and identity.

Twenty-five years ago, whilst researching a labour history, I came upon the Marxist-humanist historian E.P. Thompson's classic essay, *The Moral Economy of the English Crowd in the Eighteenth Century*. In this work, Thompson analysed the effects of the reorganization of the economy by the new ideology of laissez-faire capitalism, a form of capitalism that was 'disinfested of moral imperative' (Thompson, 1971, p. 90). Thompson was particularly interested in the way that the market for bread that had previously been structured by popular cultural notions of fairness and reciprocity, became demoralized through the institution of the free market principle of supply and demand. As I was researching this paper, it struck me that there are strong resonances between Thompson's analysis and the marketization of higher education in late twentieth century and early twenty-first century. In England, the higher education economy is no longer structured by the norms and values of academic culture committed to education as a public good. It has been reorganized by the ideology of neo-liberal capitalism. The university economy is now structured by the principle of supply and demand and the cost–benefit calculus. Academic labour is now performed in a culture of measurement (Biesta, 2010).

In the measurement culture of education questions concerning the nature and purpose of a good education have been displaced by technical and managerial questions concerning efficiency and effectiveness. The university economy is dominated by the measurement of process rather than moral purpose. The normative has been displaced by the performative:

> The rise of a culture of performativity in education – a culture in which means become ends in themselves so that targets and indicators of quality become mistaken for quality itself – has been one of the main drivers of an approach to measurement in which normative validity is being replaced by technical validity. (Biesta, 2010, p. 13)

Using Biesta's work, I argue that performativity measures only that which can be easily measured quantitatively. This has resulted in universities valuing only quantitative indicators of economic effectiveness and efficiency. For example, performativity neither measures nor values what is central to academic labour: love (Sutton, 2016a). Love defined as a 'syndrome of attitudes; that of care, responsibility, respect and knowledge' (Fromm, 1962, p. 33); as a feeling of connectedness with others; is a vital dimension of the deep, rich social relations that are necessary for the emergence of soul in academic labour. Furthermore, love is also a vital dimension of a humane moral economy. This paper then is an endeavour to reclaim the soul of academic labour that is becoming lost in performativity.

I now explore Ball's conception of performativity. Thereafter, I explore the contention that the soul is an emergent property of both human cognition and deep and rich social relations. Building upon this, the soul is conjectured to be part of human species-being. Finally, I suggest that the possibility exists for a soulful normative measure of academic labour to be developed from within the soulless technical qualitative measure of performativity.

Performativity

My interest lies in how the technology of performativity, within an increasingly marketized higher education system (Brown & Carasso, 2013), has overridden the moral purpose I believe to be central to academic labour: education as a public rather than a private good. Performativity is a quintessential dimension of the measured university. In order to critique performativity, I will use the work of the educational sociologist, Stephen J. Ball. The rationale for using Ball's (2003, 2012a, 2012b) work is that his work clearly and comprehensively addresses the perils of measurement culture in education. In addition, Ball introduces the notion of the teacher's soul into the performativity debate. However, Ball (2003) only appears to explore the 'terror' wreaked upon the 'teacher's soul' by performativity. He never defines what soul is but simply uses the work of Foucault in which the soul is a synonym for the psyche, subjectivity, personality or consciousness. In Ball's post-structuralist account, the soul is engendered by 'methods of punishment, supervision and constraint' (Foucault, 1979, p. 29); it is the medium and effect of power–knowledge relations. Thus, the soul is a product of disciplinary power. Ball's account, like many Foucauldian accounts of power, is too negative. I will negate this negation by offering a more positive account of the soul as engendered by deep and rich human social relations (see below). But before addressing the emergence of the soul from the social relations of production, it is necessary to define performativity and explore how performativity demoralizes both the institutional practices of universities and academic labour.

Performativity is a form of rationality and regulation that deploys technical judgements and comparisons to measure, incentivize and punish academics. In performativity, academic productivity is measured by largely quantitative performance indicators. For Ball, performativity, in tandem with the market and managerialism, is an educational policy technology that is neo-liberalizing higher education. This triad is changing both the nature of academic labour and identity. Ball (2012a, p. 31) offers a Foucauldian definition of performativity as 'the quintessential form of neo-liberal governmentality, which encompasses subjectivity, institutional practices, economy and government'. In this paper, I am mainly concerned with the manifestation of neo-liberal governmentality in institutional practices of higher education and academic subjectivity.

The re-ordering of institutional practices

Performativity is a 'framework of judgement' through which the efficiency and productivity of academic labour is measured (Ball, 2012a, p. 31). Pivotal to the operation of performativity is 'the translation of complex social processes and events into simple figures or categories of judgement' (Ball, 2003, p. 217). What is lost in this translation, I argue, is the quality of the complex and dynamic relationships that constitute the moral economy of academic labour. Social relationships with colleagues and students, the fulcrum of academic productivity, are reduced to de-humanized performance indicators. Performative categories of judgement are characterized by a binary opposition of quantity and quality with quality being the subordinate term. Hence, performative judgements are largely made on the basis of simplistic quantitative measures of productivity reducing the complex human processes of academic labour to simplified targets and outcome measures. For example, institutional quality assurance measures consisting of standardized bureaucratic institutional reviews and key performance indicators. Thus, the techniques of personal development review, academic development planning and so on operate to individualize and demoralize social labour by privileging quantitative measures of academic labour over the quality of that labour.

The neo-liberalizing university positions academics as 'active agents seeking to maximise their own advantage'; as individuals who are responsible for 'calculating actions and outcomes' (Rose & Miller, 1992, p. 198). Success at work requires each individual academic labourer to perpetually calculate and choose: for choice is a central tenet of neo-liberalism. Each individual is thereby 'governed through their freedom to choose' (Rose & Miller, 1992, p. 201). Choice is part of the regulatory technology of governmentality. The Foucauldian concept of governmentality can be defined as the 'internal control systems' that attempt to 're-order the collective and individual selves that make up organizational life' (Power, 1999, p. 42). I will pursue the re-ordering of the self in more detail below.

The internal control systems of universities are structured by the principles of cost effectiveness, economic efficiency and quality assurance. Performativity then is a way of making institutional and individual performance auditable through the collection of mainly quantitative forms of information. Universities have been '*colonized* by an audit process which disseminates and implants the values that underlie and support its informational demands' (Power, 1999, p. 95, emphasis in original). The effect of these informational demands is twofold. Firstly, it re-channels academic labour 'towards those activities that can be easily measured, especially as performance outcomes' (Ball, 2012a, p. 32). In this way, the more complex and difficult-to-measure 'social, emotional and moral' dimensions that are central to the soul of academic labour, but have no immediate measurable 'performative value', tend to be effaced (Ball, 2012a, p. 32). Concrete labour is thereby displaced by abstract labour, use value by exchange value.[1] Thus, the experience of academic labour becomes 'inauthentic and alienating', a commodified relationship characterized by 'active docility and depthless productivity', in which 'commitment is sacrificed for impression' (Ball, 2012a, pp. 31, 32). Secondly, performativity changes the way in which academics 'experience their work and the satisfactions they get from it' (Ball, 2012a, p. 32). For example, the complex social relationship between teacher and student is transmogrified into a simple service relationship in which the customer is always right. Furthermore, and what is highly significant for this discussion, academics' 'sense of moral purpose' is also devalued by a 'new episteme of public service' in which academic labour is restructured as a form of self-interested entrepreneurialism (Ball, 2012b, p. 20). Academics are increasingly being urged to become highly visible entrepreneurs competing to sell their goods and services in the higher education quasi-market place.

The re-ordering of self-identity

Performativity not only re-orders institutional practices it also re-orders self-identity. One of the ways in which this is accomplished is through the institutionalization of the logic of standardization: regulations and systems replace academic judgement and discretion. As stated above, this changes the experience of being an academic and tends to produce 'new mentalities, new incentives and perceptions of significance ... a new organizational actor' (Power, 1999, p. 97). The creation of this new organizational actor takes place when the technology of performativity becomes internalized: when 'academics' come to want what is wanted from them. Thus, performativity works to align academics 'moral sense' and desires with institutional demands (Ball, 2012a, p. 31).

Increasingly, universities demand that academics are in a constant state of becoming (perpetual professional development review), continually working upon themselves to improve their economic effectiveness and efficiency. Performativity also induces guilt and inadequacy if academics do not (Berg & Seeber, 2013). The collegial academic subject is being displaced by the individual neo-liberal subject acting to maximize their economic value within the academic quasi-market (Billot, 2010; Canaan, 2010). The ensemble of the social relations of production from which academic identity emerges is increasingly demoralized through the institution of individualized market-based contractual relations.

Thus, academic values and commitments are replaced by contractual duties. Performativity creates neo-liberal subjects that are 'malleable rather than committed, flexible rather than principled – essentially depthless' (Ball, 2012a, p. 31). The technology of performativity, in conjunction with marketization and managerialism, leaves little or no space for a 'shared moral language' or 'an autonomous or collective ethical self' (Ball, 2003 p. 226) necessary, I argue, for the emergence of soul.

Performativity leads to a form of demoralization through the 'commodification of the public professional' (Ball, 2012a, p. 32). This process of commodification has changed the system of rewards and sanctions in higher education and the form and content of teaching and research. The success of academic performance is no longer measured by academic but commercial values. For example, numbers of students recruited, engagement with employers and other stakeholders, and income generation (Naidoo, 2005). The power effect of being constantly measured by quantitative managerial criteria that tend to be in a constant state of flux due to ever changing market demands, leads to 'ontological insecurity' (Ball, 2003, p. 220). Academics become increasingly unsure as to whether they are 'doing enough, doing the right thing, doing as much as others, or as well as others, constantly looking to improve' (Ball, 2003, p. 220). This creates high levels of stress around resource allocation, communication and control of the labour process (Tytherleigh, Webb, Cooper, & Ricketts, 2005). At best, this has produced 'uneasy academic subjectivities' (Acker & Webber, 2016), and at worst, this has wreaked terror upon the academic's soul. However, as I observed above, Ball (2003) never adequately defines what soul is. I will address this lacuna by offering a sociological conception of the soul as the moral purpose and energy emerging from deep and rich social relatedness.

The nature and emergence of the soul

The Greek term soul is commonly translated as *psyche*, a noun, derived from the verb *psychein* which means to breathe or 'that which generates and constitutes the essential life of a being' (Goetz & Taliaferro, 2011, p. 7). My interest in the ontological dimension of academic labour and how performativity is asphyxiating academic being has prompted this paper. I want to think about academic being by conceptualizing the soul as the generative energy and constitutive power of authentic academic labour. Furthermore, I want to think about the generative energy of the human soul by using a Marxist Humanist theoretical framework. For at the heart of Marxism lies an especial emphasis on human creativity and self-creation (Williams, 1977).[2] Indeed, when reading the early Marx, one is struck by the pivotal role ascribed to creativity in social life. Creativity is what makes us human: creativity is at the centre of our species-being. It is the peculiar human ability to transform both the socio-human world and ourselves. I develop this ontological dimension of Humanist Marxism by exploring the possibility that the soul is an integral dimension of species-being that emerges from within the 'ensemble of social relations' (Marx, 1997, p. 402). To explain this contention, I draw on an essay by Brown (1998) which provides a very useful way to begin theorizing the conditions of possibility for the emergence of soul.

Brown (1998, p. 100) argues that the soul signifies a 'unique human capacity and experience', associated with the exercise of agency, self-consciousness, love and transcendence. Soulfulness is a moral relatedness to self, others and God. In my social ontology of the soul, God is displaced by society, or more properly sociality (society as dialectical process). It is sociality, and specifically the social relations of production, that reaches deeply into the essence of our human being. Brown (1998) continues by arguing that the soul is an emergent property of 'deep, rich experiences of personal relatedness', which in turn are 'an *emergent property* of certain critical cognitive abilities' (Brown, 1998, p. 102, emphasis in original).

I understand deep rich personal relatedness as relationships that are founded upon love (care, responsibility, respect and knowledge), in which social interdependence is both acknowledged and valued. Deep rich personal relatedness then involves taking responsibility for both ourselves and others and positioning others as an end in themselves, rather than a means to an end. Such relationships generate a sense of identity and belonging (Whyte, 2001), a sense of ontological security. Such relationships are rooted in community or collegiality rather than contract. The depthless nature of academic labour engendered by performativity is obviously anathema to the depth required for the emergence of soul.

Brown argues that an emergent property is made possible by an increase in the capacity of lower level abilities and their interactions. The soul's 'emergenesis' depends upon, but is not reducible to those properties. In sum, 'human experiences of soul are conditioned by but cannot be reduced to the underlying mental processes from which they emerge' (Brown, 1998, p. 103). Soul, therefore, is something different from mind or consciousness.

Next, Brown (1998) identifies six interdependent critical cognitive capacities that enable the emergence of soul: language, memory, future orientation, a theory of mind, emotional modulation and agency, Language is the uniquely human capacity to communicate and understand complex abstract ideas and emotional states. This 'makes possible important dimensions of personal relatedness that could not exist independent of language' (Brown, 1998, p. 107). Social communication through language is a necessary condition for deep personal relatedness.

In Marxist Humanism, language is conceptualized as 'practical consciousness' which arises from the need to produce 'material life itself' – food, clothing, shelter, etc. (Marx, 1997, pp. 421, 419). Language emerges from the human need to communicate with others in social labour and this requires cooperative social relationships with other people. However, I further extend Marx's conceptualization to argue that language is not only practical but spiritual, and that the spiritual and the practical are both necessary dimensions of the production of the conditions necessary for life to flourish. Therefore, a shared moral language is a necessary dimension of the social relations of production from which the soul emerges. Furthermore, language is an essential dimension of the process of human self-creation (Williams, 1977) and is one of the conditions of possibility of the emergence of soul.

Language in turn is necessary for another critical cognitive capacity: episodic or autobiographical memory. Autobiographical memory creates a historical and continuous store of memories of events, places and people (Brown, 1998). It connects the past with the present and is crucial for the development of both a stable identity and personal relatedness. Language combined with memory enables the construction of stocks of collectively accessible knowledge and understanding needed to direct future thinking, being and doing (Harvey, 2000). Brown (1998) calls this the ability to imagine possible futures. I call it the utopian imaginary and, drawing on Freire and Bloch, I argue that this is central not only to my own academic identity but also to the emancipatory purpose of higher education (Sutton, 2015).

Language and memory also enable the development of another crucial cognitive ability: a theory of mind. This is the capacity to recognize the thoughts and feelings of self and other. I would add that such recognition facilitates compassion which for me is the essence of any moral economy. A theory of mind makes possible 'emotional modulation': the 'complex social and contextual cognition' that enables people to make appropriate emotional responses and decisions (Brown, 1998, p. 103). This ability is vital for the creation and maintenance of personal relatedness. The final critical cognitive ability essential for the emergenesis of the soul is 'conscious top-down agency' (Brown, 1998, p. 117). Humans do not simply react to stimuli, our behaviour is not simply the product of conditioning, but rather is the product of agency. Therefore, the emergence of soul requires a significant degree of freedom to exercise, what Marx (1997, p. 294) terms 'will and consciousness'.

In sum, the complex interaction of these six critical cognitive powers and capacities creates the conditions necessary for the deep and rich social relatedness from which the soul emerges. However, what is not fully acknowledged in Brown's emergenesis theory are the material conditions and social relations of production necessary for the evolution of critical cognitive powers. As Marx (1997) argues, human as a species needed to organize labour collectively in order to survive. This defines their 'species-being'. I now explore the concept of species-being and argue that the soul is an integral dimension thereof.

Species-being and the spiritual dimension of social labour

Species-being is a value-laden concept used by Marx to understand the peculiarities of the human condition. It is a 'normative' rather than a simply descriptive concept of social being (Markovic, 1974, p. 53). Species-being signifies the human ability to 'transform the world through labour and thereby transform ourselves' (Harvey, 2000, p. 206). What is often not made explicit in accounts of species-being is that it is the ability to transform self and society for the good of all. But what is species-being? Species-being is constituted through a 'combination of self-consciousness, material capacity, and collective organisation' (Dyer-Witherford, 2004, p. 5). It therefore signifies that there are mental, material and mutual dimensions to the human condition. However, I would go further and add that there is an essential metaphysical dimension to the human condition: the soul.

Marx developed the concept of species-being as a critique of alienation: what he saw as capitalism's appropriation of the human ability to transform self and other through social labour. In the 1844 *Economic and Philosophical Manuscripts*, the concept of species-being emerges from Marx's discussion of alienated labour. After discussing the alienation of the worker from the product of labour, and from the production process, Marx then discusses the emergence of self-alienation. The discussion begins with the introduction of the concept of species-being. Species-being is the power to 'practically and theoretically' make 'life activity itself into an object of will and consciousness' (Marx, 1997, pp. 293, 294). Note the emphasis on will here. The collective creation of the socio-human world through labour requires both 'moral energy' (Marx, 1997, p. 381) and moral purpose: it requires soul. Building on this idea, Kosik (1976) refers to human survival as the 'spiritual-practical' production and reproduction of the reality through social labour.[3] It is my contention that the spiritual dimension of labour is often overlooked in Marxist theory. Furthermore, I speculate that the term spiritual can be fruitfully interpreted as connoting the soul, and that the soul is an essential dimension of the collective creation of the socio-human world.

Marx did not use the term soul but he did use the term spiritual.[4] He wrote of 'the physical and the spiritual life' of human beings and of the 'physical' and 'spiritual energy' used by workers in the labour process (Marx, 1997, p. 293). Marx's (1997, p. 295) discussion of alienation continues stating that under capitalism, the labourer's loss of control over the process of production and the product of their labour engenders a self-alienation in which human 'spiritual nature' is lost. Capitalist relations of production abstract the individual from their collective species-being and in that abstraction, the connection that the labourer experiences to work is lost. Thereby, the spiritual dimension of labour disappears. Labour is reduced to the means to satisfy the needs of individual physical existence. It ceases to be creative, ceases to be 'free conscious activity ... life begetting life', and becomes 'alienated externalized labour' (Marx, 1997, pp. 294, 296). In the measured university, the demoralization of academic labour under performativity creates a similar spiritual alienation in which the soul is lost.

The capitalist social relations of production that create alienation from the product and process, from self and spirit also creates alienation from other humans (Marx, 1997). This results in the commodification of species-being. So too in contemporary neo-liberalizing universities, species-being is commodified. Performativity, managerialism and the market result in the loss of the deep rich social relations which create and sustain the soul. For me, performativity is not only a reductive epistemology or mode of knowing and measuring academic labour, it is also a reductive ontology in which academics are alienated from the spiritual dimension of their species-being. Performativity is a form of positivism in which the unity of the practical and the spiritual in human labour is ruptured.

The antithesis to this reductive positivism can be found in a dialectical humanist approach that restores the complexity and interrelatedness of the spiritual and the practical.[5] The soul emerges from their dynamic interplay in academic labour. Dialectics is a way of understanding and explaining academic labour as part of the 'dialectical whole'. It is a theoretical method that proceeds 'from the whole to its parts and from the parts to the whole, from phenomena to essence and from essence to phenomena' (Kosik, 1976, pp. 18, 23). This dialectical conception captures the complexity of the social relations of academic labour that is lost in the positivism of performativity.

In sum, the soul is part of the human essence, part of species-being that emerges from deep, rich human relationships. Soul emerges from human consciousness and will, and provides both the moral energy and purpose central to soulful academic labour. Soulful academic labour is premised upon 'a moral obligation to students and colleagues, regardless of the direct or indirect career benefits' (Macfarlane, 2005, p. 172). But how might the soulfulness of academic labour be measured?

Towards a dialectical measure of academic labour

> ... alienation could not even be seen, and condemned of robbing people of their freedom and depriving the world of its soul, if there did not exist some measure of its opposite, of that possible coming-to-oneself... (Bloch, 1964, cited in Holloway, 2010, pp. 170–171)

It is my view that the measurement of academic labour is a given; it has become embedded in the institutional practices of universities. The measured university is here to stay. Nevertheless, I think it is possible for the dominance of technical performative measures to be challenged by normative measures concerned with moral purpose. The alienation caused by severing the relationship between the practical and the spiritual dimensions of academic labour can be overcome. For, in the 'paradoxical logic' of dialectical humanism, opposites are interrelated (Fromm, 1962, p. 120). What does this mean? This means that within the performative quantitative measure of academic labour resides its normative qualitative opposite. What Biesta (2010, p. 13) refers to as 'quality itself', rather than the targets and indicators of quality. Thus, although the meaning of quality is denoted and measured quantitatively, an opposite qualitative connotative meaning of quality is contained within performativity, albeit in a subordinated form. This opposite meaning provides an opening within the language of measurement for the transformation of quantity into quality. This dialectical process is called development through contradiction or negation. Furthermore, a dialectical measurement of academic labour would consist of both quantitative and qualitative measurements, and possess both technical and the normative validity.

It is beyond the scope of this paper to offer a fully developed normative model for the measurement of soul in academic labour. However, a possible starting point for such a model is to be found in the New Economics Foundation [NEF] (2014) dynamic model of well-being at work. The NEF uses an array of qualitative indicators to measure the *hedonic, eudaimonic and evaluative* dimensions of labour. The hedonic dimension measures academics' level of engagement with their work, how worthwhile it is considered to be and how happy or anxious they feel. The eudaimonic dimension measures academics' sense of meaning and moral purpose in their work, opportunities for creativity, a sense of achievement and autonomy. The autonomy so central to soulful academic labour signifies 'the ability to select tasks and research projects; time and space for thinking and research; the opportunity to engage in socially useful critique; and self- management within disciplinary departments' (Robinson, 2016, p. 27). The evaluative indicator measures overall job satisfaction. Thus, the hedonic, eudaimonic and evaluative measures are a fruitful place to begin the quest to measure soul. Adapting the well-being at work model to this end could act as the antithesis of performativity: a dialectical negation of the negation that re-valorizes the moral dimensions of academic labour.

Conclusion

> ... even the driest of his [Marx's] descriptions contain an implicit moral connotation. (Markovic, 1974, p. 59)

Like Neary and Winn (2016), my aim has been to understand alienated academic labour and identity in order that they may be transformed. However, I offer a different kind of Marxist analysis, one that foregrounds the need for a moral as well as a political economy of academic labour. In my analysis, I have worked in-against-and-beyond academic labour and identity through an exploration of the moral connotations of the concept of species-being. I argued that academic labour is an expression of human species-being. That the soulful dimension of species-being emerges from deep, rich social relations of production that are an essential dimension of the creative spiritual-practical reproduction of social life. I also speculated that the soul, conceptualized as moral energy and purpose, is an essential dimension of that species-being.

However, the regime of performativity that dominates the measured university I argued is a limiting form of positivism. Performativity deploys narrow technical measures that fail to capture the soul of academic labour. This results in demoralization. The soulfulness central to the social relations of academic production and the moral economy of the university as a public good are not measured and thereby are not valued in performativity. A re-valorization of the moral purpose at the heart of higher education is therefore necessary.

This re-valorization may be achieved through a dialectical humanist analysis. By positing a dynamic interrelationship between the technical and the normative, the quantitative and the qualitative, the limitations of performative measurement may be transcended. A qualitative normative measure of academic labour based upon the NEF dynamic model of well-being at work, I suggest, provides a starting point for the development of new moral economy of academic labour. For it is only by re-uniting the spiritual and the practical measurements of academic labour that the soul of the labourer, and indeed the university itself, can be reclaimed.

Notes

1. For a detailed discussion of the Marxian concepts of abstract and concrete labour and the associated concepts of use and exchange value, see Sutton (2016b).
2. See also Markovic (1974, pp. 73–74) who states that: 'One of the most distinctive characteristics of man (sic) is his creativity. In contrast to all other living beings man constantly evolves his tools, his methods of work, his needs, his objectives, his criteria of evaluation.' Part of the

purpose of this paper is to begin to explore the possibilities of alternatives to performative criteria of the evaluation of academic labour.
3. On the dialectical nature of cognition in Marxist Humanism, see Kosik (1976, Chapter 1).
4. In Bottomore's popular translation of the Economic and Philosophical Manuscripts (Fromm, 2011), the term 'spiritual' is translated as 'mental'. Yet, in Kosik (1976) and Marx (1997) translated by Easton and Guddat, the term spiritual is used. This does raise interesting questions concerning the politics of interpretation. In my endeavour to put the metaphysical back into Marxism, I find the latter translation more sympathetic.
5. Kosik (1976) defines dialectics as a form of critical thinking that attempts to understand and explain the human being's place in the universe by penetrating beneath surface appearances to the essence of phenomena. Dialectical thinking understands socio-human reality as a structured but evolving whole.

Acknowledgements

I would like to thank the reviewers and the editor for their critical constructive feedback. Such a rigorous but humane collegial review process is in itself a negation of the negation of de-moralizing performativity.

Disclosure statement

No potential conflict of interest was reported by the author.

References

Acker, S., & Webber, M. (2016). Uneasy academic subjectivities in the contemporary Ontario university. In J. Smith, J. Rattray, T. Peseta, & D. Loads (Eds.), *Identity work in the contemporary university. Exploring an uneasy profession* (pp. 61–76). Rotterdam: Sense.
Ball, S. J. (2003). The teacher's soul and the terrors of performativity. *Journal of Education Policy*, 18(2), 215–228.
Ball, S. J. (2012a). *Global Education Inc. New policy networks and the neo-liberal imaginary*. London: Routledge.
Ball, S. J. (2012b). Performativity, commodification and commitment: An I-spy guide to the neoliberal university. *British Journal of Educational Studies*, 60(1), 17–28.
Berg, M., & Seeber, K. (2013). The slow professor: Challenging the culture of speed in the academy. *Transformative Dialogues: Teaching and Learning Journal*, 6(3), 1–7.
Biesta, G. (2010). *Good education in an age of measurement*. Boulder, CO: Paradigm.
Billot, J. (2010). The imagined and the real: Identifying the tensions for academic identity. *Higher Education Research & Development*, 29(6), 709–721. doi:10.1080/07294360.2010.487201
Brown, R., & Carasso, H. (2013). *Everything for sale? The marketization of UK higher education*. London: Routledge.
Brown, W. S. (1998). Cognitive contributions to soul. In W. S. Brown, N. Murphey, & H. N. Malony (Eds.), *Whatever happened to the soul? Scientific and theological portraits of human nature* (pp. 99–125). Minneapolis, MN: Fortress Press.
Canaan, J. (2010). Analysing a 'neoliberal moment' in English higher education today. *Learning & Teaching*, 3(2), 55–72.
Dyer-Witherford, N. (2004). 1844/2004/2044: The return of species-being. *Historical Materialism*, 12(4), 3–25.
Foucault, M. (1979). *Discipline and punish. The birth of the prison*. London: Penguin.
Fromm, E. (1962). *Beyond the chains of illusion. My encounters with Marx and Freud*. New York, NY: Simon and Schuster.

Fromm, E. (2011). *Marx's concept of man*. (With a Translation from Marx's Economic and Philosophical Manuscripts by T.B. Bottomore). New York, NY: Frederick Ungar.

Goetz, S., & Taliaferro, C. (2011). *A brief history of the soul*. Chichester: John Wiley & Sons.

Harvey, D. (2000). *Spaces of hope*. Edinburgh: Edinburgh University Press.

Holloway, J. (2010). *Crack capitalism*. London: Pluto.

Kosik, K. (1976). *Dialectics of the concrete, a study on problems of man and world*. Dordrecht: D. Reidel Publishing.

Macfarlane, B. (2005). Placing service in academic life. In R. Barnett (Ed.), *Reshaping the university. New relationships between research, scholarship and teaching* (pp. 165–177). Maidenhead: OU Press.

Markovic, M. (1974). *From affluence to praxis. Philosophy and social criticism*. Ann Arbor: University of Michigan Press.

Marx, K. (1997). *Writings of the young Marx on philosophy and society*. (L.D. Easton & K.H. Guddat, Ed. and Trans.). Cambridge: Hackett.

Naidoo, R. (2005). Universities in the marketplace: The distortion of teaching and research. In R. Barnett (Ed.), *Reshaping the university. New relationships between research, scholarship and teaching* (pp. 27–36). Maidenhead: OU Press.

Neary, M., & Winn, J. (2016). Against academic identity. *Higher Education Research & Development, 35*(2), 409–412. doi:10.1080/07294360.2015.1094201

New Economics Foundation. (2014). *Well-being at work. A review of the literature*. Retrieved from http://www.neweconomics.org/publications/entry/well-being-at-work

Power, M. (1999). *The audit society. Rituals of verification*. Oxford: Oxford University Press.

Robinson, S. R. (2016). Forging academic identities from within; lessons from the ancient world. In J. Smith, J. Rattray, T. Peseta, & D. Loads (Eds.), *Identity work in the contemporary university. Exploring an uneasy profession* (pp. 17–32). Rotterdam: Sense.

Rose, N., & Miller, P. (1992). Political power beyond the state: Problematics of government. *British Journal of Sociology, 43*(2), 173–205.

Sayer, A. (2007). Moral economy as critique. *New Political Economy, 12*(2), 261–270.

Sutton, P. (2015). A paradoxical identity. Fate utopia and critical hope. *Teaching in Higher Education, 20*(1), 37–47. doi:10.1080/13562517.2014.957265

Sutton, P. (2016a). A labour of love? Curiosity, alienation and the constitution of academic character. In J. Smith, J. Rattray, T. Peseta, & D. Loads (Eds.), *Identity work in the contemporary university. Exploring an uneasy profession* (pp. 33–44). Rotterdam: Sense.

Sutton, P. (2016b). The strategic approach to studying, and the value of assessment. *Practitioner Research in Higher Education, Assessment Special Edition, 10*(1), 3–12.

Thompson, E. P. (1971). The moral economy of the English crowd in the eighteenth century. *Past and Present, 50*(1), 76–136.

Tytherleigh, M. Y., Webb, C., Cooper, C. L., & Ricketts, C. (2005). Occupational stress in UK higher education institutions: A comparative study of all staff categories. *Higher Education Research & Development, 24*(1), 41–61. doi:10.1080/0729436052000318569

Whyte, D. (2001). *Crossing the unknown sea: Work as a pilgrimage of identity*. New York: Riverhead Books.

Williams, R. (1977). *Marxism & literature*. Oxford: Oxford University Press.

Index

Note: Page numbers in *italics* refer to figures
Page numbers in **bold** refer to tables
Page numbers with 'n' refer to notes

Aboriginals *see* Indigenous studies, in Australia
abstract labour 176
academic collaboration *see* collaboration
academic excellence 48–49, 76
academic friendship 24–25
academic good life 35, 38, 40, 43
Academic Identities Conference (2016) 1, 75, 83, 84
academic identity 26, 60–62, 78, 90, 103–104, 161, 164, 167, 169, 173–174, 177; identity-trajectory 148–149, 151, 155–156; *see also* academic probation, of early career academics (UK)
academic induction 4, 161, 163, 166–168, 170
academic labour, dialectical measure of 181–182
academic labour, demoralization of 4, 173–183; demoralized economy 173–175; dialectical measure 181–182; institutional practices, re-ordering of 175–177; performativity 175; self-identity, reordering of 177; soul, nature and emergence of 178–179; species-being and spiritual dimension of social labour 179–181
academic management 63
academic probation, of early career academics (UK) 4, 145–146; ambitions 149, 152, 155, 156; challenges to identity development 154–155; codes of signification 150, 154–155; discursive repertoires 150, 153–154; domestication *vs.* liberation 156–157; exploring ECA's experiences 150–152; identity-trajectory 148–149, 151, 155–156; incrementalism 154; individuation 145, 153, 155; measurement culture in UK universities 146, 148; narrative analysis *vs.* analysis of narratives 151; networks 149; objective and subjective career success 146, 156; paperwork 148, 152; policy 152; power relations 150, 152; principled, personal autonomy 153; surveillance 146, 149, 152; target-setting 145, 148, 150, 151, 152, 154, 155; teaching and learning regimes 149–150, 151, 153; teaching and research-related required reporting mechanisms **147**
academic use-values 10–11
academics *see specific types*
accelerated development programmes (ADPs) 47, 50–56
achievement, relative to opportunity 41–43
Acker, Sandra 3, 4, 89
'active affects' 13
Adams, J. 79
agency 149, 178, 179; and research impact 108–109, 113
Ahmed, Sarah 12, 42
Ako Aronui professional development programme 118, 122, 126; creation of 123–124, *124*; embedding manaaki in 125; *see also* manaaki
alienated labour 180, 182
alienation 11–12, 13, 180
Amit, Vered 43
Amsler, S. S. 56
Amundsen, C. 90
Anderson, G. 77
anecdotes 36–37, 38
Angervall, P. 97
Aotearoa *see* manaaki
Archer, M. 149
arts: creative, use in higher education research 78–79; -enriched research approach 79; *see also* arts-informed postcards project
arts-informed postcards project 3, 74–76, 84–85; academic work in measured university 76–77; context and methodology of 79–80; dissent 83–84; drama 83, 84; micro-resistance 77–78, 79, 83–84; readers' theatre and mark-making 83–84; reformulation of research 76; rendering pain and paradox 81–83, *82–83*; rendering pleasure 81, *81*; use of creative arts in higher education research 78–79; wide-awakeness 75, 78–79, 84

INDEX

Auckland University of Technology (AUT) 122, 123–124; Centre for Learning and Teaching (CFLAT) 123, 125
audit culture 148; anticipatory audits 154; and early career academics in Canadian universities 89–90, 98; and impact agenda 106
Australia: Fair Work Commission (FWC) 60, 62, 65; gender equity for academic women *see* gender equity, for academic women in Australian universities; impact agendas *see* emotional responses, to impact agendas in UK and Australia; Indigenous studies *see* Indigenous studies, in Australia; National Tertiary Education Union (NTEU) 60, 62; research evaluation in 27; universities, HDR programmes in 9, 14–16; work allocation processes *see* workload models
Australian Academy of Technology and Engineering (ATSE) 105
Australian National University (ANU) 122, 125
Australian Research Council (ARC) 41, 105, 106
Australian University Teaching Criteria and Standards Framework 122
authorship *see* co-authorship; collaboration
autobiographical memory 179
autonomy of academics 65–66, 106, 109, 153, 155, 181–182

Back, Les 4
Ball, Stephen J. 3, 12, 60, 61–62, 69, 145, 146, 156, 175, 177
Bansel, Peter 14
Barcan, Ruth 14, 63, 70, 76–77, 81
Barone, T. 78
Baudrillard, J. 62
Beard, C. 104
Bennett, D. 92
Benske, K. 79
Berg, Lawrence 37
Berg, Maggie 4
Bergson, Henri 16
Berlant, Lauren 35, 36, 37, 38
Bernstein, B. 56
'better-off-overall-test' 60
Biesta, Gert 2, 174, 181
Billot, Jennie 4, 150, 152, 153, 154, 155, 160, 169
black academics *see* historically white universities (HWUs), black academics in
Bochner, A. 77
Bolden, R. 168
Bolsmann, C. 56
Booi, Masixole 46
Bottomore, T. B. 183n4
Bourdieu, Pierre 28, 48, 49, 50, 51–52, 56
Boyd, L. 61
Bozeman, B. 23, 26
Brexit 1
Brown, R. 178, 179
Brown, S. 78

Buissink, Nell 4, 117
Bullen, Jonathan 4, 131
Burrows, Roger 10–11, 12
Buthelezi, T. 80
Butin, D. 77

Cahill, C. 80
Canadian university workplace, early career academics in 3, 89–90, 98–99; academe and tensions of tenure 91–92; annual reviews 93, 94, 98; audit culture 89–90, 98; early academic career 90–91; made-to-measure product 98–99; measuring up 94–95; promotion 91, 99; reconciling 97–98; research method 93–94; romanticizing and criticizing 96–97; strategizing 95; *see also* tenure, of early career academics
capitalism 180; cybernetic 74; laissez-faire 174; neo-liberal 174
career scaffolding 169
Carr, P. L. 28
Changing Academic Profession (CAP) survey 92
Charteris, Jennifer 39
Chrislip, D. D. 21
Chubb, Jennifer 3, 103
citation 'rings'/'cartels' 29
Clarke, John 13–14
Clase, Piet 57n5
Clegg, S. 148, 153
Coates, H. 65
co-authorship 22–23, 27, 30; lack of acknowledgement 29; *see also* collaboration
co-citation, cronyism via 29
codes of signification 149, 150, 154–155
cognitive cronyism 29
collaboration 3, 20–22; benefits of 20; as communication 26–27; and creative conflict 24; as cronyism 28–29; definition of 21, 23; and disinterestedness 21; first author 28; with inexperienced/newer academics 23–24; as intellectual generosity 24–26; international 22; inter-personal criticism 23; and lack of acknowledgement 29; as mentorship 26; as moral continuum 24–30, **25**; as parasitism 29–30; as performativity 27–28; power relations between collaborators 23; problematising 22–24; quantitative/qualitative methods for measuring 23; realpolitik of 23
Collins, B. 78
commensuration 10–11, 12
commodification of public professional 177
communication, collaboration as 26–27
communism, and collaboration 25
concrete labour 176
Cook, C. 104
Cooper, A. 149, 150, 152, 153
cooperative inquiry 78
Corley, C. 26
corporate social capital 49

INDEX

corporatization 11, 12
corpus analysis: of academic induction 162–164, 167, 168, 170n1–3, 170n5–7; defined 161–182
cost–benefit analysis 174
cost effectiveness 176
Cousin, G. 80
creative arts, use in higher education research 78–79; *see also* arts-informed postcards project
creative conflict 24
creative inquiry 78
Crick, Francis 26
'crisis of ordinariness' 35, 39–40
critical pedagogy, and visual culture 75, 79
cronyism, collaboration as 28–29
'cruel optimism', and gender equity for academic women 35, 36–37, 43
C.U.D.O.S. 25
cultural capability/competence, and Indigenous studies 132
cultural capital 49, 52–56
cultural interface, and Indigenous studies 134, 135, 136–140
cultural reproduction 48, 49, 55
cultural resistance 75, 84
Cunningham, C. 79
cybernetic capitalism 74
cynical compliance 146, 156

Darwin, Charles 25
data chains 9
Daunton, L. 104
Davies, A. 77
'Dawkins revolution' 63
D'Cruz, K. 161
Degn, L. 90
DeLang, N. 80
demographic equity *see* historically white universities (HWUs), black academics in
Derrida, J. 134
dialectics: defined 183n5; humanism 181; as measure of academic labour 181–182
Diamond, Piki 117, 118, 119, 120
discursive repertoires 150, 153–154
disinterestedness, and collaboration 21
doctoral programmes 7; in Australian universities 14–16; benefits to embedded measurement practices 14–15; failures 16; and neo-liberalism 12; singular qualities 16; temporality of 16
Drakich, J. 92
drama 83, 84
Drozdzewski, Danielle 40, 41
Du Bois, W. E. B. 48, 57n4
Duncombe, S. 75, 84

early career academics (ECAs): in Canada *see* Canadian university workplace, early career academics in; and collaboration 23–24, 28; induction of 161, 162, 168; parasitism 29–30; performance appraisals 39; in United Kingdom *see* academic probation, of early career academics (UK)
Easton, L. D. 183n4
'ecologies of knowledges' 48
economic capital 49
economic efficiency 169, 176
Efe, I. 170n3
Eisner, E. 78
Elizabeth, V. 90, 99
Ellis, S. 79
emergenesis theory 178, 179
Emmeche, C. 28
emotional labour 137
emotional modulation 178, 179
emotional responses, to impact agendas in UK and Australia 3–4, 103–105; academic agency and personhood 108–109; female academics 111; flexians 104–105, 112; humanities researchers 110; impact, definition of 105; impact agendas in UK and Australia 105–106; ivory tower theory 110; job security 110–111; knowledge exchange 111–112; loss of control and identity 109–112; mind-set barrier 111; physical sciences researchers 110; public accountability and performance-related auditability 113; public intellectual 113; research methods 107; scholarly reactions to impact 106–107; sense of privilege 108; sense of purpose 112–113; type of research 108
emotions *see* arts-informed postcards project
Ennals, P. 161
'entrepreneurial knowledge managers' 76
episodic memory 179
Equity Index 46–47, 56
equity paradox 38
European Commission 21
Ewing, R. 80
excellence *see* academic excellence
Excellence Innovation Australia (EIA) 105–106
Excellence in Research Australia (ERA) 9, 38, 76, 106, 146

fairness 70, 174
Fair Work Act 2009 (Australia) 60
Fair Work Commission (FWC), Australia 60, 62, 65; review of modern awards 60
fallist student movement 48, 57n3
Fanghanel, J. 63
female academics *see* gender equity, for academic women in Australian universities
field 49, 50, 52–56
first authors, and collaboration 28
Fitzmaurice, M. 161
Flavell, Helen 4, 131
Flew, Terry 10
flexians 104–105, 112
Fortune, T. 161, 170
Foucault, Michel 10, 75, 77–78
Franklin, Rosalind 26

INDEX

freedom 31, 84, 92, 93, 99, 106, 109
free sharing of ideas *see* intellectual generosity, collaboration as
friendship, academic 24–25
friendly hostile co-operation, collaboration as 23, 25

Gannon, Susanne 39
gender equity, for academic women in Australian universities 3, 34–36; anecdotes 37; crisis of ordinariness 35, 39–40; cruel optimism 35, 36–37, 43; gender equity policies as empty referents 37–38; grants 41–43; ideal academic 38; language of diversity 42; maternity leave 40–41; optimistic objects 38; paradox of academic women's participation 37–38; performance appraisals 39; policies 42–43; publication record 40; quality assurance measures 38, 40; relative to opportunity 41–43; research outputs 38–41
Gill, Rosalind 11, 12
Giroux, Henry A. 11, 12
globalisation 121, 146
Goedegebuure, L. 65
good governance 42
'good life, the' 35; academic 35, 38, 40, 43
Gornall, J. 104
Gosling, J. 168
Gould, Stephen Jay 70–71
governmentality 176; neo-liberal 175
Govinder, K. S. 46–47
Grant, B. M. 90, 99
grants: for female academics 41–43; and impact agendas 105–106
Gravestock, P. 92
Grbich, C. 80
Grealy, Liam 2, 3, 6
Great University Gamble 146
Green, Pam 14
Greene, M. 75, 78–79, 84–85
Greenleaf, E. 92
Grey, Asa 25
Groundwater-Smith, S. 80
Group of Eight 65
groupthink 24
Guddat, K. H. 183n4

habitus 49, 50–52, 55
hākarī 126
Halberstam, J. Jack 16
Hallas, Julia 117
Halse, Christine 14
Hanna, B. E. 162
hard sciences 35
Harvey, David 10
Hazelkorn, E. 168
Health Workforce Australia, Aboriginal and Torres Strait Islander Curriculum Framework project 137–138
Hemer, S. 150
Hemmings, B. 167, 169
Hey, V. 104
higher degree research (HDR) programmes, neo-liberal metrics in 3, 6–8; alienation 11–12, 13; 'at risk' projects, identifying 15; Australian universities 14–16; commensuration 10–11, 12; corporatization 11, 12; critiques of neo-liberalism 10–14; fast supervision 14; incentivization 11, 12; intelligence and giftedness 14–15; joyful affects 14; market signals 13; measurement and higher education 8–10; neo-liberal subjectivity 17; ordinal rankings 9; outcomes-oriented model of supervision 14; passive affects *vs.* active affects 13; research training and student support 14–15; selection processes for candidates 15–16; social worlds 15; structural conflicts between stakeholders 8–9
higher education, transformation of 46–47
Higher Education Academy (HEA), UK 4, 118, 122, 123–124; Fellowship Scheme 4
Higher Education (Academic Staff) Award 2010 (Australia) 60
higher education institutions (HEIs), induction process 160, 161, 168
H-Index 11
Hinton, L. 62
historically black universities (HBUs) 47, 56–57n1
historically white universities (HWUs), black academics in 3, 46–48, 55–56, 56–57n1; academic excellence 48–49; approving right type of black academics 50–52; data analysis 50; decision-making processes 53–54; group identity 51; informal recruitment practices 51; middle-class backgrounds 51, 55; networking power 55; older established academics 53; problem of the color-line 48, 57n4; rejection, exclusion, and invisibility 52–55; social relationships 51, 52; theoretical framework 48–50
Hofbauer, J. 90
Hong Kong, authorship order in 30
Hooker, Joseph Dalton 25
Horn, M. 91
Hornibrook, S. 68
Hughes, J. 80
Hull, R. 61, 62
Humanist Marxism 178; *see also* Marxist Humanism
humanities 35
Hunter, Ian 11
Hunter, Shona 42

ideal academics 38
identity: academic *see* academic identity; identity-trajectory 148–149, 151, 155–156; organisational 145–146; professional 161, 166, 168; shared 168

INDEX

impact agendas *see* emotional responses, to impact agendas in UK and Australia
incentivization 11, 12, 89
Indigenous epistemes 134, 141
indigenous knowledge *see* manaaki
Indigenous studies, in Australia 4, 131–133; coordinating Indigenous studies units 138–139; emotional labour 137; gifts 134, 135, 138, 140, 141; hospitality 134, 140–141; identity 132, 137; implications for community 139–140; interprofessional unit 135; learning and teaching at cultural interface 136–140; ontological pluralism 135, 140; reciprocity 134, 136, 140–141; students 136–137; student satisfaction 134, 137, 139, 140; teaching staff 137–138; theoretical framework 134–135; transactional approach 136, 140; transformational learning 136, 137, 138, 139; unlearning 136, 138
induction *see* academic induction
Ingersoll, L. 69
institutional depression 77
institutional sustainability 168
intellectual generosity, collaboration as 24–26
international collaboration 22

Jawitz, J. 166
Jenkins, Fiona 38, 43
job security: and publication record 40; and research impact 110–111
Jung, J. 145, 146, 148, 150, 156

Keamy, (Ron) Kim 74
Kenny, J. 69
Key Performance Indicators (KPIs) 6, 9, 11, 13, 132, 141
King, Virginia 4, 78, 80, 160, 169
Klocker, Natascha 40, 41
Knight, P. 149, 152, 155, 166–168
koretake 121–122
Kosik, K. 180, 183n3–5
Kreissl, K. 90
Kuokkanen, Rauna 4, 134, 140
Kwok, L. S. 29–30

labour: abstract 176; alienated 180, 182; concrete 176; academic, dialectical measure of 181–182; emotional 137; social, spiritual dimension of 179–181; *see also* academic labour, demoralization of; workload models
laissez-faire capitalism 174
Lamont, A. 62
Land, R. 151–152, 156
language 178–179
Larson, C. E. 21
Laurie, Tim 2, 3, 6
Lawrence, R. 80
league tables 146, 156
Leathwood, Carole 39, 104
Leavy, P. 80

Lee, S. 23
Liccardo, Sabrina 3, 46
Lipton, Briony 3, 34
Loads, D. 78
Locke, W. 166, 168
love 174–175, 178
Lynch, K. 154
Lyons, M. 69

McAlpine, L. 90, 93, 148, 149, 152, 155, 156
McCaughan, E. J. 79
Macfarlane, Bruce 3, 20, 151, 154
McGettigan, A. 146, 155
Macleod, C. 57n1
Makgoba, M. W. 46–47
Mampaey, J. 170n3
mana 120, 121, 126
manaaki 4, 117–118, 127–128; Ako Aronui professional development programme 123–124, *124*; being careful with how we nurture and look after people 125–126; embedding in Ako Aronui 125; place in measured university 120–122; power of words 126–127; research setting 122–123; taking care of and enhancing mana 126; Te Tiriti o Waitangi 118–119; understanding 119–120
manaakitanga 120, 123–124, 125
managerialism 77, 108, 177, 180; and workload modelling 63, 69
Manathunga, Catherine 3, 74
Māori *see* manaaki
Marginson, S. 56
marketization 63, 177; of higher education 11, 174
mark-making 75, 83–84
Markovic, M. 182n2
Marx, Karl 4, 13, 174, 178–180, 183n4
Marxism 7
Marxist Humanism 179, 183n3; *see also* Humanist Marxism
maternity leave, and research output 40–41
Mathieson, S. 166, 168
Matthew effect 28
Mayes, Eve 39
Mazenod, A. 166
measurement practices 2–3; objections 2; and purpose 2–3; quality *vs.* quantity 8
memory 178, 179; autobiographical 179; episodic 179
mentorship, collaboration as 23–24, 26
merit, and gender equity 37–38, 39
Merkely, C. 92
Merton, R. K. 21, 23, 25
'mesearch' 104
'metricization', of academy 11, 12
Michaels, Mike 37
'micro-physics' of power 75, 77–78
micro-resistance, of academics 77–78, 79, 83–84
mind-set barrier, and research impact 111
Mitchell, C. 80

INDEX

Mockler, N. 80
Module Evaluation Questionnaire (MEQ) 148, 150
Moed, H. F. 29
Molestane, R. 80
moral continuum, collaboration as 24–30, **25**
Morley, Louise 38, 39
Morrish, L. 154
Morrow, R. 54

Naidoo, R. 48
Nakata, Martin 4, 134, 139
National Tertiary Education Union (NTEU), Australia 60, 62
naturalism 7
Neary, M. 173, 174, 182
neo-liberal capitalism 174
neo-liberal governmentality 175
neo-liberalism 6–7, 77, 104, 176; and audits of research quality 27; and Foucalt 10; and gender equity for academic women 40; and HDR programmes *see* higher degree research (HDR) programmes, neo-liberal metrics in; measurement, critiques 10–14; university reform 89
neo-liberal subjectivity 17
New Economics Foundation (NEF), dynamic model of well-being at work 181–182
new managerialism 35, 42, 49, 106
New Public Management 146
Newton, Issac 27
New Zealand *see* manaaki
New Zealand Qualifications Authority 119
Nixon, J. 29
Norris, J. 84
Norton, A. 70
Nye, Adele 39
Nygaard, L. 90, 97

O'Brien, A. 168
Ocean, J. 2
ontological insecurity 12, 177
ontological pluralism 135, 140
opportunity *see* achievement, relative to opportunity
organisational identity 145–146
organisational socialisation 163, 167
Ornstein, M. 92
other-regarding (other-oriented) behaviour 24, 26
outcomes-oriented model, of supervision 14
Oxford English Dictionary (OED) 21
Ozer, O. 170n3

Page, S. 140
Papadopoulos, Angelika 3, 59
parasitism, collaboration as 29–30
Parker, L. 121
'passive affects' 13
Pausé, C. 78

Performance Based Research Fund (PBRF), New Zealand 76, 78, 91, 146
performativity 174–178; collaboration as 27–28; of early career academics during probation 150, 156; and field 56; positivism of 180–182; and reordering of self-identity 177
personhood, and research impact 108–109, 112, 113
Peseta, Tai 4, 5
PhDs *see* doctoral programmes
Pilcher, N. 162
Pio, E. 121
politics of belonging 53
'politics of reinscription' 75, 84
Polkinghorne, D. E. 151
Popper, K. R. 23, 25
positivism of performativity 180–182
postcards *see* arts-informed postcards project
power–knowledge relations 175
power relations: and academic probation, of early career academics 150, 152; and approval of black academics 50, 51, 52, 53, 55, 56; between collaborators 23; and participation of academic women 37
probabilistic inferences 8
'problem of the color-line' 48, 57n4
productivity, academic 175, 176; and collaboration 27, 46–47; and decision-making 90; of early career academics in Canada 94; of female academics 38
professional development *see* Ako Aronui professional development programme
professional identity 161, 166, 168
protest movements, role of art in 79, 84
proxy indicators 8, 11
publication record 40
Puwar, Nirmal 38, 42

quality, of research: assurance, measures 176; audits 27; and impact 105, 106; reporting 38

Rambur, B. 25, 28
Rasheed, A. 121
rational–emotional dilemma 104
rationality 12, 17, 103, 175
Read, Barbara 39
readers' theatres 75, 83–84
Readings, B. 76
reciprocity 134, 136, 140–141, 174
Reconciliation Action Plans 132
Remmik, M. 167
Research Assessment Exercise (UK) 27, 146
research centres, for collaboration 21
Research Council UK (RCUK) 105, 106
research evaluation 27
Research Excellence Framework (REF), UK 40, 76, 105, 146

INDEX

research outputs: of female academics 38–41; maternity leave and 40–41; workload models 63, 65, 67
resistance, of academics: to impact agendas 106, 112; micro-resistance 77–78
review rings, and cronyism 29
Richards, K. 162
Riemer, Andrew 15
RMIT University 9
Roberts-Holmes, Guy 9
Robus, D. 57n1
Royal Society (UK) 15
Ryan, Y. 62

Sadler, K. 80
Sadler, Kirsten 74
Salisbury, J. 104
Sauer, B. 90
Sciascia, Acushla Dee 117
sciences 35
scientific research, collaboration in 22
Scopus™ database 162, 170n4
Scott, J. 77
Sedgwick, Eve 6, 12
Seeber, Barbara K. 4
self-alienation 180
self-identity reordering, and performativity 177
self-regarding (self-oriented) behaviour 24
self-surveillance, in academic probation 149
Selkrig, Mark 74
sensemaking, and organizational changes 90–91
shared identity 168
'shared moral language' 177
Sheridan, V. 161
Shin, J. C. 145, 146, 148, 150, 156
simulacra, workload models as 62, 70–71
Skelton, A. 148, 155
Skourdoumbis, A. 2
Smith, H. 166
Smith, Jan 4, 145, 166
Smith, K. 104
social beings 179–180
social capital 49, 50–52, 55
social justice 42, 48
social labour, spiritual dimension of 179–181
social networks 49–50, 55
social order, in Indigenous communities 134
social relations of production 180
social reproduction 48, 49
social sciences 35
socio-emotional entities, academics as 23
Soudien, C. 48
soul 173–183; nature and emergence of 178–179; soulfulness 178, 181
South Africa *see* historically white universities (HWUs), black academics in
species-being 174, 175, 178, 182; and spiritual dimension of social labour 179–181
Spinoza, Baruch 13, 14

Stensaker, B. 145–146, 149, 155
Stephenson, Lauren 39
Stewart, P. 92
Stoneman McNichol, J. 92
Strathern, M. 148
Striedinger, A. 90
strong theories 6–7, 12
Stuart, J. 80
student satisfaction 2, 75, 134, 137, 139
surveillance 7, 89; and academic probation 146, 149, 152
Sutherland, K. 146, 148, 156, 168
Sutton, Paul 3, 4, 173, 182n1
Swann, Jennie 117
'symbolic capital of renown' 28

Tang, J. 28
target-setting culture *see* academic probation, of early career academics (UK)
Tavin, K. 79
teaching and learning regimes (TLRs) 149–150, 151, 153
Teaching Excellence Framework (TEF), UK 76, 146
'teaching for openings' 75
Tegetmeier, William Bernhard 25
tenure, of early career academics 89, 91–92, 94–99
Te Tiriti o Waitangi 118–119
Te Whāriki 121
theory of mind 178, 179
Thomas, B. 104
Thomas, R. 77
Thompson, E. P. 174
Thornton, M. 38
Tipuna, K. 121
Tomkins, Silvan 6, 12
Torres, C. 54
Torres Strait Islanders *see* Indigenous studies, in Australia
transformational learning 136, 137, 138, 139
transformation of higher education 46–47
Tremaine, M. 78
trimester system, and workload models 66, 69
Trowler, P. 149, 150, 152, 153, 155, 166–168
Turner, G. 90
Tynan, B. 62, 68

United Kingdom (UK): academic probation in *see* academic probation, of early career academics (UK); Higher Education Academy (HEA) 4, 118, 122, 123–124; impact agendas *see* emotional responses, to impact agendas in UK and Australia; Research Assessment Exercise 27, 146; Research Council UK (RCUK) 105, 106; research evaluation 27; Research Excellence Framework (REF) 40, 76, 105, 146; Royal Society 15; Teaching Excellence Framework (TEF) 76, 146; universities, measurement culture in 146, **147**, 148

INDEX

United Kingdom Professional Standards Framework (UKPSF) 118, 122
United States, tenure of early career academics 92
University College London 21
university–industry partnerships 21
university rankings 49, 56
Usher, Robin 14

Vardi, I. 61
Verran, H. 35
Vincent, Louise 46
visual culture, and critical pedagogy 75, 79; *see also* arts-informed postcards project
Vitae Researcher Development Framework 168
Voyant Tools™ corpus analysis 162, 170n7

Waitere, H. 78
Wakeling, Paul 103
Watermeyer, Richard 103
Watson, James 26
weak theories 12–13
Webber, Michelle 3, 89
Weber, M. 25–26
Weber, S. 80
well-being at work, dynamic model of 181–182
Wenger, E. 167
Whitchurch, C. 166
White, Julie 35
'White bull effect' 30
'wide-awakeness' 75, 78–79, 84
Williams, A. 161
Williams, P. 168

Wilson, L. 166
Wilson, M. 168
Winn, J. 173, 174, 182
women *see* gender equity, for academic women in Australian universities
working hours, regulation of 60
workload models 3, 59–62; allocation of research time 63, 70; Australian university system 63; autonomy of academics 65–66; benchmarks 63, 65; boundary between teaching and non-teaching time 66; categorisation of activities 61; caveats 63; and change 69–70; conceptualisations of academic labour 65–67; current practices 63, 65; and equity 68–69; first order measures 62; managers 63, 69; and measurement 67–68; modes of teaching delivery 67; multiple teaching sessions 66; non-teaching weeks 66; overloads 68; perceptions of 67–70; reasonableness 66, 70, 71; reception of 61; research funding, and teaching income 70; research method and informational sources 62; research outputs 63, 65, 67; as simulacra 62, 70–71; structural conditions 66, 67, 69; supervision of research students 65, 66; teaching practice 67–68; transparency 60, 61, 67, 70; variations **64**
Wright, J. 78
Wright, M. 141

Yeo, M. 92
Yuval-Davis, N. 53

Zondo, N. P. 46–47

For Product Safety Concerns and Information please contact our EU representative GPSR@taylorandfrancis.com Taylor & Francis Verlag GmbH, Kaufingerstraße 24, 80331 München, Germany

Printed and bound by CPI Group (UK) Ltd, Croydon, CR0 4YY
29/07/2025
01926870-0012